Sex & Relationships

An Anthology

John P. Elia, Ph.D.

Ivy Chen, MPH

San Francisco State University

KENDALL/HUNT PUBLISHING COMPANY

4050 Westmark Drive P.O. Box 1840 Dubuque, Iowa 52004-1840

Contents

Preface

Various kinds of sexual, romantic relationships have received much attention in the media. Popular radio and television talk shows have devoted countless hours to this topic. The popular press has generated literally thousands of articles on sex and relationships. Mental health professionals have long claimed that sexual, romantic relationships are one of the most important aspects of our lives. Besides the coverage of this important area in the popular culture genre, the academic study of sex and relationships is a growing inter-disciplinary field. While there are countless research efforts and scholarly writings in this area, there continues to be a need for more work on this topic. However, both the amount of published work in this area and the number of perspectives are daunting. This pre-sented a challenge in terms of selecting which previously published works to include in this anthology. Ultimately, what resulted is a collection of writings from the popular press and academic studies. This volume covers a wide range of issues and addresses the com-plexities of sexual, romantic relationships.

This anthology begins with a brief section on contextualizing the complexity of sexual relationships, and then moves on to exploring various ways in which relationships are initiated. Next, there is a section on falling in love. Following this section is one on maintaining intimacy, and then various aspects of life decisions regarding sexual relation-ships are covered. The anthology then turns to a section on various types of conflict— and resolutions to discord—that emerge in intimate, romantic, sexual relationships. Fi-nally, the volume is concluded with a section on terminating relationships. While a number of excellent and thought-provoking pieces in this volume deal with a wide range of topics and issues, this book is not intended to be a comprehensive treatment of sexual relation-ships. However, it is intended to provide a broad coverage of important issues that are likely to be thought provoking, spark discussion, and perhaps even help some readers to improve their own relationships.

Ultimately, readers will find that this book provides not only a treatment of various aspects of sexual, romantic relationships, but also it contains disparate points of view. Many books are either too simplistic or hopelessly too academic. There is rarely the per-fect book. However, our hope is that this volume is accessible and that it has much poten-tial for practical applicability. Readers will undoubtedly see the personal relevance of this book. An added benefit of this volume is that it is accompanied by a *Students' Guide*, which is designed to get readers actively involved in each chapter by completing a number of exercises. We hope that by reading this anthology and completing the *Students' Guide*, various relationship-oriented questions will be both raised and answered, not to mention that the text and *Students' Guide* will facilitate understanding and insights, clarify values, and ultimately help individuals achieve satisfying and fulfilling sexual, romantic relationships.

Editing a volume is a tremendous amount of work and involves a plethora of details to be worked out, and can entail a countless number of logistical difficulties. John Elia thanks his co-editor, Ivy Chen, for her many hours of work on this second edition of *Sex & Relationships: An Anthology*, and for authoring the *Students' Guide*. This volume is far better because of her involvement as co-editor and co-author. In many ways, this volume reflects her expertise as a sexuality educator. John Elia also expresses his gratitude to John Woo, the research assistant for this project, who worked tirelessly to see this project come to fruition.

John Elia also thanks numerous friends who have been not only enormously supportive of him, but also who have shared his commitment to human sexuality studies, including sexuality education. He thanks Albert Angelo, Jim Brogan, John De Cecco, Amanda Goldberg, Roma Guy, Richard Hoffman, Mike Kurokawa, Wenshu Lee, Lisa Moore, Michael Quimpo, Daniel (Danny) Silver, Dee Dee Stout, Bruce Whaley, and Gust Yep.

John Elia dedicates this book to his life partner, Gina Bloom, and to her son, Brian. They have been incredible sources of love, learning, and inspiration to him. Creating a family with them continues to be a tremendous daily reminder of the importance of relationships.

Ivy Chen dedicates this book to her mother and father, Crystal and Paul, her stepmother, Judy, her sister Karen and her brother-in-law, Brian.

John P. Elia, Ph.D.
San Francisco, CA
October, 2004

Ivy Chen, MPH
Oakland, CA
October, 2004

Introduction: The Complexities of Sex and Relationships

John P. Elia, Ph.D. and Ivy Chen, MPH

There are many views about sex and relationships. Many people have finite ideas about what constitutes a bona fide, legitimate sexual relationship. A limited view of sex or relationships is likely to foreclose the possibility of having satisfying experiences with others. In an effort to articulate the breadth and depth of sex and relationships, this chapter will challenge traditional conceptions of sex and relationships in an effort to explore new and expanded vistas of an area of our lives that many of us cherish.

An Expanded View of Sexuality

Each semester the *Sex and Relationships* class at San Francisco State University is begun by asking students to define both "sex" and "relationships." We begin the discussion by wrestling with what "sex" means. Invariably, the first thing students refer to is sexual intercourse. Eventually, various and sundry activities are mentioned (e.g., masturbation, oral-genital contact, anal play, etc.). It is not surprising, however, that many people are quick to associate sex with heterosexual intercourse. Historically speaking, this has been the form of sexual expression that has been socially sanctioned, as innumerable religious and medical tracts have been reinforcing the legitimacy of it for centuries. They perpetuate the notion that the best and most supreme form of sexual expression is to take place in the marital bedroom to produce babies. A quick glance at any English dictionary also reflects this idea. For example, the *Webster's New Collegiate Dictionary* defines sex as "(1) either of two divisions of organisms distinguished respectfully as male or female. (2) the sum of the structural, functional, and behavioral characteristics of living beings that subserve reproduction by two interacting parents and that distinguish males and females. (3) a: sexually motivated phenomena or behavior. b: SEXUAL INTERCOURSE. (4) GENITALIA" (p. 1062). This definition reveals a few things. It reveals that the focus is not only on the act of sexual intercourse for procreation but also that sex is reduced to a discussion of physical activities that involve the genitals. And, indeed, the majority of people conceptualize sex in just this way. Year after year students continue to define sex along these lines. This does not speak poorly of them or others who view sex in such terms. The point is that this notion has been perpetuated without much criticism. Most people do not stop and think about the implications of such a narrow concept of sex.

Even though people often carry on sexually with others in far more complicated ways than the dictionary definition would have us believe, it is nonetheless symbolic of the form of sexuality that is held in high esteem. Other forms of sexual expression are viewed as somehow inferior or simply "not the real thing." This kind of thinking has far-reaching implications. First, it implies that if people do not engage in heterosexual sexual intercourse, for whatever reasons, their sexual relationships are somehow wrong, deficient, or lacking. Second, within heterosexual encounters, it creates a sexual hierarchy; intercourse becomes the ultimate sexual act.

While sexuality obviously includes the physical and reproductive dimensions, it also has ethical, psychological, socio-cultural, and political aspects that are equally important. Sexuality is a complicated concept and its complexity cannot be captured in a simple definition.

If we wish to enhance our sexual relationships, we must think about sexuality broadly. A broad view of human sexuality captures the breadth of experiences people consider to be sexual. Bruess and Greenberg (1988) break sexuality down into four dimensions, viz. ethical, cultural, biological, and psychological aspects. The ethical area includes ideals, religious beliefs, moral opinions, and values. The Cultural aspects of sexuality include: customs, laws, sanctions and institutions. Biological dimensions are: reproduction, fertility control, sexual motivation, expressiveness, learned attitudes, and behavior. But while Bruess and Greenberg provide a multitude of dimensions that may be connected in some way to sexuality, they fail to provide us with a tangible notion of sexuality itself.

In a philosophical essay that does not take for granted its readers' assumptions of what is meant by "sexuality," Alan Goldman (1977/1991) points out that the concept itself needs to be understood and explored. He implies that not only should the conceptions constituting sexuality be extended far beyond the boundaries of heterosexual intercourse but also he questions an even more fundamental assumption: that sexuality and orgasm must be inextricably linked. He states that sexual desire and behavior (sexuality in general) should not be viewed categorically as having orgasm as an ultimate goal or end. Often sexuality is characterized as involving orgasm as a necessary ingredient to serve as some sort of testimonial that "it" was not only in fact a sexual act but also the "real thing." This view artificially reduces sexuality and robs it of its richness and diversity.

The assumption that sexuality is a "means to an end" (orgasm) is problematic for a number of reasons. It discounts types of sexuality that do not conclude in orgasm. Also, holding such an assumption may lead one to seek orgasm with such energy and effort that the aesthetic value of the sexual process is lost. In essence, sexuality cannot be characterized as the presence of orgasm. Finally, it makes the assumption that sexuality is a physical and observable practice.

In an essay, "Sexual Behavior: Another Position," Janice Moulton (1976/1991) makes the case that sexuality transcends the physical, as she states that the seduction, flirtation, courtship, and even the anticipation of a date or sexual contact not only can be considered a part of sexuality but also can be more sexually gratifying than the physical experiences themselves.

Sexuality is a general concept of which many things are a part. Sexual behaviors range from a seductive wink of an eye, to genital-genital or oral-genital contact, to solo or mutual masturbation. The psychological aspect of sexuality includes sexual desires, sexual fantasies, sexual dreams, and sexual motives. Also, in this realm is how one defines oneself sexually, including her or his sexual identity, and how one perceives oneself sexually in general (and in relation to other aspects, as outlined above in Bruess and Greenberg, 1988).

Sexuality often cannot be identified as a palpable, monolithic thing due to its complexity and multiple meanings. Literature does a wonderful job of illustrating the varying degrees of complexity and subtlety of sexuality. In her book on lesbianism, JoAnn Loulan (1987) recounts an experience of one of the characters in her book:

> Remember the first time…the first time you felt that flush of love for a woman. For me it was for Mrs. McAndrews in second grade. I would just sit and stare for hours. She was tall, with tightly curled grey hair, and beautiful smooth skin. I was in heaven. That's lesbian magic (p. 32).

Edith Wharton (1918) in her novel, *Summer*, describes a scene depicting female heterosexuality:

> Since the day before, she had known exactly what she would feel if Harney should take her in his arms: the melting of palm into palm and mouth onto mouth, and the long flame burning from head to foot (p. 106).

An example of male homosexuality is depicted by E.M. Forster (1914) in his novel *Maurice*:

> He would not deceive himself so much. He would not—and this was the test—pretend to care about women when the only sex that attracted him was his own. He loved men and had always loved them. He longed to embrace them and mingle his being with theirs…(p. 62).

The examples above illustrate how individuals express their sexualities and interpret them in a variety of ways and contexts. Clearly, sexuality is highly individualistic and subjective.

Sexuality is so complicated and subjective that it is possible that a person can be sexual with another person without this latter person knowing about it. Let's use the example of massage. A platonic friend invites you to her or his place to visit. In the midst of your conversation, your friend indicates that he or she has had a tough week and that her or his neck, shoulder, and back muscles are tight and knotted. You think highly of your friend and want to offer some relief so you offer a massage. Your friend accepts your offer, and to get to the affected areas he or she partially disrobes. At the time, both of you think nothing of this at least as far as sexuality is concerned. Your thoughts remain platonic and your friend is only too glad at the possibility of relief from muscular tension. However, as you begin to rub your friend's muscles, you begin to admire her or his physique, curves in the shoulders and back. You gradually become aware of your sexual feelings. You begin to admire your friend in a new light. Here you are kneading your friend's muscles and he or she is uttering sounds of bliss as the tension begins melting away. Your friend is not thinking about sex. However, you are quite conscious of your sexual feelings. Your physical contact became sexualized in your mind without your friend sharing such feelings. Depending on the nature of your friendship, you may or may not choose to reveal this to her or him. The point is that sexual expression is highly varied, complicated, and nuanced. Various experiences hold the potential of becoming sexual ones.

In keeping with the notion that sexuality covers a vast area of human experiences, the Sexuality Information and Education Council of the United States (SIECUS) maintains that "sexuality" encompasses "the sexual knowledge, beliefs, feelings, attitudes, values, intentions, and behaviors of individuals" (Barthalow-Koch, 1992; see also SIECUS, 1990).

Sexual Relationships Broadly Conceived

As with sex and sexuality, most people think about relationships in very narrow and specific terms. Most books on intimate and sexual relationships perpetuate this notion and have not been helpful in providing an all-inclusive view of sexual relationships. Most cover traditional relationships and the issues therein, and virtually ignore the myriad forms of relationships that exist. For instance, Brehm (1992) identifies various types of relationships by stating that "[p]eople have all kinds of relationships with each other. They have parents and/ or children; they work with people on the job and/or at school; they encounter grocery clerks, physicians and office receptionists; they have friends; they may be dating, living with a lover, or married. Out of this vast array of relationships, this book will concentrate on the last two categories" (p. 4). Brehm is not alone in providing readers with a narrow—even an exclusive—focus. There are a number of works that focus on traditional forms of sexual relationship (see, for example, Hendrick and Hendrick, 1992; Scharff, 1982). While these works have indeed made solid contributions to the field, they not only neglect to address various relationship styles but also to challenge traditional conceptions of what constitutes a healthy and satisfying sexual relationship. The trade book market has been flooded with books like John Gray's (1992) *Men Are From Mars and Women Are From Venus*, which focus on traditional heterosexual relationships and continue to reinforce traditional gender roles. Of course, such books serve the purpose of addressing the issues faced by stereotypical heterosexual relationships. The problem is that these books imply that there is a monolithic standard with which to judge whether or not a relationship is valuable, healthy, or worthwhile.

Brehm (1992) states that many definitions of intimate relationships emphasize three characteristics: (1) behavioral interdependence; (2) psychological need fulfillment; and (3) emotional attachment. Behavioral interdependence refers to intimates who have intertwined lives. Psychological need fulfillment includes such needs as: intimacy (being able to share a wide variety of feelings), social integration (having an outlet to share concerns and worries), nurturance (playing the role of caretaker), assistance (receiving help), and assurance (having our value reaffirmed). Emotional attachment refers to the love and affection partners feel for each other. Although it is true that many people find comfort and functionality in having sexual relationships in which the above-mentioned aspects are a part, there are fully functional and fulfilling sexual relationships that do not fit the standard description.

As mentioned earlier, when characterizing and defining "sex," over the years our students have defined "sexual relationships" along very traditional lines as well. When we ask them what is the first thing that comes to mind when thinking about what characterizes sexual relationships, they mention various qualities: sexual contact (usually intercourse) between members of the opposite sex, love, monogamy, marriage, intimacy, long-term association, etc. It hardly needs to be mentioned that many happy, healthy, and fulfilling relationships are comprised of the qualities mentioned above. To this extent, writings of all sorts focusing on traditional notions or relationships have affirmed these relationship styles and this is, indeed, "music to the ears" of these who are engaged in such relationships.

However, untraditional relationships not only receive little scholarly treatment but also are viewed negatively. A historical investigation would quickly reveal why traditional relationship styles are held in high esteem while untraditional ones are looked upon with suspicion and are discouraged. A number of institutions, *viz.,* religion, medicine, law, and education, have reinforced traditional sexual relationships. Judeo-Christian sexual morality has encouraged and blessed marital relationships involving procreation (Bullough, 1976). Essentially, Christians have viewed any form of sexuality outside of marriage and without procreative intent as sinful (Payer, 1984). Generally speaking, bio-medial sciences supported the religions prohibition against any form of sexuality that did not lead to procreation by hypothesizing and promulgating ideas that "sexual aberrations" led to physical maladies. Such ideas began as early as the eighteenth century and traces of this mentality can still be seen in the medical establishment (particularly in psychiatry and clinical psychology). Another institution that reinforces the sanctity of traditional relationships is law. The most current laws that best illustrate intolerance of untraditional sexual relationships are the sodomy laws. These laws, until relatively recently, were enforceable in many states throughout the United States. Finally, education (at every level of schooling) has perpetuated the idea that conventional relationships are the best way to go. This notion is manifested in a few ways. First, the general curriculum tends to be heterosexist (the idea that heterosexuality is the correct and most supreme way of life) in that the teaching of English literature or history tend to focus on heterosexual aspects of life. Bisexuals, gays, and lesbians are usually completely ignored. For example, even if a high school English literature course discusses the works of E.M. Forster, Oscar Wilde, or Walt Whitman, homosexual overtones are often glossed over or not discussed at all. Second, sexuality education has been remiss in discussing various sexual lifestyles. It has been widely documented for years that most sexuality education focuses on reproductive anatomy and physiology (Elia, 1997; Elia, 2000a & 2000b). This focus implicitly gives much credence to heterosexual relationships while completely ignoring the validity of other forms of sexual relationships. It is clear then that various institutions have lent support to traditional relationships while both explicitly and implicitly discriminating against unconventional forms.

Despite the pull to conform to traditional standards for sexual relationships, many people have departed from the norm, and have chosen to engage in various types of unconventional relationships. This has come at a price. There has been much discrimination. Tax breaks, vacation discounts, and family memberships discounts and fitness centers—just to mention a few examples—are unavailable to those who are openly involved in non-traditional situations. More vicious forms of prejudice are also common, such as physical attacks, emotional abuse, name-calling, taunting, termination from employment, etc. In some cases, people are deprived of their livelihoods. In other cases, partner health insurance coverage and standard employee benefits are often not provided due to their unconventional lifestyles.

If our society is to endorse democratic values and pluralism, as it often claims, then we can no longer tolerate such discrimination. Personal and social harm result from such a lack of tolerance/acceptance. We have always been curious about why people become so enraged and threatened by even the thought of others engaging in different sexual relationships than they choose. Of course, myriad psychological and sociological theories attempt to explain such a phenomenon, but at the most basic level it remains a mystery as to why people become obsessed, incensed, outraged, vicious, and generally pugnacious about how others decide to live their lives. If a person decides to be in a consensual bisexual, three way sexual relationship that is non-monogamous, how does this negatively impact other people's lives? People often have "knee jerk reactions" to these kinds of situations, without thinking.

Assumptions about Sexual Relationships

There are many assumptions about what constitutes a healthy and worthwhile sexual relationship. Unfortunately, most people are quick to criticize unconventional sexual relationships without really thinking through their negative reactions, and providing an intelligent, or at least a thoughtful, response. Because many of the chapters in this anthology address some of the following assumptions fully, and due to a lack of space, an exhaustive treatment will not be undertaken here. Let's, however, identify some assumptions and raise some questions.

One major assumption is that heterosexual relationships are better than and superior to other types of relationships (e.g., bisexual, gay or lesbian, or transgender). How could such a claim be made? Within heterosexual relationships, marriage is seen as the ultimate expression. Why is marriage necessarily better than non-marital relationships (e.g., cohabitive or non-cohabitive situations)? Monogamy is assumed to be more noble than non-monogamy. Why is monogamy given such high status? Can we really expect that one person can fulfill all of our sexual needs? How about two or more people who agree to open up their relationship to include more people sexually? Relationships that involve two individuals are seen as the norm no matter what their sexual preferences/orientations.

How about involving more than two people in a sexual relationship? Given various circumstances, could not a relationship that involved more than two people be more beneficial, fulfilling, exciting, rewarding, and/or convenient? Long-term relationships are viewed as more valuable than short-term ones. Have not most of us had short-term relationships that have been ultimately more valuable than long-term ones in terms of fun, excitement, hot sex, personal insights, and quality? How about sexual relationships that are almost entirely based on a sexual connection—as with "fuck buddies"—and are devoid of qualities that have long been considered the hallmarks of healthy sexual relationships such as love, deep emotional attachment, mutual self-disclosure, intellectual compatibility, shared interest (besides sex), etc? Innumerable assumptions are held and promulgated without being seriously questioned or challenged. It is time that these types of assumptions be questioned and challenged for us to be able to explore the full potential of, and most optimal forms of, sexual relationships.

The Mission of This Book

This book is intended to answer and raise questions about sex and relationships. It is divided into a variety of sections dealing with various aspects of sexual, romantic relationships. The first section deals with the initiation of intimate sexual relationships. The second section covers falling in love. The third section deals with the development and maintenance of intimacy in sexual relationships. The fourth part explores life decisions. The fifth section contains several chapters on conflict and trouble in sexual relationships. Finally, there is a brief section on terminating relationships.

Given the limitless size of the interdisciplinary sub-field of intimate and sexual relationships, this book does not attempt to be comprehensive. Rather, it provides readers with a number of chapters on disparate subjects about various aspects of sexual relationships. Also, this book offers a balanced perspective. While a number of chapters challenge traditional perspectives about relationships, many others are written along conventional lines. There is something in this book for nearly everyone!

References

Barthalow-Koch, Patricia. "Integrating Cognitive, Affective, and Behavioral Approaches into Learning Experiences for Sexuality Education." In James Sears's (ed.) *Sexuality and the Curriculum: The Politics and Practices of Sexuality Education.* New York: Teachers College Press, Columbia University, 1992: 253-266.

Brehm, Sharon. *Intimate Relationships.* 2nd ed. New York: McGraw-Hill, 1992.

Bruess, Clint E. and Greenberg, Jerold S. *Sexuality Education: Theory and Practice.* 2nd ed. New York: MacMillan Publishers, 1988.

Bullough, Vern. *Sexual Variance in Society and History.* Chicago. University of Chicago press, 1976.

Carroll, Janell L. and Wolpe, Paul. *Sexuality and Gender in Society.* New York: HarperCollins, 1996.

Elia, John P. *Sexuality Education: A Challenge for the Schools.* Unpublished Doctoral Dissertation. University of California, Davis, 1997.

Elia, J. P. (2000a). The necessity of comprehensive sexuality education in the schools. *The Educational Forum,* 64(4), 340-347.

Elia, J. P. (2000b). Democratic sexuality education: A departure from sexual ideologies and traditional schooling. *Journal of Sex Education and Therapy,* 25(2&3), 122-129.

Forster, E.M. *Maurice.* New York and London. W.W. Norton, 1971 (Originally published in 1914).

Goldman, Alan. "Plain Sex." In Alan Soble's (ed.) *The Philosophy of Sex: Contemporary Readings.* 2nd ed. Savage: Littlefield Adams Quality Paperbacks, 1991: 73-92.

Gray, John. *Men Are From Mars And Women Are From Venus.* New York: HarperCollins, 1992.

Hendrick, Susan and Hendrick, Clyde. *Liking, Loving, & Relating.* 2nd ed. Pacific Grove, CA: Brooks/Cole Publishers, 1992.

Loulan, JoAnn. *Lesbian Passion: Loving Ourselves and Each Other.* San Francisco: Spinsters/Aunt Lute, 1987.

Moulton, Janice. "Sexual Behavior: Another Position." In Alan Soble's (ed.) *The Philosophy of Sex: Contemporary Readings.* 2nd ed. Savage: Littlefield Adams Quality Paperbacks, 1991: 63-72.

Payer, Pierre J. *Sex and the Penitentials: The Development of Sexual Code, 550-1150.* Toronto: University of Toronto Press, 1984.

Scharff, David. *The Sexual Relationship.* Boston: Routledge & Kegan Paul, 1982.

Sexuality Education Council of the United States (SIECUS). "Position Statement 1990." *SIECUS Report* 4 (4), (1990): 10-12.

Webster's New Collegiate Dictionary. Springfield, MA: G. & C. Merriam Company, 1974.

Wharton, Edith. *Summer.* New York: Perennial Library/Harper & Row, 1979 (Originally published in 1918).

Part

Learning about Relationships

Relationships 101: Is a Classroom the Place to Learn About Love?

CHAPTER

Some College and High School Students Are Finding Out

Rebecca Winters

"O.K. now I'm going to show you how to complain," says Marline Pearson to a class of 15 unusually attentive college students. Pearson, a sociologist, is teaching a course called Couples Relationships at Madison Area Technical College in Madison, Wisconsin. When one of her students mentions that her boyfriend is always, like, falling asleep when they're supposed to do stuff, Pearson seizes what feels like a teachable moment. She suggests the student zero in on a specific time when her boyfriend dozed off and tell him how it made her feel. "Stay away from 'You always' and 'You never,'" she advises. "Even if you think the person does it always."

This new breed of romantic counseling—equal parts sex ed, social science and Dear Abby—is now being offered as formal courses at colleges and high schools across the country. Over two weekends, Pearson's students learn methods developed by researchers at the University of Denver and used for marital counseling in churches and in the military. They watch videos of fighting couples and discuss how conflicts can spiral out of control. They learn tidy formulas for success and failure in love: the three characteristics of successful couples (one is a man who can accept influence from a woman), the four behaviors that spell doom (constant criticism is a biggie). Each time Pearson rattles off a list of rules, her students start furiously taking notes, not because they'll be tested—they won't—but because they're truly dying to know.

"There's a great hunger for understanding relationships, not just body parts," says Sarah Brown, president of the National Campaign to Prevent Teen Pregnancy. "Young people tell us they're almost drowning in information about AIDS, condoms, pregnancy. But they want to know, 'How do I break up with my boyfriend without hurting his feelings?'" One recent study of college students' use of counseling services at Kansas State University showed that the percentage of students seeking help for relationship problems rose from 34% in 1989 to 60% in 2001. School counselors say courses like Pearson's—as well as more than half a dozen national relationship-curriculum programs in high schools—are filling a void. They offer healthy models of love for children of divorce and a middle ground in the wake of the culture wars that polarized sex education in the 1980s, with emotionless biology classes at one end and preachy abstinence lectures at the other.

Young love has always been traumatic. But the anxious, euphoric stage these programs address used to be a lot shorter. In 1960 the average age of first marriage was 20 for women, 23 for men; today, it's 25 for women, 27 for men. With dating starting at around 15, says David Popenoe of the National Marriage Project at Rutgers University, "now you have 10 or 15 years of figuring out what to do with the opposite sex when marriage isn't uppermost in your mind." It may take them longer to get there, but most high school seniors—65% of girls and 58% of boys, according to a University of Michigan study—still say it's "very likely" they will stay married to the same person for life, numbers that are up slightly from 15 years ago.

Of course there's no guarantee that taking a course will help teens and young adults achieve the kind of relationships they say they ultimately want. The last time the U.S. threw itself into teaching young people about love was in the 1950s, when social scientists at colleges offered marriage education. By the '60s, many of those classes were being laughed off campuses as rigid and sexist, or as faulty attempts to stamp the mysteries of emotion with the imprimatur of science. "There's always going to be this sense of the imponderables," says Beth Bailey, author of *From Front Porch to Back Seat: Courtship in 20th Century America.* "People fall in love. It's not something where you can go down a checklist and match people up by scientific formulas."

There are reasons to expect that this movement may be different, however. It's more flexible about the roles of men and women and, at least in some secular classes, it makes room for homosexual relationships. Each course is unique, but the emphasis today is more on developing communication skills and less on establishing moral absolutes. "If we have the right tools, then maybe we'll have a better shot of making our relationships work," says Rebecca Olson, 22, who took Pearson's course last winter with her boyfriend, Aaron Edge, 23, to help her avoid repeating the mistakes her divorced parents had made. Last month Olson and Edge got engaged.

Pearson has decided that teenagers need to get the message before they hit college. So she's publishing a curriculum for high school students. "All their experience tells these young people to be cynical," she says. "And yet part of their spirit says, 'I want it to be different for me.'" You don't have to be an incurable romantic to hope they succeed.

Part

Initiating a Relationship

Environment Plays a Large Part in Finding a Mate

CHAPTER 2

Hannah Lodwick

I've often wondered whether people have one true love or if any number of romantic partners will do as a potential mate. After considerable contemplation and observation, I've decided that, rather than individuals predestined to complement exactly one other person, soul mates develop over time, and they come from a pool of potentially ideal and initially equal suitors.

When I was young, I had the overly romanticized notion that each human has one person destined for his or her perfect match. I also disagreed with those who dated only one or two people from their hometown before marrying their high school sweetheart. It seemed those marriages came through default or convenience, not because of a once-in-a-lifetime connection.

While I felt content and even excited with the idea of living a single life for some time, I still hoped my future would eventually include a special other-someone. As "journeys end in lovers meeting," I thought fate would have to bring us together. After that, fireworks would explode, and I'd know I had met destiny, or so I thought.

These days, I realize the error of my ways. Environment plays a large part in forming values, beliefs, hobbies and even personality, so it stands to reason most people will have more in common with someone from the same country than with others. Commonalities usually translate into stronger relationships, so I generally eliminated the possibility that I should travel to India to meet my one perfect match. Environmental similarities do, however, open a select pool of people who share the same background. From that group, any number of people could work as a romantic partner.

Aside from the fact that most people marry someone who has lived relatively close to them, many personality types complement each other. This means any number of people could satisfactorily marry each other and live happy, fulfilled lives. That's where the soul mate stuff comes in—it appears after a prolonged relationship.

At the beginning of an association between people who share commonalities, the liaison can terminate at any time with little to no harm to either party. If, however, the affiliation continues for a significant time, each party grows increasingly closer to the other, and their lives intertwine, creating a near-irreversible association. This is best seen in couples who have been married many years—they have developed into each other's true love. Shakespeare put it best when he wrote, "So they lov'd as love in twain; Had the essence but in one; Two distinct, divisions none."

What a Girl (and Boy) Wants

3

CHAPTER

John Fetto and Rebecca Gardyn

Scoping the singles scene for the road rules of dating

When it comes to finding the perfect mate, there's a widely held belief that men and women are looking for completely different things. Not so, according to the findings of an exclusive Quick Query survey conducted for American Demographics by online market research firm Harris Interactive. In fact, when nearly 1,500 single men and women were asked to rate the characteristics they most desire in a partner, their final lists were a perfect match.

"Intelligence" beat out all other traits, as being an extremely or very important characteristic in a significant other, with 79 percent of total respondents in agreement. Next on everyone's list is "funny" (70 percent), "attractive" (34 percent), "athletic" (12 percent), and "wealthy" (6 percent). This hierarchy holds true across not only sex, but every other demographic segment, including age, income, level of education, race, and ethnicity.

Because what single Americans look for in a future mate is so uncannily similar, we consulted noted psychologist Dr. Joyce Brothers for her expert opinion. Is she surprised at the findings? "Not in the slightest," she says. While she admits that—island or no island—men and women are both prone to give in to temptations of the flesh, "it's that feeling of mutual intelligence that is most important for the long term." What she does find interesting is the fact that "wealth" scores so low among women. "Ten years ago—when it was more important for a woman to have money to bring up children—'wealthy' and 'attractive' might have switched places," says Dr. Brothers. "Now that women have status, they can look for attractiveness, just like men."

So now that we know what singles are looking for in a future mate, where do they look for their future date? According to our survey, which allowed for multiple answers, 65 percent of singles say they commonly meet potential dates through friends, co-workers, or family. Other notable venues for hooking up are: work (36 percent); school (27 percent); online (26 percent); and bars or coffee shops (26 percent). Fewer than 20 percent of all singles meet at church (or another place of worship), in line at the grocery store, at libraries or bookstores, or at the gym.

Not surprisingly, there is little difference across gender lines where singles meet—typically, where a man meets a woman, a woman also meets a man—yet there are some remarkable differences across other demographic groups. For instance, a significantly higher rate of blacks than whites meet other singles in church (28 percent vs. 16 percent), waiting in line (21 percent vs. 12 percent), and at the gym (13 percent vs. 4 percent). Those making a second go of it (divorced or widowed singles) are significantly more likely than singles who've never married to meet dates on the Internet (42 percent vs. 22 percent). But this group tends to shy away from romantic encounters at libraries and bookstores, where only 4 percent of them meet potential dates, compared with 12 percent of the never-marrieds.

When it comes to prepping and primping for a date, men and women have slightly different agendas. Dabbing a little eau de toilette behind the ear is more of a girl thing—76 percent do so, compared with 58 percent of men. Women are also significantly more likely than men to buy new clothes before a date (38 percent vs. 12 percent), put on special undergarments (33 percent vs. 13 percent), and clean their house or apartment (58 percent vs. 52 percent). As for the gents, 69 percent stop off at the bank or ATM for some extra cash prior to a date. But so do 54 percent of women (you can't make any assumptions these days). Forty-two percent of men wash their car, and 25 percent buy flowers or candy. If after all that the guy is still left waiting for his date, it could be because she's plotting an escape route: 22 percent of women develop a plan to get out of a bad date, compared with only 11 percent of men. Important differences also exist between racial and ethnic groups when it comes to getting ready for a date. For instance, Hispanics and blacks are considerably more likely than whites to buy new clothes, 35 percent and 43 percent, respectively, compared with 21 percent of whites. Hispanics are also more likely than whites to buy flowers or candy before a date (21 percent vs. 14 percent).

When it comes to who should call whom after a good first date, the etiquette jury is still out: 71 percent of women say they've no qualms about making the first call. But even those who decide to play coy won't have long to wait. The majority of guys (64 percent) say they'll call within a day, 29 percent will call two to three days afterward, and 2 percent will wait a full four days before calling. Still it's better (emotionally) to play it safe than sorry. As Dr. Brothers points out, "Many men who have no intention of calling say they will, thinking that's being polite. But if the woman really likes the man, that's the worst kind of torture."

Shall We?

Which of the following would you most prefer to do on a special date?			
	ALL	**MEN**	**WOMEN**
Eat at a nice restaurant	43%	46%	39%
Go to a concert, movie, theater	23%	21%	26%
Make dinner at home or go on a picnic	16%	18%	13%
Go to an amusement park, mini-golf, go-carts, or arcade	10%	6%	14%
Go to a bar or coffee shop	4%	4%	3%
Go watch a live sporting event	3%	2%	4%
Participate in a physical activity (hiking, tennis, biking, etc.)	3%	4%	1%

Source: Harris Interactive

Meet the Quirkyalones

Sam Hurwitt

Valentine's Day, San Francisco. There's a line of cop cars arriving outside the Bill Graham Civic Auditorium, where some kind of love rave is going on, and a line of gay couples outside City Hall waiting to be married. "I should find a girl here and get married, just on principle," Kaya Oakes says as we walk past. Problem is, she's already married. Kaya's musician husband was playing a gig that night, so she opted to leave the comfort of her Berkeley digs and head over to the Rickshaw, a new club on Fell Street off Van Ness, where we find a bustling crowd in full flirtation mode, chatting in clumps with drinks in hand and playing party games to break the ice. In one corner, a few guys and gals sit around a crafts table making valentines. It could be mistaken for a V-Day singles scene, except that these people are here to celebrate the fact that they don't need a romantic partner at all.

They call themselves quirkyalones, and this is their second annual bash—the International Quirkyalone Day Party—complete with an "Ask a Quirkyalone" advice booth, questionnaires to encourage socializing (call 'em QA Q&As), and cute theme drinks. The quirkytini, which involves currant vodka and Japanese plum wine, tastes like a pep rally. At the mic set up at the far end of the large main room, next to the crafts table, singer-songwriter Stephanie Bernstein starts in on a rambling song she wrote especially for the occasion—um, actually she'd intended to finish it in time for last year's event—about getting over your fairy-tale Prince Charmings and that "once-upon-a-time state of mind." Kaya, meanwhile, spots what was advertised as the "Alone-Time Table," but is actually swarming with people piled on each other's laps—"a mini-orgy," she calls it. A disproportionate number of these assembled hipsters are writers, at least according to the first of many guys who try to chat up Kaya, herself a 33-year-old poet, essayist, and writing instructor at UC Berkeley. To further illustrate the guy's point, one roving reporter we run into immediately launches in with the tough questions: "Is this just a meat market pretending not to be a meat market?"

"It's not even trying that hard!" her friend adds.

The contradiction isn't as marked as it appears. Just because these people don't "need" significant others doesn't mean they won't go for a little TLC. It's not that they aren't open to the potential of romance, nor even that they prefer being alone. What makes quirkyalones quirkyalone is that they refuse to be in relationships for the sake of being in relationships. They chafe at the perception that they're supposed to be with somebody in order to feel whole, and are unwilling to compromise their sense of self for anyone. Because of these exacting romantic standards, they may spend long stretches of time single, and that's fine with them, because they enjoy their own company, and that of friends.

"People still seem to get tripped up on the 'alone' part and think that we're loners or asocial recluses," says Sasha Cagen, the thirty-year-old Rhode Island native and Mission District denizen who coined the term that spawned this budding movement. "The whole concept is about resisting social obligation or formula, but it's not about inhibiting your own legitimate desires. Nothing in what I've put forward I feel is exclusive of domestic relationships."

Cagen first unleashed her idea with an essay titled "People Like Us: The Quirkyalones" in the inaugural issue of her independent magazine *To-Do List* in July 2000. In it she posited a whole separate class of singletons, true romantics who would not sacrifice a whit of their personalities or their standards simply for the sake of snagging a significant other. The quirkyalone movement is envisioned as an alternative to the spinster/old maid model of lifelong singledom—a response to the conventional message, to women especially, that a coupled state is the norm and that to be alone is to be lonely.

But in coming to terms with her own experience as a "deeply single" person, Cagen had little reason to believe she would start a revolution. To be sure, she played up the concept in her magazine, but it's so sporadically published—only three issues to date, and on extended hiatus because of lack of time and funds—that it seemed more than likely the idea would end there.

What's remarkable about the quirkyalone concept is how it has managed to spread, essentially through word of mouth, from the ephemeral pages of an underground national magazine with a circulation of 2,000 to Internet ubiquity. It certainly didn't hurt that Cagen's essay was reprinted in the September 2000 Utne Reader and on her magazine's Web site, which included an "Are You a Quirkyalone?" quiz. (Web junkies love personality quizzes.) Soon, sizable quirkyalone communities were springing up on popular Web sites, including LiveJournal.com and Bay Area-based Tribe.net, in addition to the more official forum at Quirkyalone.net.

The idea, in fact, spread as an online memo nine months before the essay was even published. "When I first finished a draft of the piece, I forwarded it to a friend of mine just for her to give me initial feedback," Cagen explains. "She sent it on to some of her friends without asking me, so then over the next few days I started to get e-mails back from people that I didn't know. It had taken on a life of its own already as an e-mail forward. And that's when I started to get those e-mails, like, 'Thank you, I thought I was the only one on the planet who felt this way.'"

It was through this overwhelming response from unexpected quarters that Cagen's sense of what it meant to be quirkyalone expanded from her own experience as a single, urban-dwelling woman in her twenties to encompass male and female quirkyalones, gay and straight, rural and suburban, teens and septuagenarians, innate "womb" quirkyalones and "born-again" converts, and even married quirkyalones, dubbed quirkytogethers. (Quirkytogether means different things to different people, but is best defined as a long-term relationship that caters to one's quirkyalone tendencies, whether that involves separate bedrooms or just the freedom to run off to pursue one's own projects.)

"The first roundtable discussion we had for the first issue of *To-Do List* was me and [senior editor] Annie Decker, and Lisa Jervis and Andi Zeisler from 'Bitch' magazine," Cagen recalls. "It was weird for me, because they were chiming in with their own thoughts about what it meant to be quirkyalone, and it was different than my exact experience, and I felt very protective of it then. I was like, 'No, you have to have had exactly this experience in junior high and high school, and only this many relationships and X amount of time single.' It was just totally personal at that point, and now I've learned that that's boring, because that would just be me, and it's been more interesting to let other people define it and hear what they have to say. The married people, the born-again people. I mean, it started off that there were only born quirkyalones, and then the born-again people were a total revelation to me because I really didn't anticipate them identifying."

Cagen originally conceived of the quirkyalone as an innate core identity, affecting an undercurrent of people who just didn't need what they were told to need. She speculated they make up about 5 percent of the population. "You know, it's too bad we can't put quirkyalone on the US census," she says a teensy bit defensively when asked whether she stands by that number today, and then confesses she came up with the figure by thinking about how many people she could relate to in high school.

It's an open question whether quirkyalones really represent a breed apart or simply an unusually healthy way of thinking about the relatively common situation of being single, but it was clear to Cagen that she'd touched a nerve with all sorts of people, and that quirkyalone was more than just an identity—it was a movement, one that would even hijack Valentine's Day, renaming it "International Quirkyalone Day."

So she started collecting people's experiences and broad discussions of what it means to be quirkyalone for a slim, lighthearted user manual issued by HarperSanFrancisco in January. It must be said that *Quirkyalone: A Manifesto for Uncompromising Romantics* is, well, a quirky book, full of checklists, photo-booth strips, cute illustrations, more lists, profiles, quotations, affirmations, sections on self-matrimony and romantic obsession, homemade pie charts, still more lists, great quirkyalones in history, and some relevant Cagen juvenilia. But considering how far the idea has already spread, the book is liable to add more fuel to the fire rather than be the last word on the subject.

One person drawn to that fire was 38-year-old Megan Lynch, who read an article about the movement and later joined the quirkyalone "tribe" on Tribe.net, the SF-based networking site that combines Friendster-like profiles and Craigslist-like listings with interest-related message boards. A quirkyalone community may sound like a contradiction, but Cagen emphasizes the importance of finding your own urban tribe of like-minded souls—"significant others, plural," she calls them. Besides, it's not as though you actually meet anyone in these online communities; you merely swap ideas and experiences from the safety of your keyboard.

Megan got involved not because she thought she necessarily fit the profile, but because she felt she had something to learn from it. "I'm actually someone who was very much raised with the 'You're nobody till somebody loves you' thing," she says over corned beef and cabbage at the Starry Plough, a Berkeley pub where her friend is Irish dancing that night. "This is the reason I joined the tribe—lately I've been trying to fight my own tendencies to look for fulfillment from somebody else.

"It's not like I have ultimate power over that," she admits, "but I have a lot more power over changing that than I think I do. So for me, subscribing to that tribe was a way to get a window into people who naturally feel that self-sufficient and see what their secret is."

The Berkeley-based singer, who goes by Spidra Webster online, has long dark hair and a natural intensity that commands attention—"I'm the eldest of fifteen kids, so I'm used to jockeying for attention," she explains—and is at once amiable and reserved. She speaks slowly and deliberately.

"I think part of it is tapping into this real need that people either have to get an echo for something they already strongly believe is right—and they're looking for their tribe, so to speak—or people like me who fight with intellectually knowing that it's true but maybe in their hearts still having trouble feeling confident about that," Megan says. "Because some of the social 'shoulds' are not keeping pace with what society's actually becoming like. There are, I gather, more people like me who are staying single and childless later in life. However, the way society approaches us, pressure-wise, is still very much like my parents' generation, where you're getting married in your twenties and having kids, finding your fulfillment in this perfect partnership.

"I think people are looking for some validation," she continues. "And I think somebody giving a word to it, whether or not that concept perfectly covers the way they feel about it or not, gives them something to hold onto and go, 'Yeah, I knew I couldn't be the only one.'"

Cagen, too, emphasizes the importance of just putting the word out there, though she is uneasy with the suggestion that words such as "movement" and "manifesto" might lead people to interpret quirkyalone as something that can be learned, as opposed to a state of existence. "The first intention was just to name this way of being and to point out there's this whole huge population out there in the United States and even beyond that has never been identified before," she says. "And to name something is powerful, because it starts a conversation that hadn't existed before. So that was the starting-off point, to gather the troops—well, not the troops, but the people who are already out there. I never had any intention of trying to convert people, but maybe that is the natural leaning of a movement and a manifesto, because ideas spread outward. I was talking to someone recently who figured out that it is a new idea that hasn't been put forward previously, and it brings forward all these positive qualities about being alone and being choosy and selective and self-determining."

Cagen is hardly the only person not entirely comfortable with the idea of quirkyalone as a movement, at least judging from the Tribe.net quirkyalones, who numbered 134 at the time of writing. (The LiveJournal quirkyalone forum is larger still with 202 members, many of them teenagers, but despite the inherent exhibitionism of online journals, or perhaps because of it, the journalers did not respond to interview requests.) Melissa Kirk is a 33-year-old Berkeley native who works as an acquisitions editor for a local publisher and is active in the quirkyalone tribe under the Web moniker Honey B. Sitting at Berkeley's Espresso Roma one week before the party, she is quiet and a bit shy, uneasy with the thought of being some kind of poster girl for quirkyaloneness.

"The funny thing about that tribe is they're really iconoclasts or something," she says. "The discussion is a lot about 'Why this movement? I don't want it to be a movement. I just want to be myself.' It's funny because they're all disassociating themselves. They don't want to be part of the hip scene or whatever—they just want a concept that they like but not Sasha's groundswell of attention. I can see that; I feel like that a little bit. But I also feel that anything that makes it more acceptable to be a single woman who's not dating for the sake of having a boyfriend—I'm glad the concept is getting out there."

She flashes a brief, conspiratorial smile. "There are lots of people who want to do their work and not worry about if they're not gonna have a date on Friday night," she says. "It's not really that abnormal, it's just not okay."

Melissa is an old-school quirkyalone, one who read the original essay in *To-Do List* and promptly hopped aboard. "It just struck me as being a really cool thing," she recalls. "I always felt that way anyway, that I don't really want the same things about a relationship that other people I know do—get married and have kids and blah de blah. If I meet somebody cool that'd be good, but I'm not going to sit around and worry about it." She actually has a cameo in the book, in one of the many questionnaire profiles scattered throughout, although she doesn't make it much of a point of pride. "I feel like such a goober. I'm really not this groupie person, you know. I just filled out their little questionnaire on a whim because I saw it on Craigslist. I wasn't like, 'Oh, I really want to have my picture in this crazy book!'"

But at the party the following week, Melissa is in top form, decked out in an evening gown and long white gloves. "I'm having fun," she says. "Everyone's really friendly. Usually I'm the one at parties nobody wants to talk to. I didn't think I'd stay so long." She rushes off to mingle some more.

Kaya, on the other hand, is being mingled way too much. Despite clearly being a quirkytogether—she's wearing her wedding ring, although she'd fretted beforehand about whether it would seem insensitive—she keeps running across guys who are here because they heard there would be a lot of single women, and who are looking to get quirkylaid tonight.

In truth, there's nothing verboten about quirkyalones having a casual hookup: Cagen even created the term "quirkyslut"—someone "who maintains high standards for a romantic relationship but becomes more flexible for the Saturday or even Tuesday night encounter"—and says it's not uncommon for a respectable quirkyalone to turn quirkyslut every now and again. At this party everyone is given nametags on which they're to indicate if they're quirkyalone, quirkytogether, quirkyslut, or "in support of quirkyalones," which would perhaps facilitate prowling.

Versions of this very party are taking place in at least a dozen cities tonight—London, Seattle, St. Paul, and Madison, Wisconsin, to name a few. The San Francisco bash is getting increasingly crowded as the night wears on—Cagen later reports that there were more than 350 revelers. "It seems like it's about 50/50 men and women," Kaya estimates during the party. "I had a feeling it'd be all women."

There's no question quirkyalone is a ladies-first philosophy. It's perfectly possible for men to be quirkyalone, but the movement isn't targeted at them precisely because it's always been okay for men not to wrap up their self-worth in a relationship. In Quirkyalone, Cagen writes, "Our culture is already rife with archetypes for male loners: Odysseus, Western cowboy, geek, James Dean, solitary indie-rock boy, and so forth. The scant few labels that describe a woman alone are pejorative: spinster and old maid."

That it is even economically possible for a woman to live alone is a very new thing in this country, and by no means the norm elsewhere in the world. But as both Megan and Melissa point out, prevailing social attitudes haven't really caught up with this reality, and are still rooted in the sense that a woman is supposed to go from the safety of her family to the care of her husband with as little time in between as possible.

"The fact that women entered the workforce in the last fifty years is changing our ideas about how relationships are structured, or what being single is like, in ways we don't even understand yet," Cagen later agrees. "We can be more romantic in our relationships because women have financial independence. And I think it's a positive thing to name that choosiness that hasn't been available to previous generations because the stigmas were so unbearable. Most women, at least middle-class women, were trapped in marriage. We're going through a social revolution, and all of this is new."

But even as some things change, others never do. Though the quirkyalone aspect gives the IQA Day party a fun, casual air as singles scenes go, there's the usual contingent of pretty people posing to be seen, and at least some seemingly creepy older guys on the prowl. A gal named Kate, who appears to be in her mid-twenties, has the name "Christina Ricci" pinned to her back. She says she's supposed to ask people questions to find out who she is, but it turns out she doesn't really watch movies or TV so she's at a distinct disadvantage. Even when she figures out who she's supposed to be, she hasn't the slightest idea what her name is. An older bearded guy named Dave walks up and joins the conversation. "I think they assign us people we look like," he says, turning around to show us "Janet Reno" on his back. He has a point. Kate does resemble Ricci around the eyes. At first he seems like one of the aforementioned creepy guys, but then it turns out he was at last year's party and knows what this is all about, unlike Kate, whose roommate told her about it just today. "I think this idea is really going to take off," Dave says with enthusiasm. Then, as soon as Kate wanders off, he turns to Kaya and asks with great urgency, "Did she come with you?"

At Cafe Macondo in the Mission a few days after the party, Cagen conducts a post-mortem. "Yeah, there were a lot of people who knew about quirkyalone and already had the book and were really excited and came up to me and that kind of thing," she says. "And then I think there were a number of people there who really didn't know anything much about quirkyalone at all and had just heard that it would be a singles party on February 14. And not to stereotype a single group, but it seemed to me there were a number of older men that were maybe more in that category. I did hear of one hookup, which was different from last year—I didn't have any hookups last year."

Cagen is friendly, with an easy laugh and a slight interrogative lilt, as though checking to make sure she is being understood. She has chin-length blonde hair and a loose black sweater, and is wielding a blue backpack and a paper cup of coffee she brought in with her. She has been run ragged lately promoting the book and shoehorning five interviews a day around her job as a proofreader. A few weeks ago she sounded pretty much at the end of her rope, but now she is more relaxed.

Even now, the crown doesn't always rest easy on the queen bee of the quirkyalones. The trouble with writing about relationships, even in a playful or breezy way, Cagen says, is that people expect her to be more of an authority on the subject than she really is. "A lot of people ask me for advice at these readings, like, 'Well, I'm in my fifties, and what do I do if most of my friends are married now?'" she says. "And I'm like, well, maybe make new friends? Find some other quirkyalones or quirkytogethers? It's so hard for me to say, because I am not a self-help guru. I don't want to write an advice column; that's not who I am. I wrote an essay, it struck a nerve, and then I brought these stories together. People want advice, they want a sort of pronouncement on whether they're quirkyalone or not, and that's hard for me to give, and it's not really my job to do that anyway."

Her job, as she sees it, is to write personal essays. "You know, I write from my experience," Cagen says. "I'm not a sociologist; I'm not even a journalist. I compiled everyone's stories as much as I could into this book. The reason for the book was the phenomenal response. It wasn't because it was my plan to write one. But ultimately I have to do things through the prism of my experience because that's the way that I write, that's how my best writing comes about."

Her experience may dictate her writing, but she'll be damned if she'll let her writing dictate her experience. "The main thing is, I don't know what most of these people expect in terms of me being single forever, but I don't think that is my responsibility in any way," she says. "There has to be a separation between the private and the public in this instance. It's not unquirkyalone to want to meet someone or to fall in love or even to get married if that's what you want to do. Not that getting married is my priority, but there's no quid pro quo with me being single, and there shouldn't be."

The trouble with coining a new word doesn't stop with people expecting its inventor to embody their misinterpretations of its meaning. People latch onto these terms, but in a much more simplistic way than Cagen would like. "Another thing that's sort of frustrating is that now it gets cast as like a fad," the writer says, "like this year's metrosexual or something. Which is not really what it is because I don't think metrosexuals set up online groups to talk about being metrosexual; there's no metrosexual philosophy. It's not a complicated term. Quirkyalone is very hard to sum up in one sentence in a way that I think metrosexual is not."

If the quirkyalone ideal could be summed up in one person, it might be Rebecca Lippert, who goes by SugarBunni on Tribe.net and is an active member of the quirkyalone forum and scores of others. She is as close to the ideal of a happy, highly social, self-fulfilled quirkyalone as a person could ask for. A 28-year-old performance artist with a shock of pink hair on an otherwise shaved head—a recent development—Rebecca exudes confidence and a strong sense of self, and is about as far from shy and retiring as is humanly possible. She performs in a women's wrestling troupe and creates conceptual fashion shows that always involve nudity of some sort. As for her alone time, she doesn't really know what the big deal is.

"I find it interesting that there's been so much written about the quirkyalone thing, because I can't comprehend what's to write about other than some people like to be alone and are okay with it," she says, hanging around at the Starry Plough the night after Megan's interview. Rebecca, too, had a friend performing—at an open mic in this case—so our conversation is punctuated by hoots and hollers, the occasional electric act, and insistent requests for "Rubber Ducky." To the various truisms and affirmations in Cagen's book ("Quirkyalones have vibrators." "We are sociable people.") we can now add this one: Quirkyalones like the Starry Plough.

Rebecca's quirkyalone identity is so innate, in fact, that she has little time for the concept. "Maybe there are people who take it very seriously and really identify with it, but for me it's just like another word," she says. "'Movement' to me implies it's going somewhere, and I guess in some regards it could branch out and encompass other people and teach other people it's okay to be alone. But I can't see this quirkyalone movement taking me anywhere, because we just all like to be alone and that's okay. I mean, okay, best-case scenario, I meet another quirkyalone and get married! Hahahahaha, I'm joking. And have babies!"

She actually yells this last part, she finds it so hilarious.

"I think I like it better just as this little floating concept than a whole movement," she says. "I'm putting it in a word category with weirdo. Weirdo is a word I identify with very much. Am I going to start a weirdo community and weirdo support group? No. You know if you're a weirdo or not—you just are. And I think you know if you're a quirkyalone or not—you just are."

Rebecca speculates on what the Quirkyalone Day party will be like: "Are these alone communities full of extroverts who also like being alone, like me?" she wonders. "I can't imagine the introverts really bothering with coming out for something. It will be interesting, especially given the whole Valentine's Day-ness. Like if it turns into some weird meat market, I'm gonna have to bust heads."

No heads got busted, if only because Rebecca wound up missing the Quirkyalone Day bash. She'd planned to drop by the party early in the evening—mostly because she wanted to meet Honey B.—and then head over to a circus act and DJ night elsewhere, but ended up helping with a Valentine's Day party in her building instead, even though she usually shrugs off the holiday as "invented bullshit."

And so, to the list of truisms, we can perhaps add this one as well: A truly self-realized quirkyalone need have no fear of traditional Hallmark holidays.

Are You a Quirkyalone?

This simple personality test, courtesy of Quirkyalone.net, is designed to help determine whether you are quirky, alone, quirkyalone, or possibly even normal! Keep score, then see results at the bottom of the quiz.

1. Do you like walking (alone) at night?
   A. Yes, I'm fascinated by the interactions between strangers. (10)
   B. I think of walking alone in utilitarian terms: It's a matter of getting from A to B. (5)
   C. Long walks alone at night don't appeal to me. They seem dangerous and/or boring. (2)

2. Has anyone ever called you quirky?
   A. Yes, people often do. (10)
   B. Once or twice. (6)
   C. No. (0)

3. Which do you have more of, numerically speaking?
   A. Past boy/girlfriends. (0)
   B. Current amigos. (10)

4. Did you go to your senior prom?
   A. Yes. I went in with a date. (0)
   B. Yes. I went alone/with friends. (10)
   C. No. No prom for me. (10)

5. How often do you pursue extracurricular activities?
   A. I write, draw, organize, throw pottery, sing, or cycle a few times a week. (10)
   B. I take classes every so often. (6)
   C. Not so much these days. (2)

6. What kind of movie would you most like to see?

   A. Romantic comedy. (6)
   B. Indie movie about a fucked-up family. (10)
   C. Action thriller. (4)

7. What is your chosen family?

   A. Friends. (10)
   B. Significant other. (2)
   C. Pets. (8)

8. Would you rather be lonely alone or lonely together?

   A. Lonely alone. (10)
   B. Lonely together. (0)

9. Would you rather have a predictable vibrator or an inconsistent partner? (Assume you are a woman.)

   A. Vibrators are a woman's best friend. Vibrator, please. (10)
   B. Inconsistent partner. I prefer the human touch—even if he/she isn't that dextrous. (0)

10. Have you ever gone to a movie alone?

    A. Never. (0)
    B. No, but I would try. (5)
    C. A few times. (8)
    D. More than a few times. (10)

11. What is the longest you have gone without a significant other?

    A. 1 - 3 months. (0)
    B. 4 - 8 months. (5)
    C. 8 months - 2 years. (5)
    D. Two years plus. (10)

12. When you go to a bar to meet somebody, whom are you looking for?

    A. A nice person to talk to. (5)
    B. Your next boy/girlfriend. (5)
    C. A certain feeling of possibility. (10)

13. You spot a perfect J.Crew couple holding hands. What do you feel?
    A. Nothing. (5)
    B. That's nice. (0)
    C. It must be so easy for you. (10)

Quiz Results Score

YOUR QUIRKY STATUS

(15-39) **Not quirkyalone:** And that's okay. Just remember that coupledom and quirkyalonedom are equally complicated states of being; don't let society lull you into that smug, superior attitude that gives some normals a bad name.

(40-85) **Somewhat quirkyalone (otherwise known as quirkytogether):** You are probably part of a mysterious group of people, the quirkytogethers. You share many of our quirky qualities, but you manage to find yourself, on a regular basis, in a coupled situation. Interesting.

(86-129) **Very quirkyalone:** Relatives may give you quizzical looks, and so may friends, but you know in your heart of hearts that you are following your inner voice. Though you may not be romancing a single person, you are romancing the world.

(130) **Loner:** Hang yourself!

Office Romances

Tim Moynihan and Alan Jones

Most people have had a romantic relationship with a colleague and half of those admitted it had affected their work, a new survey revealed today.

Three out of five people (61%) admit to having had a romantic relationship at work.

In a third of cases (32%), one or both of the partners was already married.

In almost half of the relationships (46%), one partner was more senior than the other, and in 51% of cases, both partners were part of the same team or department.

Three in 10 people have enjoyed physical intimacy in their workplace, with the favourite spots being lift or stairwell (8%) and work stations (8%).

Half admit that the relationship had an impact on their work, with one in 10 moving teams or departments and a similar proportion leaving the organization of their own accord as a result.

Three in five people believe workplace romances are a perfectly normal part of working life.

Seven in 10 believe organizations should leave it up to the individual to decide.

The leisure and tourism industry is a hotbed for workplace romance, with eight in 10 having had a relationship at work.

Healthcaremedical workers are the least likely to have relationships at work.

Four in 10 respondents describe the relationship they had as lasting more than three months, with flings (17%) and one night stands (14%) being less common.

Secrecy is the norm with only one third of workplace relationships being completely open.

Two thirds of people (66%) would 'keep quiet and leave them to it' if they discovered two colleagues were having a relationship.

Almost 30% would not be able to resist telling one or two people.

Men are twice as likely to gossip about workplace relationships as women.

The vast majority of workers are very unlikely to tell managers or the HR department about a colleague or colleagues' relationship.

But they would be two thirds more likely to do so if they believed the relationship was affecting the lovers' or their team's work.

The findings were from a poll of 1,000 workers for employment law advisers Human and Legal Resources.

Mind May Make Net Pal Too Perfect

Sue Vorenberg

E-mail romantics, beware: You might see more in your partner than is really there.

Scientists at the University of Central Florida have studied how people perceive each other when their only communication is through e-mail or in chat rooms.

They found that people often put their online partner above themselves, said Michael Rabby, a communication professor who conducted the study.

"What we found was that people tended to rate their partner with more socially desirable characteristics than they gave themselves," Rabby said. "They said of their partners that they practice what they preach, they go out of their way to help people, are always courteous."

Rabby and his graduate student, Amanda Coho, will present their findings Monday in Albuquerque at the Western States Communication Association annual conference.

Rabby and Coho have studied three groups of students so far, making them talk to each other only online for three weeks. After the three weeks, they had to write a biography of their partner and fill out forms about their impressions of them.

"Why do they rate their online partners so highly?," Rabby asked. "We're not sure. It could be because the partners don't know each other well, and we tend to give people the benefit of the doubt and we're harder on ourselves. The other thing it may be is that it's an attribute of computer communication."

Another thing the researchers found is that with little information to go on, people tend to assume that their partners are similar to them, Coho said.

"They may think, 'Well, I don't know exactly how they are, but I'm a nice person so they must be a nice person, too,'" she said.

It might sound frivolous, but this type of information could actually help businesses better target their communications to customers or employees. It could also help online chatters and daters learn whether they should trust each other, Rabby said.

"In business I think we'd like to know what statements seem most genuine," Rabby said. "I think the next stage of all this will be to look at specific statements and see what made people believe certain things about their partners."

One hint: If you're trying to impress your online honey, don't reply to their e-mails immediately, he added.

"Connected to this, I have a friend who's dating online, and we're looking at the pattern of how time is communicated," Rabby said. "If I respond quickly to e-mail, my partner might think I'm just hanging out on the computer and that I don't have a life."

So should you even bother with online dating? Yes, but keep your eyes and finger open, Rabby and Coho advise.

"I'd call it a buyer beware," Rabby said. "It's becoming much more common to meet people online, and the success rates are growing. Through that medium it's a lot easier to transmit good parts of one's self. It's a lot easier to focus on the good than the bad online because it's much easier to control information."

Getting to know somebody online first can be a fine thing, but there's still a long way to go from that to a real relationship, Coho added.

"I don't know that you can ever truly know somebody by just typing messages to them," Coho said. "Personally I've met a lot of people online including my boyfriend. I guess you just have to look at what kind of details people are willing to give you. Will they give you personal details or will they give you vague impressions? Instincts usually are a good guide even in the online environment."

Understanding how technology is changing society is a major undertaking. But it could be critical in learning how to find a balance in people's lives, Rabby added.

"The technology pulls us apart, but it can also bring us together and make things more personal," he added.

Mating Strategies of Young Women

7 CHAPTER

Devendra Singh

One of the most robust and reliable findings in the scientific literature on interpersonal attraction is the overwhelming role played by physical attractiveness in defining the ideal romantic partner (Hatfield & Sprecher, 1986; Jackson, 1992). Both men and women express marked preference for an attractive partner in a noncommitted short-term (casual, one night stand) relationship (Buss & Schmitt, 1993). For committed long-term relationships, females appear to be willing to relax their demand for a partner's attractiveness, especially for males with high social status or good financial prospects (for a review see Buss, 1999). Males also look for various personality qualities (kindness, understanding, good parental skills) in their search for long-term mating partners, but unlike females, they assign disproportionately greater importance to attractiveness compared to other personal qualities (Buss, 1999). The paramount importance of attractiveness in males' mate choices has been recently demonstrated by using the distinction between necessities (i.e., essential needs, such as food and shelter) and luxuries (i.e., objects that are sought after essential needs have been satisfied, such as a yacht or expensive car) made by economists. Using this method, Li, Bailey, Kenrick, and Linsenmeier (2002) reported that males treat female attractiveness as a necessity in romantic relationships; given a limited "mating budget," males allocate the largest proportion of their budget to physical attractiveness rather than to other attributes such as an exciting personality, liveliness, and sense of humor.

Why do males assign so much importance to attractiveness that when constrained (limited mating budget), they ignore personal attributes that appear to be critical for the viability of a long-term romantic relationship? Many desirable personal qualities may be reliably linked to and covary with attractiveness. If so, attending to attractiveness would provide sufficient information, thereby rendering additional information about the personal qualities redundant. Consider the stereotype "what is beautiful is good" (Dion, Bersheid, & Walster, 1972). Social theorists propose that the belief that attractive people are socially skilled and popular (based on media portrayals and/or cultural myths) shapes the reactions and behaviors of other people towards them, inducing attractive people to internalize stereotypic qualities in their self-concept and behave accordingly (Cooley, 1990 Darley & Fazio, 1980). Indeed, the review of the literature on the stereotype reveals that attractive people are more popular with the opposite sex, less lonely, less socially anxious, and more socially skilled than less-attractive people (for a meta-analytic review, see Feingold, 1992; Langlois et al., 2000).

A major drawback of explanations based on social theories is that they do not specify why people in diverse societies assign great importance to attractiveness in the first place. What is so unique about physical attractiveness that people develop a positive impression of people possessing attractiveness? Evolution-based theories of human mating propose that physical attractiveness reliably signals genotypic and phenotypic qualities and viability of an individual (Buss, 1999; Thornhill & Gangestad, 1993). In the case of females, attractiveness can also act as a cue for fertility and reproductive potential. Therefore, female attractiveness at a glance provides a multitude of information essential for a male's reproductive success (Buss, 1999; Singh, 2000, 2002; Symons, 1979). Because attractiveness signals attributes that are crucial for reproductive success, attractive people are pursued by many as potential mates, inculcating and reinforcing their beliefs about their greater desirability compared to unattractive people. The possession of highly sought-after traits would allow attractive people to be choosy, demanding, and less compromising in relationships, as well as to seek extra-pair relationships and to readily replace mates. If attractive people exhibit such behaviors more often than unattractive people, the attractiveness stereotype would contain such characterizations.

There is, indeed, some data to support this reasoning. Consider the "darker side of beauty" that was first reported by Dermer and Thiel (1975). These investigators found that both male and female participants assigned many positive attributes such as poised, interesting, sincere, etc., to facial photographs of attractive women as would be expected on the basis of the "what is attractive is good" stereotype, but also assigned many negative attributes such as status-seeking, snobbish, likely to request divorce, and prone to extra-marital affairs. Ashmore, Solomon, and Longo (1996) reported similar findings using full body photographs: Attractive women were perceived to be vain, dishonest, less moral, to have a lack of concern for others, and to be more sexually provocative than less-attractive females. Such a cluster of negative attributes or a "darker side" of the attractiveness stereotype is difficult to explain on the basis of social theories of stereotype formation, which suggest that attractive women internalize such attributes based on other people's expectations and behave accordingly. People typically deny the existence of negative attributes in themselves to maintain a positive self-image; there is no reason to believe that attractive females would not want to do likewise.

An alternative explanation would be that attractive females do, at least occasionally, engage in behaviors that are not held in high regard, thereby giving the "darker side of beauty" some basis in truth (e.g., Alley & Hildebrandt, 1988). Attractive females, compared to unattractive females, would be pursued by a greater number of males and thus have greater opportunity for courtship with different males. They would also have a greater ability to replace a mate if he failed to live up to expectations or if their personal needs or situations changed, and if needed they would have greater opportunities to engage in extra-marital relationships. Indeed, a meta-analysis of studies in attractiveness and behavior revealed that attractive females date more frequently, have more sexually permissive attitudes, engage in a greater variety of sexual activity, and have sexual intercourse at an earlier age than do unattractive females (Feingold, 1992). Some studies have also reported a positive relationship between physical attractiveness and number of sexual partners (Mikach & Bailey, 1999; Stelzer, Desmond, & Price, 1987; Wiederman & Hurst, 1998).

All these findings, however, are based on U.S. population samples, and it could be that they merely document a culture-specific phenomenon. If the "darker side" of the attractiveness stereotype is truly reflective of attractiveness-mediated sexual attitudes and behaviors, this stereotype should be evident in other cultures as well. In this paper, I present evidence indicating that men and women from diverse societies (Azore Island, Guinea-Bissau, Indonesia, and the U.S.) judge attractive female figures to be interesting, intelligent, and desirable companions but not very faithful. This cross-culture stereotype consensus suggests that the "darker side" of the attractiveness stereotype may be based on a kernel of truth. It could be that attractive women in various cultures engage in some behaviors which lead to the perception of not being very faithful. To explore this possibility, I examined some mate attraction tactics used by females differing in attractiveness. Data from young U.S. females show that compared to less-attractive females, attractive females report higher frequencies of using attractiveness enhancement tactics (e.g., wearing makeup), flirting with other males to make a date jealous, and acting possessively. These findings, taken together, suggest that the "darker side" of the attractiveness stereotype may be partly due to the types of mating strategies chosen by females differing in attractiveness.

Study 1: Cross-Cultural Evidence for the "Darker Side" of the Attractiveness Stereotype

The assumption of evolution-based mate selection theories is that female attractiveness reliably signals health, reproductive age, and fertility and mandates that males, across cultures, should assign a great deal of importance to attractiveness for selecting mating partners to ensure their reproductive success. Additionally, judgments about what is beautiful should not vary substantially across cultures; bodily features that are indicators of health, reproductive age, and fertility should be judged as attractive cross-culturally. There are empirical data supporting both of these expectations. Buss (1989), based on a large cross-cultural study conducted in 37 cultures on six continents and five islands, found that female attractiveness or "good looks" was rated very high for mate choice in all the cultures. A cross-cultural study by Cunningham, Roberts, Wu, Barbee, and Druen (1995) found a highly significant consensus in attractiveness judgments for facial photographs of Asian, Hispanic, Black, and White women. A recent meta-analytic study revealed exceptionally high consensus across ethnicities and cultures for judgments of attractiveness (Langlois et al., 2000). Female facial features such as a thinner jaw, short distance between mouth and chin, and fullness of lips are reliable indicators of youthfulness and hormonal status (Fink & Penton-Voak, 2002; Johnston & Franklin, 1993). It could be that cross-cultural consensus in attractiveness judgments is due to people using these features to arrive at such judgment.

Like faces, body size and body shape affect attractiveness judgments and are reliable indicators of female hormone profile, reproductive age, fecundity, and risk for major disease (Bjorntorp, 1997; Kissebah & Krakower, 1994). Body size is typically described as thin, normal, or overweight, and in the majority of epidemiological studies, body mass index (BMI) is used for body size classification (Seidell & Flegal, 1997). BMI is calculated by dividing body weight (kg) by height (m) squared. The World Health Organization (WHO) defines people with 18.5 or below BMI as underweight, 18.5 to 24.9 as normal weight, 25 to 29.9 as overweight, and 30 or greater as obese (Seidell & Flegal, 1997). As BMI is based on overall body weight and height, knowledge that a person has a BMI of 19 cannot be used to figure out the age (prepubertal, reproductive, or postmenopausal) or even the sex of the person.

The body shape differences between the sexes are largely determined by the nature of fat distribution or the anatomical location of fat deposit. The anatomical location of body fat is regulated by sex hormone levels, and change in production in sex hormones induces sexual dimorphism in body shape as well as age-related (prepubertal, reproductive, menopausal) changes in female body shape. Simply stated, estrogen facilitates fat deposits on lower body parts (hips, buttocks, and thighs) and inhibits fat deposits on upper body parts (stomach, shoulders, nape of the neck), thus creating a "pear-shaped" body. Testosterone, on the other hand, inhibits fat deposits on lower body parts and facilitates fat deposits on upper body parts, creating an "apple-shaped" body (Bjorntorp, 1987, 1991; Rebuffe-Scrive, 1987). At puberty, an increase in sex hormones promotes differential fat deposits and gives rise to sex-specific body shapes: Females develop pear-shaped and males apple-shaped bodies.

One commonly used method for quantifying differences in body fat distribution is to measure and compute the ratio of the waist circumference to the hip circumference (WHR). WHR has a bimodal distribution with relatively little overlap between the sexes. The range of WHR for healthy premenopausal Caucasian women is .67 to .80 and in the range of .85 to .95 for healthy Caucasian men (Jones, Hunt, Brown, & Norgan, 1986 Marti et al., 1991). Women typically maintain a lower WHR than men throughout adulthood, although after menopause, WHR approaches the masculine range due to the reduction of estrogen levels (Kirschner & Samojlik, 1991). The link between the size of WHR and estrogen levels is clearly demonstrated in women undergoing treatment for polycystic ovarian disorder (PCO), which is marked by impaired estrogen production. When these women are administered an estrogen-progestagen compound, their WHRs (which are higher than nonpatients) become lower overtime in absence of any reduction of their BMIs (Pasquali et al., 1999). WHR, independent of BMI, is also negatively correlated with ease of becoming pregnant in artificial insemination (Zaadstra et al., 1993) and in-vitro fertilization-embryo transfer programs (Waas, Waldenstrom, Rossner, & Hellberg, 1997). Thus, unlike body size or BMI, WHR systematically covaries with female sex hormone profile and fertility.

It should be stressed, however, that BMI and WHR are positively correlated and BMI does affect the size of WHR, especially in instances of very low and high BMI. For example, low BMI leads to typical gynoid patterns of fat distribution (low WHR), whereas high BMI results in android patterns of fat distribution (high WHR) in women (Kirchengast et al., 1998). It is, therefore, common practice in clinical research to measure both BMI and WHR if the subject population represents a wide range of BMI. For accurately evaluating the role of WHR, BMI is divided into lower, middle, and upper terciles and the relative contribution of BMI and WHR is examined within each tercile (Lev-Ran, 2001). For drawing any valid conclusion about the role of body weight and body shape on health or fertility, interaction between WHR and BMI is critical.

The interaction between body weight and body shape is also evident in judgment of female attractiveness. In the initial study on the relationship between female attractiveness and WHR, line drawings of female figures with four sizes of WHRs (0.7, 0.8, 0.9, and 1.0) were developed and were depicted within three levels of body weight (underweight, normal, and overweight). Since all figures were drawn to show identical height, these three levels of body weight represented three levels of BMI (Singh 1993a, 1993b). As there was a significant interaction between WHR and body weight, the relationship between WHR and attractiveness ratings was computed with each of the three body weight or BMI levels. Results show that the female figure with 0.7 WHR in the normal weight range was judged to be more attractive than other figures. However, the overweight female figure with 0.7 WHR was not judged to be attractive. Thus, the inverse relationship between WHR and attractiveness was strongest for normal weight figures followed by underweight figures and absent in overweight figures. These findings were clearly stated in the original research: "Neither body weight [BMI] nor WHR alone can explain attractiveness. To be attractive, women must have a low WHR and deviate little from normal weight" (Singh, 1993b).

Recently, Tovee and his colleagues (Tovee, Maisey, Emery, & Cornelissen, 1999; Tovee, Reinhardt, Emery, & Cornelissen, 1998), ignoring this interaction between BMI and WHR, have reported that BMI explains significantly more variance of attractiveness data than WHR. If BMI is treated as an independent variable and a wide range of BMI is used (emaciated BMI of 15 to obese BMI of 30), BMI would indeed account for far greater variance than WHR or any reported indicator of attractiveness such as facial symmetry, small chin, or full lips. It is more important to identify indicators of attractiveness and their adaptive significance than to demonstrate that some variables such as age (using 10- to 80-year-old range) or obesity account for more variance than, for example, fluctuating asymmetry does.

The original finding that normal weight female figures are judged to be more attractive than figures with higher WHRs has been replicated with Australian (Connolly, Mealey, & Slaughter, 2000), British (Furnham, Tan, & McManus, 1997), German (Henss, 1995), Indonesian (Singh & Luis, 1995), and Kenyan (Furnham, Moutafi, & Baguma, 2002) participants. Similar findings have been reported when digitally altered photographs of attractive women instead of line drawings are used (Henss, 2000; Singh, 1994; Streeter & McBurney, 2003).[1] On the basis of these cross-cultural findings, I hypothesized that people from non-Western societies will also judge normal weight figures with low WHR as most attractive and share attractiveness stereotypes as reported for U.S. participants.

METHOD

Participants. Participants came from two cultural groups with minimal exposure to commercial television. The first group of participants (males n = 46 females n = 32 age range 19-60 years) was from the Azore Islands. The Azore Islands, located in the North Atlantic Ocean (30[degrees] longitude, 40[degrees] latitude), are inhabited by Caucasian people of European descent who originally came to these islands to provide provisions to ships sailing from Europe to American colonies. After the introduction of the steamship, the

Azore Islands became isolated and had very limited contact with Western societies until recently. Television was introduced by the government in 1986, and currently only one channel is available for public viewing and it does not air commercials (M. H. de Azevedo, personal communication, January 8, 1996). Azore Islanders are the only known Caucasian people without any sociocultural pressure to diet and lose body weight for cosmetic reasons (de Azevedo & Ferreira, 1992).

The second group of participants (males n = 72 females n = 37 age range 20-55 years) was from Guinea-Bissau, a former Portuguese colony in West Africa. Guinea-Bissau is one of the poorest countries in the world (average monthly income is estimated to be less than 10 U.S. dollars) with a minimum degree of urbanization. An experimental television service was started in 1989, which operates for about 6 hours a day without any commercials (M. H. de Azevedo, personal communication, January 8, 1996).

Materials and procedure. Participants from the Azore Islands and Guinea-Bissau individually rated the 12 female figures that have been used in past research. Each rater was given a sheet showing 12 female figures, each with an assigned identifying letter so the rater could examine all 12 figures simultaneously. All instructions for rating figures for various attributes were in Portuguese and raters were told to indicate their highest three and lowest three rankings for each of the following attributes in order: good health, youthfulness, attractiveness, sexiness, desire for children, capability for having children, interesting to talk to, good companion, intelligence, ambition, aggressiveness, sense of humor, kindness and understanding, faithfulness, and desirability for long-term romantic (marriage) relationship. Raters were not allowed to give tied rankings.[2] Methodological justifications for obtaining only top three and bottom three rankings, instead of ranking for each figure, have been previously reported (Singh, 1993a).

RESULTS

To examine which attribute(s) raters associated with each stimulus figure, the ranking data for males and females from both societies were separately subjected to multidimensional unfolding (MDU) analysis. MDU is a multidimensional scaling analysis in which two separate sets of stimuli (in the current analysis, figures and personal attributes) may be scaled simultaneously into the same dimensional solution space (Davison, 1983). This technique enables one to examine (a) whether raters perceive various attributes as interrelated and (b) whether they assign these attributes, such as attractiveness, youthfulness, etc., to particular figures. The strength of the relationship among attributes or between an attribute and a figure is inferred by how close or how far apart they are located from each other in the solution space. If raters perceive a figure to possess certain attributes, then those attributes would be located close to that figure in the solution space. Conversely, if raters perceive that a figure does not possess certain attributes, then those attributes would be located away from that figure in the solution space.[3]

MDU analysis revealed two dimensions (Dimension I representing WHR and Dimension II representing body weight) for figures and attributes for both Azore Islanders and Guinea-Bissau raters. Results from MDU analysis are as follows: male Azore Island raters, stress = 0.151, [R.sup.2] (squared multiple correlation indicating the proportion of variance of ranking data accounted for by the MDS solution space) = 0.978; Female Azore Island raters, stress = 0.162, [R.sup.2] = 0.958; Male Guinea-Bissau raters, stress = 0.180, [R.sup.2] = 0.970; Female Guinea-Bissau raters, stress = 0.162, [R.sup.2] = 0.994. As reported in previous studies, there was no significant sex difference in ranking of various personal attributes assigned to stimulus figures.

First, it should be pointed out that there was significant consensus among groups for attractive judgments (Kendall concordance coefficient W for males across four groups, W = 0.89 and for females across four groups, W = 0.89). These findings suggest that the cross-cultural consensus based on facial beauty (Cunningham et al., 1995) is also evident for body shape, as defined by WHR and body weight. Both body weight and WHR influenced the location of attractiveness within solution space. Normal weight figures with low WHR (0.7 and 0.8) were located close to attractiveness except for within the Azore Island group (who perceived the normal weight figure with 0.9 WHR as more attractive than the normal weight figure with 0.8 WHR), whereas the normal weight figure with 1.0 WHR was located far away from attractiveness. A similar interaction between WHR and body weight was evident for underweight figures. Underweight figures with low WHR (0.7 and 0.8) were located close to attractiveness but underweight figures with high WHR (0.9 and 1.0) were not. This was true for youthfulness also, as underweight figures with low WHRs were perceived as youthful but underweight figures with high WHRs were located farther away from youthfulness.

It should, however, be stressed that the location of attributes associated with a stimulus figure in the solution space is affected by the number of stimulus figures that significantly differ on many attributes. For example, youthfulness is primarily associated with adolescence, and thus a youthful adult woman would be located away from the attribute of youthfulness and located close to an adolescent girl. If youthfulness is important for a long-term relationship but is also the hallmark of adolescent girls, then youthfulness would be located slightly away from the woman desired for a long-term relationship. Ideally, only one stimulus figure should be used to determine the location of multiple attributes perceived to be associated with the figure. In this study, however, 12 figures differing in body weight and WHR were ranked to ascertain cross-cultural consensus for judgments of attractiveness and the attributes associated with female attractiveness. When 12 figures that differ significantly in their attractiveness are examined, it appears that neither youthfulness nor capacity to have children are highly desirable attributes for long-term relationships. Another way to determine what males seek in a long-term relationship is to examine the relationship of various personal attributes desired in a long-term mate. Table 7.1 presents correlations (Spearman rho) between desirability for long-term relationship and personal attributes.

As is evident, males in all the groups associate healthiness, attractiveness, youthfulness, and intelligence with desirability for long-term relationships. The relationship between capacity to have children is positive, but not very strong. One of the reasons for this finding is that even a slight reduction in attractiveness impacts the evaluation of female reproductive capability. For example, the highest mean rankings for attractiveness and for

Table 7.1

Spearman Correlations (Rho) Between Desirability for Long-Term Relationship and Various Attributes				
	U.S. CAUCASIAN	AZORE ISLANDS	INDONESIAN	GUINEA-BISSAU
Healthy	0.96	0.97	0.79	0.88
Attractive	0.93	0.87	0.59	0.81
Youthful	0.84	0.53	0.73	0.68
Intelligent	0.66	0.70	0.73	0.88
Capacity for having children	0.39	0.43	0.07 (a)	0.55
Interesting	0.79	0.89	0.70	0.64
Sense of humor	0.24 (a)	0.71	—	0.76
Good companion	0.81	0.94	—	0.69
Ambitious	0.82	0.21	—	0.79
Aggressive	0.80	-0.19 (a)	—	-0.46
Kind and understanding	-0.36	0.80	-0.23 (a)	0.87
Faithful	-0.69	-0.59	-0.67	-0.53

(a) Nonsignificant

capacity to have children were assigned to the normal weight figure with 0.7 WHR by Indonesian males and females. However, in MDU analysis, based on 12 figures, the capacity to have children was located away from attractiveness (Singh & Luis, 1995). In the present study, highest mean rankings for attractiveness and desirability for long-term relationships were also assigned to the normal weight figure with 0.7 WHR, and the mean rankings for capacity to have children were high (mean rank of 1 by Indonesian and U.S. groups; mean rank of 2 by Azore Island group; mean rank of 3 by Guinea-Bissau group).

More central to the present investigation was the relationship between attractiveness and faithfulness. All groups located faithfulness farther away from attractiveness, which is suggestive of the belief that attractive females are not faithful; still, they preferred attractive figures for a long-term relationship and companionship. This "darker side" of attractiveness was not dependent on the sex of the rater, as the negative link between female attractiveness and faithfulness was evident in all female groups. Spearman correlations (rho) were significantly negative between the ranking of attractiveness and faithfulness (Azore Island, $r = -0.61$; Guinea-Bissau, $r = -0.59$; Indonesia, $r = -0.84$; U.S., $r = -0.87$) for all four female groups. It is remarkable that the "darker side" of attractiveness stereotype initially discovered in U.S. undergraduate students (Dermer & Theil, 1975) is evident in adult males and females from diverse cultures.

DISCUSSION

It is quite impressive that participants from such diverse cultures judged normal weight figures much more attractive and desirable for a long-term relationship rather than underweight and overweight figures. It is commonly assumed that people in poor countries prefer overweight women whereas in Western countries underweight figures are preferred. The present data, however, show a high degree of consensus across cultures for normal weight figures. The preference for normal weight women with female-typical WHR would be expected from an evolutionary perspective. In an ancestral hunter-gatherer population, an extremely thin woman (low BMI) would signal malnutrition or sickness; such a woman would have been excluded as a potential mate without any further examination of her WHR. Similarly, an obese woman (high BMI) would arguably be uncommon (due to unpredictable food supply and physical work) and hence obesity would be a sign of a pathological condition; such a woman would have also been excluded as a potential mate without any further examination of her WHR. From an evolutionary perspective, attractiveness indicators should be examined within the context of an evolutionarily relevant range of occurrence. If the majority of women were within the range of normal weight and if the occurrence of extreme thinness or obesity was rare, attending to WHR would have allowed our male ancestors to reliably infer the health and fertility of their potential mates.

The stereotypical belief that attractive women are not very faithful, although consistent with the findings of the darker side of attractiveness, creates a puzzle as attractive women are also rated as most desirable for a long-term relationship. This finding is at odds with the reported importance that U.S. males assign to faithfulness in their long-term partners (Buss, 1999). One reason for such a discrepancy could be the different methods used. Previous studies have used surveys requiring participants to indicate the importance of or to rank desired traits one at a time, without any information about how different traits are related to each other. Many traits come in clusters (Li et al., 2002), and in the present study, participants saw attractive figures and ranked various personal attributes in relation to attractiveness. Such a technique allows us to infer clusters of personal attributes—a stereotype—that contain some negative and some positive attributes. For instance, an extremely attractive woman such as Jennifer Lopez could be judged as arrogant, conceited, and unkind and yet as a desirable mate by many men. It is also quite possible that some of the negative attributes may be based on reactions of the others towards the evaluated individual rather than possession of the attribute by the individual. For example, the reason for locking and guarding an expensive car is not based on "unfaithfulness" of the car, but rather on the possibility that others may steal the car because of its high desirability. A similar phenomenon could explain perceived unfaithfulness of attractive females.

Of course, another possibility for such a cross-culturally persistent "darker side" of the attractiveness stereotype is that it is based on a kernel of truth. Some researchers have proposed that, on average, many stereotypes are accurate (e.g., Japanese are industrious, scientists are absent-minded, the American Republican party favors big business) but lose their accuracy when over-generalized or applied to particular cases (Lee, Jussim, & McCauley, 1995). Thus, it could be that some of the attractive females in many societies are less faithful than their less-attractive counterparts. Because males assign such great importance to attractiveness, attractive females are exposed to greater opportunity for using "trial liaisons" in selecting long-term mates, and in many instances, replacing mates (the Elizabeth Taylor or Jennifer Lopez effect).

This, however, does not directly explain why unattractive females are perceived as faithful. Unattractive females may be perceived as more faithful simply by default in comparison to more attractive women, or they may, in actuality, be more faithful. Faithfulness alone is not enough; to be judged attractive the female must offer some other qualities as well. One way to evaluate these alternatives would be to examine mate attraction tactics of less-attractive females. Some evolutionary theorists have proposed that when personal attributes desired by potential mates, such as one's own attractiveness with respect to potential competitors, are low, such individuals engage in alternate strategies to attract mates (for theoretical details, see Gangestad & Simpson, 2000). Unattractive females can demonstrate that they offer qualities (such as cooperativeness, devotion, similarity in interest, and social values) that males desire in long-term romantic relationships in addition to physical attractiveness. Such trade-offs can provide opportunities for mate attraction for less-attractive females. If so, then mate attraction tactics should be different for attractive and less-attractive females.

Study 2: Nature of Behavioral Tactics Used in Mate Attraction

One of the essential conditions for human mate selection is that both males and females should know what mate attributes are sought by the other sex. If males seek attractive mates then females must be aware of such preference and share the knowledge about what morphological features males find attractive. There is ample evidence for consensus between the sexes for female facial attractiveness (Cunningham et al., 1995) as well as for attractive female bodies as defined by the size of WHR (Furnham, Tan, & McManus, 1997 Henss, 1995 Singh, 1993b). Such shared knowledge allows a female to evaluate her potential competitors, to assess her own attractiveness relative to theirs, and in many instances to use deceptions (e.g., corsets, padded bras, facial makeup) to enhance her attractiveness to males. Self-assessed attractiveness of a female would depend on the reaction of males to her and the history of her ability to entice males who are desirable to and pursued by other females. Females with such a history would assess their attractiveness higher than females who are unable to attract high quality males.

The self-assessed attractiveness would determine the mate attraction tactics available to the female. If self-assessed attractiveness is comparable to potential competitors, a female may opt to engage in attractiveness-enhancing tactics to gain an edge on her competitors. Research shows that females frequently enhance their physical attractiveness with the help of makeup or cosmetics and by dressing seductively, acting nice, flirting, and using various postures (such as leaning into someone, brushing against someone, and parading) to attract men (Greer & Buss, 1994 for other sources, see Mealey, 2000). The success of such tactics would be greater for attractive females than for less-attractive females. Those females who assess themselves as less attractive than potential competitors may use attractiveness-enhancing tactics less often than more attractive females.[4]

METHOD

To test this hypothesis, I examined attractiveness-enhancing tactics used for mate attraction by young Caucasian females (n = 144 age range 18-22 years). Physical measurements of each participant (weight, height, WHR) were obtained and each participant was asked to rate her own attractiveness on a 10-point scale (0 = extremely unattractive 9 = extremely attractive). Each participant completed a questionnaire dealing with dating history, participation in social organizations, and hobbies. Embedded in this questionnaire were 10 questions dealing with tactics used in dating. These questions were selected from the questionnaire used by Tooke and Camire (1991) to explore inter-sexual and intrasexual mating strategies. The selected questions dealt with attempts to look and behave more attractively to potential dates (wearing revealing clothes or facial makeup, walking with a greater swing or bounce than usual) behaviors that could increase the interest of the romantic partner (acting more friendly and social than usual, complimenting the date on his appearance, intentionally appearing vulnerable, pretending to be interested in starting a relationship) tactics to ward off potential competitors (putting arms around date more often in front of others) and attempts to make the date jealous (flirting with other guys).

It should be stressed that for this investigation, female attractiveness was defined by WHR, whereas nearly all previous studies concerning female attractiveness have focused on facial features (Cunningham, 1986; Johnston & Franklin, 1993; Jones, 1995; Langlois et al., 1987; Perrett, May, & Yoshikawa, 1994). Furthermore, in those studies that did address the body in defining attractiveness, only a thin-fat dimension was explored, and typical findings show that in Western industrialized society, thinness is equated with attractiveness (Fallon & Rozin, 1985; for a review see Jackson, 1992). However, as I have stated, thinness alone does not provide enough information about the dimension of body shape that also determines female attractiveness. A thin woman may be dissatisfied with her body image if she is not shapely. For example, Davis and Cerullo (1996) reported that very slim women (BMI = 15) are preoccupied with losing weight if they have a high WHR (0.89), but slim women (BMI = 15) with a low WHR (0.64) are satisfied with their body image and do not attempt to lose weight. When U.S. men and women are presented female figure line drawings differing on both body size and body shape (as defined by WHR), both males and females judge normal weight figures with low WHR as more attractive than thin figures (Singh, 1993b). The data presented on the "darker side" of the attractiveness stereotype in this paper replicate these findings. What is more, a female's own WHR affects her self-assessment of attractiveness.

RESULTS AND DISCUSSION

There was a significant negative correlation (Pearson r = -0.39, p < .01) between WHR and self-rated attractiveness. This finding is consistent with the reported observation of Mikash and Bailey (1999) that people judge women with low WHR as more attractive than women with high WHR. Penton-Voak & Perrett (2001) also found a negative correlation between WHR and women's self-assessed attractiveness. These findings taken together validate the inverse relationship reported for female attractiveness and

WHR based on line-drawing figures. Body weight was also negatively correlated (Pearson $r = -0.26$, $p < .01$) with self-rated attractiveness. Thus, both body weight and WHR affect self-assessed attractiveness of females.

For data analysis, participants were divided into low WHR (0.72 or below n = 74) and high WHR (0.73 or above n = 70) groups using a median split. A similar median split was used for creating low body weight (126 lbs. or below n = 70) and high body weight (127 lbs. or above n = 73) groups to investigate if females use different mating tactics that were a function of WHR or body weight. Attractive females (low WHR group) attempt to look more attractive, compliment the looks of their dates, act possessively (putting arms around the date), and flirt more often than less-attractive (high WHR group) females. When females with low and high body weight groups were compared, no significant differences in the use of these mating tactics were found.

It appears that use of attractiveness-based mating tactics by females with low WHR is effective in mate attraction. Women with low WHR report having greater numbers of sexual partners over their lifetimes than women of comparable age and body weight but higher WHR (Mikach & Bailey, 1999 Singh, Dijkstra, & Buunk, 1996). The history of being able to attract males or being pursued romantically by males would allow such attractive females to aspire to and more frequently succeed in acquiring highly desirable mates.

General Discussion

The findings that people from highly diverse cultures judge normal weight female figures with low WHR as more attractive demonstrates that WHR is a universal rather than Western-culture-specific indicator of female attractiveness. Additionally, the fact that overweight figures in spite of low WHR are not judged to be attractive by participants in any examined culture confirm the original assertion that to be judged attractive, women should not greatly deviate from normal weight (Singh, 1993b).

The most intriguing finding is that participants from these diverse cultures associate unfaithfulness with attractiveness and yet find attractive females desirable for long-term relationships. Why are attractive females cross-culturally perceived to be unfaithful? The findings of the second study suggest that such perception is probably based on differences in mating strategies used by females differing in physical attractiveness. Mating or sexual strategies are typically defined as genetically based programs or decision rules (which are not necessarily consciously formulated or under deliberate control) for selecting mates and allocating efforts to mating, reproduction, and parental care. The choice of strategy and associated behavioral tactics depend both on individuals' personal qualities (status,

Table 7.2

Behavioral Tactics Used by Women With Low WHR and Higher WHR in Mate Attraction		
BEHAVIORAL TACTICS	**LOW WHR MEAN (SD)**	**HIGH WHR MEAN (SD)**
Wearing tighter clothing to appear thinner	2.01 (1.1)	1.37 (0.87)
Using facial makeup to look nice	2.16 (1.23)	1.72 (1.12)
Complimenting date on his appearance	2.21 (1.31)	1.60 (1.04)
Acting shy and letting date have dominant role	1.39 (1.10)	0.70 (0.97)
Flirting with other guys to make date jealous	1.32 (1.01)	0.59 (0.77)
Putting arms around date in front of others	1.86 (1.10)	1.72 (1.18)

BEHAVIORAL TACTICS	**T TEST**	**EFFECT SIZE COHEN'S D**
Wearing tighter clothing to appear thinner	3.07 **	0.65
Using facial makeup to look nice	2.14 *	0.37
Complimenting date on his appearance	3.25 **	0.52
Acting shy and letting date have dominant role	4.32 **	0.67
Flirting with other guys to make date jealous	3.93 **	0.81
Putting arms around date in front of others	2.16 *	0.12

* $p < .05$.
** $p < .01$.

health, age, physical attractiveness) and specific features or cues in the environment (see Gangestad & Simpson, 2000, for detailed theoretical formulation and evidence). In other words, while sex-specific mating strategies and behavioral tactics in a given species are inherited by all the members, the choice of a given strategy depends on situational and personal variables.

One of the most convincing confirmations of this logic is the mating behavior of zebra finches that have had their attractiveness either enhanced or reduced by attaching leg bands of different colors. Burley (1986) discovered that female zebra finches preferred males with black leg bands to males with "unattractive" blue leg bands. Zebra finches mate monogamously, and both males and females share equally in parental care. After attractiveness manipulation, however, preferred males started engaging in polygamous mating (nonpreferred males continued to attempt speciestypical monogamous mating). Preferred females (black leg band) devoted less time to carrying out parental functions than is typical of their species, but still had higher reproductive success than unattractive (blue leg band) females, because the mates of attractive females devoted more time to carrying out parental functions.

These finding cannot be dismissed by arguing that such effects were obtained because these finches were bred and raised in captivity. The use of different mating strategies based on preferred personal qualities of the opposite sex has been reported for wild barnacle geese. Barnacle geese pair monogamously, and males prefer larger and heavier females. In their field studies, Choudhurry and Black (1993) found that preferred females engage in more "trial liaisons" prior to monogamous pairing than do less-preferred females. The findings concerning zebra finches suggest that an accidental increase in attractiveness enabled the newly enhanced members to activate alternative strategies that were not previously available.

A fundamental assumption of all evolution-based human mating theories is that mate preference and mating strategies evolved to solve either the specific adaptive problems encountered by the ancestral population or the specific selection pressures that occurred in the environment of evolutionary adaptiveness (Buss, 1994 Symons, 1979 Thornhill, 1997 Tooby & Cosmides, 1992). The reproductive success of ancestral human females depended on their ability to evaluate potential mates' willingness to invest in their offspring as well as their phenotypic and genetic qualities. Human females invest heavily in reproduction and in feeding, caring for, and raising their children. The reproductive success of the female, therefore, would be greatly enhanced if she could accurately assess the ability of her mate to acquire resources and his willingness to divert those resources to her and her children and to protect her children. Mortality rates for father-absent children are reported to be significantly higher than those for two-parent children (Geary, 1998).

In addition, the reproductive success of females would depend on their ability to evaluate genetic quality of their potential mates. Mates with higher genetic quality would give the gift of good health and attributes desired by others. There are some facial and bodily features that are reliable indicators of genetic quality of males. One such indicator is the degree of deviation from bilateral symmetry of faces and bodies. Males with greater facial and body symmetry are healthier and cope with emotional and physical stress more effectively than less-symmetrical males (Shackleford & Larson, 1997; Thornhill & Moeller, 1997). Thus, ideally, females should mate with males who control resources, direct such resources to their children, and possess morphological features indicative of high genetic quality.

Such males, however, are limited in number. Furthermore, given paternal uncertainty (fertilization being concealed) and risk for cuckoldry and the fact that paternal care is beneficial but not essential for offspring survival, high-genetic-quality males are able to seek out short-term mating with many females instead of investing in a long-term committed relationship. Symmetrical men report greater numbers of sex partners and are reported to invest less in relationships than nonsymmetrical men (Gangestad & Thornhill, 1997). Attractive males with optimal WHR are also perceived to be less faithful (Singh, 1995). As a result, females frequently encounter the problem of trading off between male provisioning and their genetic quality (Bellis & Baker, 1990; Cashdan, 1996; Emlen, 1995). Females have evolved mechanisms to deal with trade-offs, as is evident from the findings that ovulating women (when the probability for conception is high) more often than nonovulating women seek out extrapair copulation (Baker, 1996) and prefer mates who exhibit highly masculine facial features indicative of testosterone for short-term relationships (Johnston, Hagel, Franklin, Fink, & Grammer 2001). When the possibility of conception is low (nonovulatory period), women prefer mates with relatively feminine faces indicative of prosociability, low aggression, and willingness to invest in offspring (Gangestad & Simpson, 2000).

The probability of success in a trade-off strategy would greatly depend on the degree of female physical attractiveness, as males rank this the most desirable trait for both short- and long-term relationships. Highly attractive females may be able to obtain both higher genetic benefits and material benefits from males. Failing that, attractive females would have the option to obtain material benefits from a long-term mate and genetic benefits from short-term liaisons. Such options would be rarely available to less-attractive females. Less-attractive females should be willing to sacrifice some genetic benefit in exchange for superior material benefits provided by the mate. There is evidence to suggest that less-attractive human females seek less-masculine males for relationships. Unlike women who consider themselves attractive, less-attractive women prefer men with slightly feminized faces for relationships (Little, Burt, Penton-Voak, & Perrett, 2001). These findings have been replicated when WHR rather than self-rated attractiveness is used. Women with high WHR prefer slightly less-masculine male faces than women with low WHR (Penton-Voak & Perrett, 2001). This physical-condition-dependent mate preference has also been observed in fish. Female stickleback fish that are in poor physical condition court less-attractive males than do females in better condition (Bakker, Kunzlera, & Mazzi, 1999).

Less-attractive females would have enhanced reproductive success by seeking males who are caring and willing to invest resources in their offspring rather than by competing for high genetic quality males. Men with less competitive ability may actually perceive attractiveness differently and may find female physical attractiveness less important for sexual arousal than do males with greater competitive abilities (Symons, 1995). Males mating with less-attractive women (high WHR) would have high reproductive success, as females with higher WHRs give birth to heavier and taller babies (Brown, Potter, & Jacobs, 1996), more sons (Manning, Anderton, & Washington, 1996; Singh & Zambarano, 1997), and sons with high levels of testosterone (Manning, Trivers, Singh, & Thornhill, 1999). More importantly, mating with less-attractive females would require less need for mate guarding and higher paternal certainty as the opportunities for extra-pair copulation would be fewer than for attractive females.

There are still a number of issues that need to be investigated to gain a better understanding of the nature of human mate selection. First, the conditions in which people are willing to accept mates who are desirable in some respect but still possess some negative qualities needs to be explored (Regan, 1988). In real life, most people possess many positive and negative qualities; however, researchers so far have explored primarily the positive qualities desired in a mate. Thus, the personal qualities for which people are willing to compromise, when forced to choose, are not known. For example, would men ever choose an attractive woman who is unkind and not very faithful, or would they prefer a less-attractive woman who is very kind and faithful as a mate?

Second, the conditions that govern the rules of tradeoffs should be systematically explored. It is not known how the sex ratio of the local population, environmental conditions (pathogen prevalence, harsh economic conditions), or social customs (polygyny, bride price) affect the nature of trade-offs in mating decisions. Likewise, cost-benefit analysis of trade-offs in mating decisions, particularly as it applies to sex differences, is essential. Information about such issues is needed to help develop an accurate understanding of human mating decisions.

Acknowledgements

I am grateful to Courtney Hinton for collecting data for the second study and to Jennifer Currah, Hillary Procknow, Peter Renn, and Scott Strong for their invaluable help in various ways in finalizing this research paper.

Endnotes

1. Two studies conducted in non-Western societies have failed to replicate the negative relationship between the size of WHR and female attractiveness. Yu and Shepard (1998) tested 18 males 13 to 60 years old using only six female figure line drawings (0.7 and 0.9 in each of the three body weight categories) and found that Gombato (a tribal group in Peru) did not judge figures with low WHR as more attractive than figures with high WHR. Wetsman and Marlowe (1999), using the same six figures with men from the Hadza tribe of Tanzania, also failed to replicate the finding that figures with low WHR are judged more attractive than figures with high WHR. The use of only 6 figures representing only two levels of WHR rather than 12 figures with four levels of WHR makes comparison with cross-cultural findings of other investigators difficult.

2. I am grateful to Mafia Helena Pinto de Azevedo, M.D., Professor of Medical Psychology, Coimbra University, Portugal, for organizing research teams for data collection in the Azore Islands and Guinea-Bissau. Dr. Carlos Ferreira arranged data collection of people from the Azores and Leonice Furtado collected data from Guinea-Bissau.

3. An illustrative example of MDU would be using a U.S. map to determine the location of national parks relative to a given city. One would be able to accurately use this information from the map without needing to compute whether a given national park is significantly closer to or farther from a given city.

4. The decision for attractiveness-enhancement tactics would be affected by a woman's standing in intrasexual competition. For example, if an attractive female were competing for a man who was being chased by women less attractive than she, she would have little reason to engage in attractiveness-enhancing tactics. Similarly, if an unattractive woman were competing with women of comparable attractiveness, she may benefit by engaging in attractiveness-enhancing tactics. In essence, various factors (e.g., age, sociosexual skills, and comparative attractiveness) should enter into selection of the type and frequency of tactics of mate attraction.

References

Alley, T. R., & Hildebrandt, K. A. (1988). *Determinants and consequences of facial aesthetics.* In T. R. Alley (Ed.), *Social and applied aspects of perceiving faces* (pp. 101-140). Hillsdale, NJ: Erlbaum.

Ashmore, R. D., Solomon, M. R., & Longo, L. C. (1996). "Thinking about fashion models: A multidimensional approach to the structure of perceived physical attractiveness." *Personality and Social Psychology Bulletin, 22,* 1083-1104.

Baker, R. (1996). *Sperm wars: The science of sex.* New York: Basic Books.

Bakker, T. C., Kunzler, R., & Mazzi, K. (1999). "Condition-related mate choice in sticklebacks." *Nature, 40,* 234.

Bellis, M. A., & Baker, R. R. (1990). "Do females promote sperm competition? Data for humans." *Animal Behavior, 40,* 997-999.

Bjorntorp, P. (1987). *Fat cell distribution and metabolism.* In R. L Wurtman & J. J. Wurtman (Eds), *Human obesity* (pp. 66-72). New York: New York Academy of Science.

Bjorntorp, P. (1991). "Adipose tissue distribution and functions." *International Journal of Obesity, 15,* 67-87.

Bjorntorp, E (1997). "Fat distribution, insulin resistance and metabolic diseases." *Nutrition, 12,* 795-803.

Brown, J. E., Potter, J. D., & Jacobs, D. R. (1996). "Maternal waist-to-hip ratio as a predictor of newborn size: Results of the Diana Project." *Epidemiology, 7,* 62-66.

Burley, N. (1986). "Sexual selection for aesthetic traits in species with bio-parental care." *American Naturalist, 127,* 415-445.

Buss, D. M. (1989). "Sex difference in human mate preferences: Evolutionary hypotheses testing in 37 cultures." *Behavioral and Brain Sciences, 12,* 1-49.

Buss, D. M. (1994). *The evolution of desire: Strategies of human mating.* New York: Basic Books.

Buss, D. M. (1999). *Evolutionary psychology. The new science of the mind.* Boston: Allyn and Bacon.

Buss, D. M., & Schmitt, D. E (1993). "Sexual Strategies Theory: An evolutionary perspective on human mating." *Psychological Review, 100,* 204-232.

Cashdan, E. (1996). "Women's mating strategies." *Evolutionary Anthropology, 5,* 134-143.

Choudhurry, S., & Black, J. M. (1993). "Mate-selection behaviour and sampling strategies in geese." *Animal Behavior, 46,* 747-757.

Connolly, J., Mealey, L., & Slaughter, V. P. (2000). "Development of preferences for body shape." *Perspectives in Human Biology, 5*, 19-29.

Cooley, C. H. (1990). *Human nature in the social order.* New York: Scribner's.

Cunningham, M. R. (1986). "Measuring the physical in physical attractiveness: Quasi-experiments on the sociobiology of female facial beauty." *Journal of Personality and Social Psychology, 50*, 925-935.

Cunningham, M. R., Roberts, A. R., Wu, C. H., Barbee, A. E., & Druen, E. B. (1995). "Their ideas of beauty are, on the whole, the same as ours: Consistency and variability in the cross-cultural perception of female attractiveness." *Journal of Personality and Social Psychology, 68*, 261-279.

Darley, J. M., & Fazio, R. H. (1980). "Expectancy confirmation processes arising in the social interaction sequence." *American Psychologist, 35*, 867-881.

Davis, C., & Cerullo, D. (1996). "Fat distribution in young women: Association and interaction with behavioral, physical and psychological factors." *Psychology, Health and Medicine, 1*, 159-167.

Davison, M. L. (1983). *Multidimensional scaling.* New York: Wiley.

de Azvedo, M. H., & Ferreira, C. E (1992). "Anorexia nervosa and bulimia: A prevalence study." *Acta Psychiatrica Scandinavica, 86*, 432-436.

Dermer, M., & Thiel, D. L. (1975). "When beauty may fail." *Journal of Personality and Social Psychology, 31*, 1168-1176.

Dion, K. K., Berscheid, E., & Walster, E. (1972). "What is beautiful is good." *Journal of Personality and Social Psychology, 24*, 285-290.

Emlen, S. T. (1995). "An evolutionary theory of family." *Proceedings of the National Academy of Sciences USA, 92*, 8092-8099.

Fallon, A., & Rozin, P. (1985). "Sex differences in perception of desirable body shape." *Journal of Abnormal Psychology, 94*, 102-105.

Feingold, A. (1992). "Good-looking people are not what we think." *Psychological Bulletin, 111*, 304-341.

Fink, B., Penton-Voak, I. (2002). "Evolutionary psychology of facial attractiveness." *Current Directions in Psychological Science, 11*, 154-158.

Furnham, A., Moutafi, J., & Baguma, P. (2002). "A cross-cultural study on the role of weight and waist-to-hip ratio on female attractiveness." *Personality and Individual Differences, 32*, 729-745.

Furnham, A., Tan, T., & McManus, C. (1997). "Waist-to-hip ratio and preferences for body shape: A replication and extension." *Personality and Individual Differences, 22*, 289-294.

Gangestad, S. W., & Simpson, J. A. (2000). "The evolution of human mating: Trade-offs and strategic pluralism." *Behavioral and Brain Sciences, 23,* 573-644.

Gangestad, S. W., & Thornhill, R. (1997). *Human sexual selection and developmental stability.* In J. A. Simpson & D. T. Kenrick (Eds.), *Evolutionary social psychology* (pp. 169-195). Mahwah, N J: Erlbaum.

Geary, D. C. (1998). *Male, female: The evolution of human sex differences.* Washington, DC: American Psychological Association.

Greer, A. E., & Buss, D. M. (1994). "Tactics for promoting sexual encounters." *The Journal of Sex Research, 31,* 185-201.

Hatfield, E., & Sprecher, S. (1986). *Mirror, mirror: The importance of looks in everyday life.* Albany, NY: SUNY Press.

Henss, R. (1995). "Waist-to-hip ratio and attractiveness: A replication and extension." *Personality and Individual Differences, 19,* 479-488.

Henss, R. (2000). "WHR and female attractiveness: Evidence from photographic stimuli and methodological considerations." *Personality and Individual Differences, 28,* 501-513.

Jackson, L. A. (1992). *Physical appearance and gender. Sociobiological and sociocultural perspectives.* Albany, NY: SUNY Press.

Johnston, V. S., & Franklin, M. (1993). "Is beauty in the eye of the beholder?" *Ethology and Sociobiology, 14,* 183-199.

Johnston, V. S., Hagel, R., Franklin, M., Fink, B., & Grammer, K. (2001). "Male facial attractiveness: Evidence for hormone mediated adaptive design." *Evolution and Human Behavior, 22,* 251-267.

Jones, D. (1995). "Sexual selection, physical attractiveness, and facial nesting: Cross-cultural evidence and implications." *Current Anthropology, 36,* 723-748.

Jones, P. R. M., Hunt, M. J., Brown, T. P., & Norgan, N. G. (1986). "Waisthip circumference ratio and its relation to age and overweight in British men." *Human Nutrition: Clinical Nutrition, 40c,* 239-244.

Kirchengast, S., Gruber, D., Sator, M., Knogler, W., & Huber, J. (1998). "The impact of nutritional status on body fat distribution patterns in pre- and postmenopausal females." *Journal of Biosocial Sciences, 30,* 145-154.

Kirschner, M., & Samojlik, E. (1991). "Sex hormone metabolism in upper and lower body obesity." *International Journal of Obesity, 15,* 101-108.

Kissebah, A. H., & Krakower, G. R. (1994). "Regional adiposity and mortality." *Physiological Review, 74,* 761-811.

Langlois, J. H., Kalakanis, L., Rubenstein, A. J., Lavson, A., Hallam, M., & Smoot, M. (2000). "Maxims or myths of beauty? A meta-analytic and theoretical review." *Psychological Bulletin, 126,* 390-423.

Langlois, J. H., Roggman, L. A., Casey, R. J., Ritter, J. M., Rieser-Danner, L. A., & Jenkins, V. Y. (1987). "Infant preference for attractive faces: Rudiments of a stereotype." *Developmental Psychology, 23*, 363-369.

Lee, Y. T., Jussim, L. J., & McCauley, C. R. (Eds.). (1995). *Stereotypic accuracy: Toward appreciating group differences.* Washington, DC: American Psychological Association.

Lev-Ran, A. (2001). "Human obesity: An evolutionary approach to understanding our bulging waistline." *Diabetes and Metabolic Research Review, 17*, 347-362.

Li, N. P., Bailey, J. M., Kenrick, D. T., & Linsenmeier, J. A. W. (2002). "The necessities and luxuries of mate preference: Testing the tradeoffs." *Journal of Personality and Social Psychology, 82*, 947-955.

Little, A. C., Burr, D. M., Penton-Voak, I. S., & Perrett, D. I. (2001). "Self-perceived attractiveness influences human preferences for sexual dimorphism and symmetry in male faces." *Proceedings of the Royal Society of London B, 268*, 39-44.

Manning, J. T., Anderton, R., & Washington, S. M. (1996). "Women's waist and the sex ratio of their progeny: Evolutionary aspects of the ideal female shape." *Journal of Human Evolution, 31*, 41-47.

Manning, J. T., Trivers, R. L., Singh, D., & Thornhill, R. (1999). "The mystery of female beauty." *Nature, 339*, 214-215.

Marti, B., Tomilehto, J., Saloman, V., Kartovaara, L., Korhonen, H. J., & Pietiner, P. (1991). "Body fat distribution in the Finnish population: Environmental determinants and predictive power for cardiovascular risk factor levels." *Journal of Epidemiology and Community Health, 45*, 131-137.

Mealey, L. (2000). *Sex differences: Development and evolutionary strategies.* San Diego, CA: Academic Press.

Mikash, S. H., & Bailey, J. M. (1999). "What distinguished women with high numbers of sex partners?" *Evolution and Human Behavior, 20*, 141-150.

Pasquali, R., Gambineri, A., Anconetani, B., Vicennati, V., Colita, D., Caramelli, E., et al. (1999). "The natural history of the metabolic syndrome in young women with the polycystic ovary syndrome and the effect on long-term oestrogen-progestagen treatment." *Clinical Endocrinology, 50*, 517-527.

Penton-Voak, I. S., & Perrett, D. I. (2001). *Male facial attractiveness: Perceived personality and shifting female preference for male traits across the menstrual cycle.* In P. J. B. Slater & J. S. Rosenblatt (Eds.), *Advances in the study of behavior* (pp. 219-259). San Diego, CA: Academic Press.

Perrett, D. I., May, K. A., & Yoshikawa, S. (1994). "Facial shape and judgments of female attractiveness." *Nature, 368*, 239-242.

Rebuffe-Scrive, M. (1987). "Regional adipose tissue metabolism in men and women during menstrual cycle, pregnancy, lactation and menopause." *International Journal of Obesity, 11,* 347-355.

Regan, E. C. (1998). "What if you can't get what you want? Willingness to compromise ideal mate selection standards as a function of sex, mate value, and relationship context." *Personality and Social Psychology Bulletin, 24,* 1294-1303.

Seidell, J. C., & Flegal, K. M. (1997). "Assessing obesity: Classification and epidemiology." *British Medical Bulletin, 53,* 238-252.

Shackelford, K., & Larsen, R. J. (1997). "Facial asymmetry as indicator of psychological, emotional, and physiological distress." *Journal of Personality and Social Psychology, 72,* 456-466.

Singh, D. (1993a). "Adaptive significance of female physical attractiveness: Role of waist-to-hip ratio." *Journal of Personality and Social Psychology, 65,* 293-307.

Singh, D. (1993b). "Body shape and women's attractiveness: The critical role of waist-to-hip ratio." *Human Nature, 4,* 297-321.

Singh, D. (1994). "Is thin really beautiful and good? Relationship between waist-to-hip ratio (WHR) and female attractiveness." *Personality and Individual Differences, 16,* 123.

Singh, D. (1995). "Female judgments of male attractiveness and desirability for relationships: Role of waist-to-hip ratio and financial status." *Journal of Personality and Social Psychology, 69,* 1089-1101.

Singh, D. (2000). *Waist-to-hip ratio: An indicator of female mate value.* Proceedings of Human Mate Choice and Prehistoric Marital Network International Symposium, Kyoto, Japan, 16, 79-99.

Singh, D. (2002). "Female mate value at a glance: Relationship of waist-to-hip ratio to health, fecundity and attractiveness." *Neuroendocrinology Letters Special Issue, 23*(Suppl. 4), 65-75.

Singh, D., Dijkstra, P., & Buunk, B. (1996, July). *Sexual behavior stereotypes and reality of women differing in the size of their waist-to-hip ratio.* Paper presented at the Human Behavior and Evolution Society Meeting, Davis, CA.

Singh, D., & Luis, S. (1995). "Ethnic and gender consensus for the effect of waist-to-hip ratio on judgment of women's attractiveness." *Human Nature, 6,* 51-68.

Singh, D., & Zambarano, R. J. (1997). "Offspring sex ratio in women with android body fat distribution." *Human Biology, 69,* 545-556.

Stelzer, C., Desmond, S. M., & Price, J. H. (1987). "Physical attractiveness and sexual activity of college students." *Psychological Report, 60,* 567-573.

Streeter, S. A., & McBurney, D. H. (2003). "Waist-hip ratio and attractiveness: New evidence and a critique of 'a critical test.'" *Evolution and Human Behavior, 24,* 88-98.

Symons, D. (1979). *The evolution of human sexuality.* Oxford, England: Oxford University Press.

Symons, D. (1995). *Beauty is in the adaptation of the beholder: The evolutionary psychology of human female sexual attractiveness.* In P. R. Abramson & S. D. Pinkerton (Eds.), *Sexual nature/Sexual culture* (pp. 80-118). Chicago: University of Chicago Press.

Thornhill, R. (1997). *The concept of an evolved adaptation.* In G. R. Bock & G. Cardew (Eds.), *Characterizing human psychological adaptations* (pp. 4-22). Chichester, England: Wiley.

Thornhill, R., & Gangestad, S. W. (1993). "Human facial beauty: Averageness, symmetry and parasite resistance." *Human Nature, 4,* 237-269.

Thornhill, R., & Moeller, A. E. (1997). "Developmental stability, diseases, and medicine." *Biological Review, 72,* 497-548.

Tooby, J., & Cosmides, L. (1992). *Psychological foundations of cultures.* In J. Barkow, L. Cosmides, & J. Tooby (Eds.), *The adapted mind* (pp. 19-136). New York: Oxford University Press.

Tooke, W., & Camire, L. (1991). "Pattern of deception in intersexual and intrasexual mating strategies." *Ethology and Sociobiology, 12,* 345-364.

Tovee, M. J., Maisey, D. S., Emery, J. L., & Comelissen, P. L. (1999). "Visual cues to female physical attractiveness. *Proceedings of the Royal Society of London, 266,* 211-218.

Tovee, M. J., Reinhardt, S., Emery, J. L., & Cornelissen, E. L. (1998). "Optimum body-mass index and maximum sexual attractiveness." *Lancet, 355,* 548.

Waas, E., Waldenstrom, V., Rossmer, S., & Hellber, D. (1997). "An android body fat distribution in females impairs the pregnancy rate of in-vitro fertilization-embryo transfer." *Human Reproduction, 12,* 2057-2060.

Wetsman, A., & Marlowe, G. H. (1999). "How universal are preferences for female waist-to-hip ratios? Evidence from the Hadza of Tanzania." *Evolution and Human Behavior, 20,* 219-228.

Wiederman, M. W., & Hurst, S. R. (1998). "Body size, physical attractiveness, and body image among young adult women: Relationships to sexual experience and sexual esteem." *The Journal of Sex Research, 35,* 272-281.

Yu, D. W., & Shepard, G. H. (1998). "Is beauty in the eye of the beholder?" *Nature, 396,* 321-322.

Zaadstra, B. M., Seidell, J. C., VanNoord, E. A. H., Te Velde, E. R., Habbema, J. D. E., Vrieswijk, B., et al. (1993). "Fat and female fecundity: prospective study of body fat distribution in conception rates." *British Medical Journal, 306,* 484-487.

Dating and Courtship in the Later Years

Lori J. McElhaney

A Neglected Topic of Research

Most research on families in later life centers on increasing our understanding of the continuation and termination of long-term relationships. The body of research on widowhood is substantial, and there is a growing interest in long-term marriages that end in divorce. However, there has been a paucity of research on the development of new intimate relationships—dating, courtship, and re-marriage—following widowhood or divorce in later life. Although families form and re-form across the life span, these issues are often overlooked or forgotten by researchers who study later life families.

When dating and courtship are mentioned, most people tend to think about older adolescents and young adults. This image is reflected in social science research, which typically focuses on young, never-married individuals. The dating experiences of older, previously married individuals have largely been ignored. With the growth in the older population and increases in the number of single elderly, this phenomenon may be encountered more often by professionals in the family and aging fields. The purpose of this paper is to provide an overview of the existing research on dating and courtship in later life, concentrating on estimates of the number of older adults who are dating, social attitudes, differences between younger and older adults, the ways in which older people meet dating partners, predictors of dating, motives and functions of dating, and activities of dating.

Reprinted with permission from GENERATIONS, Vol. 16, Issue 3, Summer 1992. Copyright © 1992 American Society on Aging, San Francisco, California. www.asaging.org

Number of Older Adults Who Are Dating

There is no good estimate of the number of older adults who are dating. Although her work was not restricted only to older ages, Lopata (1979) found that only 22 percent of widows reported having close male relationships since their husbands' deaths. Of those, the majority (two-thirds) reported having only one close male relationship, and many married their first "boyfriends."

More recently, Bulcroft and Bulcroft (1991) examined the prevalence of dating on the basis of a subsample of previously married single adults age 55 and over from the National Survey of Families and Households. Thirty percent (93 out of 310) of the males and 6.7 percent (77 out of 1,111) of the females reported having one or more dates during the past month. Of those dating, over half the men and almost one-third of the women reported dating more than one partner in the past year. Almost one-half of both men and women identified the relationship as "steady dating."

Social Attitudes

An extensive assessment of social attitudes toward later life dating is not easily found. McKain (1969) states that courtship among the elderly is more influenced by outside factors than it is among younger couples. Using advice books for the elderly as an indication of changes in social attitudes, Arluke, Levin and Suchwalko (1984) report that, ironically, "although sexual activity among the elderly is being encouraged more,...remarriage and dating continue to be denied or discouraged for the elderly" (p. 418). Only 10 percent of these advice books published prior to 1970 approved of dating in later life. In the post-1970 advice books, the approval rate increased, but only to 24 percent. There was no difference in approval of remarriage, which stayed at 26 percent in both pre- and post-1970 books.

In a recent analysis of network television programs in which the central characters are elderly, Bell (1992) reports that despite the increase in positive images of elderly characters, "prime-time television doesn't seem to know how (or wish) to handle a continuing intimate relationship between two elderly people of the opposite sex" (p. 310).

Differences Between Younger and Older Adults

Bernard (1956) acknowledged a difference in love between younger and older individuals. New relationships in later life can provide an opportunity to express emotions that may have been lost or suppressed during the first marriage, and love "is likely to have wider dimensions than love in youth and may perhaps be treasured even more, because the partners have experienced the deprivation of love" (p. 124).

Researchers have suggested other ways in which dating relationships are different for the two age groups. First, older daters are not experimenting with marital roles; they have most often been married before and have specific expectations for marital partners. Second, more emphasis is placed on companionship by older daters. Although less emphasis is placed on romance and sexuality, these still are a part of the dating relationship (Bulcroft and Bulcroft, 1985; Bulcroft and O'Connor, 1986; Bulcroft and Bulcroft, 1991).

Another difference is outside influences. Instead of being influenced by parents, older daters may be more influenced by the reactions of their adult children to their dating behavior (Bulcroft and Bulcroft, 1991). Sometimes the true nature of the relationship is kept hidden from children. However, Bulcroft and O'Connor (1986) suggest little influence of adult children on parent's dating but possible influence on its seriousness.

Meeting Dating and Marriage Partners

Researchers have found differences between ways that widowed women meet men they merely date and ways they meet men they end up marrying. Lopata (1979) reports that, most commonly, widows meet dating partners in public places or through introductions by friends (25% each). Few dating partners knew each other in the past or through the late husband. None of the widows met dating partners through introductions by their children. This differs from the way in which new husbands were met. New husbands were more often known in the past or known through organizations and clubs (Lopata, 1979). This type of meeting of new spouses was also found by Vinick (1978) and McKain (1969).

Bulcroft and Bulcroft (1985) reported that dating partners were more often met through formal structures rather than through friends or by chance meeting. However, this seemingly contradictory finding is not surprising since the 10 adult participants in their study were identified by their membership in a singles dub for older adults.

Predictors of Dating in Later Life

Activity level is important in meeting new people with whom to form intimate relationships. Older adults who are socially active have more opportunity to meet people who might be potential dating and marriage partners (Vinick, 1978).

Bulcroft and Bulcroft (1991) tested several predictors of whether or not older adults dated. For males and females combined, significant negative relationships were found for age and single family residence. Significant positive relationships were reported for comparative health, driving ability, organizational memberships, and contacts with siblings. Gender was also significant, with males more likely to date than females. The researchers did not find significant effects for marital history, contacts with children, disability level, or religious activities.

Motives and Functions of Later Life Dating

One of the main questions asked by the researchers is why older people date. Reasons given for dating include selection of a marital partner and maintenance of social activity. In addition, for older women, dating increases prestige. Older women who date report that other women envy their dating relationship. Dating may also serve to increase self-esteem; the women feel desirable because of their ability to attract men. For men, however, dating functions as an outlet for self-disclosure (Bulcroft and Bulcroft, 1985; Bulcroft and O'Connor, 1986). For both men and women, the roles performed in dating relationships include friend, confidant, lover, and, to a lesser extent, caregiver (Bulcroft and O'Connor, 1986).

Activities of Later Life Dating

Jacobs and Vinick (1979) report that new and developing relationships in late life tend to follow traditional gender role patterns. For example, men typically initiate and sustain the relationship. A traditional gender role pattern was also reported in a small qualitative study by Bulcroft and Bulcroft (1985).

Dating activities of widows reported in Lopata (1979) include going out to dinner, going to movies and other public places, participating in or going to sports events, and going to each other's homes. McKain (1969) describes courtship activities among retirement remarriage couples as visiting children, attending church, going to movies, attending social events, and having dinner at one partner's house. Activities reported by Bulcroft and Bulcroft (1985) included dancing, playing cards, camping and canoeing, going out or to the other's home for dinner, taking trips, and attending movies, theater, or concerts.

Conclusions

Despite the limited research on dating and courtship in later life, some implications for older adults and their families are evident. Given the imbalance in the sex ratio and the tendency for men to be involved with younger women, dating may not be a realistic option for older women. If dating is a realistic and desired activity, then staying socially active and involved in organizations increases the chance of developing new intimate relationships. The roles of other family members are not clear. Whether a person had children was not found to predict dating behavior, yet children may influence how far new relationships develop.

Given the increase in the number of single elderly people and the typical loss in social roles with aging, dating and courtship can be an important aspect of social relationships in later life. More reliable and accurate information is needed before professionals can be prepared to help families faring this issue. By ignoring the development of new intimate relationships in later life, researchers may continue to contribute to negative stereotypes of single elderly people.

References

Arluke, A., Levin, J. and Suchwalko, J., 1984. "Sexuality and Romance in Advice Books for the Elderly." *Gerontologist 24*(4): 415-18.

Bell, J., 1992. "In Search of a Discourse on Aging: The Elderly and Television." *Gerontologist 32*(3): 305-11.

Bernard, J., 1956. *Remarriage: A Study of Marriage.* New York: Dryden Press.

Bulcroft, K. and Bulcroft, R., 1985. "Dating and Courtship in Late Life: An Exploratory Study." In W. A. Peterson and J. Quadagno, eds., *Social Bands in Later Life: Aging and Interdependence.* Beverly Hills, Calif: Sage.

Bulcroft, K. and O'Connor, M., 1986. "The Importance of Dating Relationships on Quality of Life for Older Persons." *Family Relations 35*:397-401.

Bulcroft, R. and Bulcroft, K., 1991. "The Nature and Functions of Dating in Later Life." *Research on Aging 13*(2): 244-60.

Jacobs, R. H. and Vinick, B. H., 1979. *Re-engagement in Later Lift: Re-employment and Remarriage.* Stamford, Conn.: Grey-lock.

Lopata, H. Z., 1979. *Women as Widows: Support Systems.* New York: Elsevier.

McKain, W. C., 1969. *Retirement Marriage.* Storrs, Conn.: Storrs Agricultural Experiment Station.

Vinick, B. H., 1978. "Remarriage in Old Age." *Family Coordinator 27*(4): 359-63.

Part

Falling in Love

The Complex
Chemistry of Love

Colette Bancroft

CHAPTER

Romantic love really is all about chemistry, and on a brain scan it looks a lot like addiction. Evolution has hard-wired us to form long-term attachments—and to fool around. And those antidepressants that helped you get over your last romance might keep you from finding a new one.

That's just some of the news in *Why We Love: The Nature and Chemistry of Romantic Love* (Henry Holt & Co., $25) by Helen Fisher, an anthropologist and research professor at Rutgers University. Its pages are laced with poetry and romantic legends, but the book focuses on Fisher's scientific research into love.

Speaking from her home in New York City, Fisher says, "The human brain evolved about 2-million years ago, and I think romantic love really took off at that time."

Her studies of the evolution of sex, love, marriage and gender differences in the brain and behavior have been the source of four books. As part of her research for *Why We Love*, she took a look inside the brains of 20 people who identified themselves as "madly in love."

The subjects were placed in a functional magnetic resonance imaging machine, which takes pictures of blood flow to active parts of the brain. They alternately gazed at a photograph of their beloved, performed a simple math exercise and looked at a neutral photo of an acquaintance.

When Fisher and her colleagues analyzed the data, they found that certain parts of the brain's "reward circuitry" lit up like fireworks when subjects were looking at their honeys. That indicated the brain was revving up its production of powerful chemicals associated with concentration, energy and elation.

"That really blew my mind," Fisher says. "Originally I thought romantic love was an emotion, or a constellation of emotions. But when we saw what was going on in the brain, I realized it was a drive," like hunger, thirst, the maternal instinct or the sex drive.

Love at first sight is straight out of nature, Fisher says, a descendant of animal attraction.

"A squirrel has to choose another squirrel. If he finds one with a bushy tail and nice whiskers, he has to make a move. He can't spend a year talking to her about T.S. Eliot."

Although few species of animals form lasting pair bonds, many of them do make choices. "There's not a mammal on this planet who will copulate with just anybody. They all have favorites."

For humans, Fisher says, choosing favorites has evolved into a much more elaborate system of responses. We have three distinct mating drives, each with its own neurochemicals.

Lust, the craving for sexual gratification, is associated with testosterone in both sexes. Intense romantic love that idealizes a particular partner is tied to dopamine and norepinephrine, while attachment, a calm, secure union with a long-term partner, is related to the hormones oxytocin and vasopressin.

"Those three different brain systems act independently," Fisher says. "We've really inherited a very difficult design."

We expect lust to lead to romantic love and then to attachment, but they can happen in any order, Fisher says. We can even feel them for different people at the same time.

Our culture tends to put such a high value on romantic love that many people feel the attachment stage is the failure of love.

"Americans don't respect attachment. It's a very ornate and remarkable feeling. It's much more subtle, much more complex. Romantic love is just like being hit by a truck," she says.

Attachment occurs in all human cultures. And so does adultery. "I think we're wired for both.

"Ninety-seven percent of mammals do not form pair bonds to raise their young. Adultery is not the news. The news is that we bother to pair up at all."

Fisher says that both attachment and wanderlust were adaptive behaviors. The first human mothers had to carry their infants in their arms instead of on their backs like other primates, so they needed mates to help them survive.

On the open, predator-haunted plains on which early humans lived, one man couldn't effectively protect a whole harem of women and their children, but he could protect one family. So individuals who formed pair bonds were more likely to raise their young and pass on the brain circuits for attachment.

"Now, 2-million years ago, it was also adaptive for that male to slip over the hill and copulate with another woman," Fisher says. "If he fathered children with her, it doubled the number of his genes that got passed along."

Adultery was adaptive for women because it could mean extra protection and resources for their children. If a woman got pregnant by more than one man, it meant she had children with more genetic variation. And they passed on the tendency for adultery over the millennia.

Fisher says, "We've evolved a dual reproductive strategy: the tendency to pair up and the tendency for the roving eye. We're in a pickle."

Complicating matters is the intensity of romantic love, which Fisher says is as powerful as addiction to drugs—and triggers similar pleasurable neurochemicals.

"All the addictions are associated with dopamine: cocaine, heroin, alcohol, tobacco."

Your brain in love is responding to that chemistry. Fisher says romantic love has three main characteristics of addiction. "First is tolerance. First you just see the guy on Saturday. Then you see him on Saturday and Wednesday. And pretty soon you want to move in. You need more and more.

"Then there's withdrawal. If you're without this person you go through this horrible pain.

"And finally there's relapse. You think you're over it, and eight months later he calls to ask you something and you're right back in love with him."

We've adapted to getting our hearts broken, too. Fisher says rejected lovers go through a stage of protest, followed by one of resignation and despair.

When the reward of romantic love is taken away, the brain's reward system first becomes elevated, and motivation and obsession increase, according to Fisher's research. That leads to an intense effort to win back the lost love.

"It's a typical mammalian response, to win back the mother," she says. "If you put a puppy in the kitchen by itself, away from its mother, it will throw itself at the door and whine and cry."

So spurned lovers beg for another chance and often get it. "Protest is adaptive if it works, if you can win back that mating partner."

But the protest stage can also involve enormous rage, even violence. Anger can be adaptive, Fisher says. "For millions of years, it was, you've got to get on with the mating process, move on to the next potential mate. So that fury would alienate them, and it would also help you to detach from them."

Just as protest may win love back and rage may help sever the connection, depression might be adaptive too.

"Depression evolved for a lot of good reasons. It's an accurate, honest sign that things are really wrong. It signals that to your friends, your family, the people around you, so they're more likely to come around and help you.

"And depression gives you a real dose of reality. You're no longer looking through those rose-colored glasses. And, of course, you can learn something from the experience."

In the last couple of decades, science has plumbed the chemistry of depression and invented ways to treat it. One class of antidepressants, selective serotonin re-uptake inhibitors (such as Prozac and Zoloft), have become enormously popular.

Fisher says that although in the short term they can be lifesavers, the drugs may have an unanticipated effect—they could be a sort of antidote to love.

When we fall in love, dopamine and norepinephrine levels rise, and serotonin levels fall. Taking SSRIs brings up the serotonin level and suppresses dopamine. That could inhibit romantic love.

Fisher says, "Long-term use could jeopardize people's ability to fall in love, to stay in love, or even to feel attachment for the partner they've got."

Research into the chemistry of love raises the question of whether it could lead to similar enhancers, the long-sought love potion.

Fisher says romantic love is too complicated for chemical manipulation.

"You can take cocaine right now, you can take Wellbutrin right now, and elevate your dopamine. But you won't fall in love with the next person you see.

"There are just so many cultural factors."

But, she says, such research may have indirect effects. For example, one thing that triggers dopamine is a novel experience, anything from an exotic vacation to bungee jumping. That could point to a way to keep a spark of romance in a long-term attachment.

"If you understand this, you can do novel things with someone you love. It may enable us to trigger these brain systems in our own ways," Fisher says.

"Now, you'll never get back that crazy feeling, that intensity and obsession all the time. And that's good, because it's very metabolically expensive.

"But a little romance—we all want that."

Mixed-Race Relationships Aren't Black and White

CHAPTER

Julia Cole

In the 21st century, people are increasingly forming relationships across religious, race and class boundaries. Does this mean that conflict is inevitable, or are people in such partnerships simply more adept at solving differences?

Statistics suggest that inter-racial marriage is on the increase. One in ten Asian women in the UK are with a white partner. And figures from the USA suggest that there has been a 30 percent rise in the past 40 years in the number of couples marrying across the black/white boundary.

The same statistics suggest that the more educated you are, the more likely you are to choose a partner from a race different to your own. Children of a dual ethnic heritage are the fastest-growing segment of the UK population.

These figures suggest that the current generation of children will regard relationships with partners from a different ethnic background to be natural and acceptable.

In just one generation, attitudes to crossing racial barriers have changed dramatically. A recent poll by The Observer newspaper found that 80 percent of 18 to 24-year-olds would consider a mixed-race marriage, while only 27 percent of those aged over 65 would.

So, is the outlook for inter-racial relationship rosy? The Observer poll found that 14 percent of those who are or were married to someone of a different colour to them would not consider mixed marriage again due to the difficulties they had encountered.

Clearly for some people, marrying across racial boundaries had caused problems.

If you are considering a relationship with someone of a different ethnic background, here are some pointers to help you think through what you need to consider:

Who am I going out with? It is important to get to know someone from a different background very well. It is possible to make assumptions about your potential partner's interests and ideas because of their colour or religion. Talk about how they were brought up, whether they have particular religious beliefs and how they feel their ethnicity has influenced their life. Be honest about yourself, explaining the same things about your own background. Don't focus on problems and talk yourselves out of the relationship, but face any issues you think may cause difficulties. For instance, if you know your parents may find it tough to accept someone of a different religion, tell your partner as soon as you have begun the relationship.

Talk about coping strategies. If it looks as though your relationship will continue, think through how you will manage possible problems. Sadly, you may encounter racial abuse, especially if you live in an area where inter-racial relationships are unusual (in rural areas, for example).

Talk about how you might handle this. Think about typical scenarios. For instance, what will we do if someone makes a rude remark in the pub? You also need to discuss how you will introduce your partner to your family. It is crucial that you are as positive as possible, demonstrating by example that you are at ease with one another. If you antici-pate specific issues will be raised (such as religious concerns), work through what you will say to parents and friends.

For example, you may want to say that you are aware of the differences in your religions but plan to explore each other's beliefs to understand them better. Never suggest you will convert to another religion to keep the peace. Giving your partner's family this impression if you know it is unlikely is harmful to your relationship with them. Never give your partner the impression that you might join their religion unless you genuinely know it's what you want to do.

How do you view the future of the relationship? Once you are going out together and the relationship looks stable, talk about what you want for the future. For instance, if you are a Catholic with a Protestant, discuss how you will approach issues [about] contra-ception or even abortion. It may seem lacking in romance to tackle such serious concerns at such an early stage, but without this attention to detail the relationship may run into difficulties.

This can happen because your expectations are built on assumed opinions and ideas, rather than a properly understood and shared knowledge of each other.

If the relationship is serious enough to consider marriage or living together, talk about the impact of your different backgrounds on any children you may have. Read [about] the subject to help you understand more. Try *Mixed Matches: How to Create Successful Inter-racial, Inter-ethnic and Inter-faith Relationships* by Joel Crohn (Fawcett Books).

Do not forget that the joys of an inter-cultural relationship often result as much from overcoming the obstacles as from the adventure of crossing cultures.

In a recent BBC interview Ishi Harbott (a Tanzanian Muslim), wife of Glen Harbott (a white UK resident), said: "It's crazy to object to mixed-race relationships. It enriches your life rather than detracts from it."

It seems that a growing number of people in Britain agree with her: Not only can a mixed-race marriage enrich the individuals concerned, it can also enrich the society we live in, helping to break down the unhealthy barriers of race.

Part

Maintaining Intimacy

The Key to Intimacy on Paper

Beth Sherman

CHAPTER

Michelle has a solid marriage. She and her husband are committed to each other. They have similar interests and shared values. She says she loves him, and he loves her. And sex isn't a problem.

But she still feels something is missing.

"Even though I love him, I can't really talk to him," says Michelle (not her real name), a 36-year-old mother of two, who works as an executive secretary in Manhattan. "I never know what he's thinking, what he's feeling. And I don't really feel comfortable telling him what I think a lot of the time. When I'm angry at him or disappointed, I keep those feelings to myself. When I'm feeling especially close to him, I can't say it out loud."

Like many people, she has difficulty with intimacy, which the dictionary defines as "a warm friendship developed through long association" and "that which characterizes one's deepest nature." In a romantic context, psychologists say intimacy is the ability to open up to your partner, to be comfortable stating your feelings and needs, to develop a shared emotional bond.

A recent study divided intimacy into four components: feelings of warmth and love; understanding and knowledge of your partner; physical and sexual closeness; and commitment. The study revealed that though most couples' commitment level increased as they progressed from dating to marriage to parenthood, their ability to understand and know each other decreased. "It's relatively easy to achieve instant intimacy," says Andrew Schwebel, a professor of psychology at Ohio State University who conducted the study. "The problem couples have is maintaining intimacy over the long haul."

Experts say the inability to achieve intimacy may stem from a variety of reasons. Some people are afraid that by opening up, they become vulnerable to being hurt. Others don't want their partners to view them as needy, imperfect or complaining. Still others never learned how to be close emotionally, often because their parents didn't express love and affection easily.

"People fear that by opening up to their partner, he or she might get angry or hurt them or reject them," says Bernard Katz, a professor of psychology at Nassau Community College who has a private practice in Plainview. "They fear by being honest, they could damage the relationship, and the other person could respond by telling them things they don't want to hear."

Katz says when it comes to intimacy, there are three types of people. The first group has no problem communicating openly and honestly. The next group experiences certain emotions and needs, but is afraid to share them. "People will tell things to a friend, a therapist, even a stranger. But they won't confide in someone with whom they're romantically involved," says Katz.

The third group is not in touch with their inner feelings and emotions. "You say: 'What are you thinking about?' And the answer is 'Nothing.' 'What are you feeling?' 'I don't know.' And they're telling you the absolute truth," Katz says.

According to therapists, most people have within them the desire for intimacy. "The wish to be connected with other people is universal," says Harold Bernard, a clinical psychologist in Manhattan. "But with some people, the capacity for intimacy has to be developed. It's not inborn or readily available."

Psychologists say there are a variety of ways to develop closeness and intimacy. When voicing an increased need for intimacy, they say, couples should be as specific as possible. "A woman will say to her husband: 'Tell me more about yourself. Reveal to me,'" says Samuel Osherson, author of *Wrestling with Love: How Men Struggle with Intimacy with Women, Children, Parents and Each Other* (Fawcett, $20). "Her husband hears this as an open-ended task. He's put on the spot, and he can't or won't do what she demands."

A better approach, says Osherson, is to state your needs and frustrations directly. "Say: 'Look. I feel you're not really taking the time to ask me how I am, how work went for me today. I need to know I matter to you.'"

Often, however, couples have difficulty stating the behavior that bothers them and the behavior they would like to see instead. In her book, *Passage to Intimacy*, which will be published by Fireside in June, Lori H. Gordon offers a "dialogue guide"—16 starter sentences that lead from one thought to the next and are designed to facilitate communication and change. She says to start with a simple request, one that is not charged with emotion. For instance, "I notice that you constantly give me advice when I drive. I assume this means that you think I need advice about my driving. I wonder why you do that. I suspect that you're used to giving directions..." And so on, until the last sentence, which begins: "I hope that you will change your behavior because it really matters to me."

"People need to fine-tune their thoughts and feelings and present them in a non-threatening manner," says Gordon, a marriage and family therapist and director of the PAIRS Institute (Practical Application of Intimate Relationship Skills), a 16-week program to improve couples' intimacy levels.

Experts urge care to avoid repeating old patterns and blaming your current partner for a parent's lack of love and understanding. "If your father rejected you when you were young and never appeared interested in what you said or did, you might be unconsciously blaming your husband for what happened in your past," says Osherson. "Your husband might never be verbal enough because you're associating his behavior with your father's."

Ultimately, experts say, being intimate involves more than just talking about your feelings. Listening is equally important. "True intimacy involves knowing that your partner is hearing what you're saying and acknowledging that what you're expressing is important. It's telling you you're valued," says Marion Solomon, author of "Narcissism & Intimacy: Love and Marriage in an Age of Confusion" (W.W. Norton, $10.95).

Some psychologists who work with couples conduct exercises designed to improve listening skills. One partner, for instance, is instructed to share what's on his or her mind. The other partner listens and then tries to repeat what has been said, sticking as closely as possible to the original statement. "Sometimes, people have difficulty repeating it back because they feel they're being put on the spot," says Jay Buchbinder, director of the Lifeworks Men's Center in Bellmore, which holds workshops on communication and intimacy. "People behave in a hostile or defensive manner because they're reacting to what's been said rather than listening to what's been said. If you're not listening, you're not understanding. And if you're not understanding, you're not communicating.

"What you want to do," he continues, "is listen to what's being expressed. Don't criticize or evaluate the need. It doesn't help to say: 'Why do you need that? You shouldn't need that. I wouldn't need that if I were you.'"

Although some people may have difficulty expressing intimate feelings and thoughts in words, actions can be just as significant. Solomon has a client who complains that her husband doesn't see her as a person in her own right and doesn't recognize her interests and her needs. When the client became interested in art, her husband went out and bought canvases and paint for her and set up a studio in their home. "She wasn't happy about it because she felt he was taking her interest away from her and assuming control," says Solomon. "He still wasn't saying: 'Your interest in art is wonderful. You're wonderful.'

"We tend to be very narcissistic in our world view," says Solomon. "Our reality is truth, so we feel that our {husbands or wives} should fulfill our needs our way. And that's just not realistic." In *Helping Men Express Love* Steven Farmer used to have a running joke with his first wife.

She'd say: "I love you."

He'd say: "You'll get over it."

"We never talked about our feelings," says Farmer, a psychotherapist and the author of *The Wounded Male* (Ballantine, $10). "When we wanted to get close, we'd have sex."

Farmer traces his difficulty with intimacy to his family upbringing. "In our house, being close meant you weren't fighting," he says. "My father was an alcoholic, and, at times, he could be rageful and violent. I vowed I'd never be like him. So instead, when I got angry, I would pull away and withdraw."

Experts say many men have problems with intimacy. To express love and affection openly, they say, flies in the face of the "tough guy" image still fostered by society. "Women are comfortable initiating contact, starting conversation," says Jay Buchbinder, director of the Lifeworks Men's Center in Bellmore. "But men are caught up with work, with responsibilities. There's very little value placed on developing close relationships."

Men generally join his group when they are going through some kind of crisis. "Say there's a medical problem. Or a marriage just broke up. Or someone just lost his job," says Buchbinder. "When something dramatic happens, we want to reach out to someone."

Those men who want to become less closed off emotionally might try exercises meant to enhance self-expression. Some therapists recommend doing facial exercises—growling, making faces, baring your teeth, raising your eyebrows. "When we're young, we learn to put on a mask, and eventually that mask becomes permanent," says Marvin Berk, a social worker who leads weekly support groups for men in Manhattan. "Softening the facial muscles loosens the defenses."

Farmer encourages men to practice body awareness. Often, he says, physical sensations (such as feeling constricted or flushed), can cue men to what they are feeling emotionally. In one exercise, he has men pay attention to their breathing and then scan their bodies from head to foot, noticing strain, tension or numbness. "If we don't have words for our feelings, we tend to experience those feelings as tension," he says.

Still another exercise he uses is to have men write down memories of various experiences in their lives and the feelings these events evoked—grief over the loss of a parent, anger toward a friend, the first blush of love for a spouse. Reliving the painful or joyous events, he says, helps bring feelings closer to the surface.

After years of therapy and workshops devoted to personal growth and change, Farmer believes his own capacity for intimacy is greatly improved. "Occasionally, I fall back into old patterns and go into withdrawal," he notes, "but I try to catch it. And when I do, I'm willing to communicate. To say: 'I'm scared. Or I'm angry. Or I love you.'"

Opposites Attract, But Shared Values Keep Us Together

CHAPTER 12

Elizabeth Heathcote

Falling in love is a bit like being a tourist: a time for pure pleasure, focusing on the welcoming locals rather than the rubbish in the backstreets. There are so many bonkers chemicals flying around, so much hope, expectation and lust, that it can be hard to catch glimpses of the stripped-down reality of five years hence.

But as a relationship agony aunt, I have learned that reading the signals from a prospective partner can be even harder if you come from different cultures—particularly if theirs looks glam. And while it is romantic and stimulating to take the short-cut into someone else's culture that only a love affair can offer, the truth is that, long term, it can mean hard work. Relationships thrive on similarity, not difference.

"Think of each partner as a disco ball with lots of little mirrors," says Adrienne Burgess, author of *Will He Still Love Me Tomorrow?*, which analyses relationship data.

She says: "For a relationship to work, quite a lot of your mirrors have to be similar but especially in terms of values and experience. Opposites attract but they don't stay together as long."

Burgess's research rates shared values and experience as two of the most important factors in successful relationship; much more so than shared interests. It's a cliché that meeting "the one" feels like "coming home" but that is what most people are looking for: a person we can finally relax alongside; who understands what we mean and what we want and who we are. That comes from familiarity and shared assumptions.

"All of us are born into families and communities with their own belief systems, and where two different sets meet, there is always the potential for a rub," says Denise Knowles, a Relate counsellor. "Ideally, what you get is compromise, a rich cross-pollination, but it can turn into a major source of conflict, especially when children come into the picture."

This does not mean that cross-cultural relationships are never made in heaven. It is possible to have grown up in a family of a similar size with a similar feeling and values even if it was half-way across the world, or within a different race or creed.

"I know a very successful mixed-race couple whose backgrounds, on the surface, look so different," says Burgess. "But both families had a similar sort of feeling—warm and happy—with a similar number of children and similar aspirations. The couple emphasize these similarities. They are very close."

Couples Communications Getting on the Right Track

CHAPTER

J. Gibson Henderson

The most common complaint of those couples who come for counseling is not money, sex or their children but complaints about "communication problems," or lack of communication. People are bewildered that they initially had so much in common, felt so comfortable together, found it so easy to talk to each other and now frequently encounter either silence or arguments without end.

For example, Rick and Diane have been married for seven years. Rick is typically very busy at his job and in his free time, he looks for every chance he can get to play golf. Diane is very occupied with her volunteer activities. They have two small children and are devoted parents, but consequently have even less time for each other.

For years, Diane has been telling Rick she wants more time with him. She says he never talks to her and she wants him more involved with the family. He staunchly and rationally defends his right to have time to himself. He says he works hard for the family and deserves time to play golf. Diane just as rightly expresses her frustration at his distance from her and the children.

Now, Diane and Rick are coming in for counseling because Diane is interested in someone else and Rick has found out. Rick is outraged that Diane is seeing someone but at least he is coming in with her for counseling, something she has wanted for years.

What's at the heart of Diane's unfaithfulness? Sex? Not yet, although she does have passionate feelings for the other person. Intimacy? Yes! She wants—and with her new lover, has found—what's missing for her in her marriage: the closeness that comes with talking and being listened to, the intimacy that comes with sharing life together.

So many times, couples are absolutely right in the positions they communicate to each other. Rick is reasonable wanting time to himself. Diane is correct to want more communication in the marriage. Yet both also miss the point, which is not to be right but to develop some shared vision of their relationship. Rick is blind to the importance of solid communication in a marriage. He hasn't realized that what Diane wants also will make a positive difference in his life. Diane lacks strategies for getting Rick to listen to her, for putting things positively and for making small, specific and immediate requests that will give her some satisfaction. Instead, she asks for what seems like a major change in his lifestyle and scares him into defending his turf. The emotional intensity grows with each repeated encounter. It's now reached the point where it's hard to imagine that a simple weekend alone for the couple might solve at least Diane's immediate needs for contact. Much of marital communication makes mountains out of molehills on both sides.

So what do couples need to know to find their way out of these ceaseless arguments? For starters, couples need to discover the simple power of listening.

For men, it's often hard to listen because they are trained to fix things. They can't imagine that just allowing their partner to get something off her chest and letting her know they are listening can provide relief in itself. Listening will actually allow her to calm down and make a small, fulfillable request. Saying, "I understand" or "I'm sorry that happened," can make a great difference. These statements should be followed by "What can I do to help?" or "Is there something I can do right now to help?" Such questions take courage because of the imagined "mountains" that will be asked.

For a women, it's often hard to ask for what she wants. Most women have been trained to take care of others first, themselves later (only later never seems to come). A woman doesn't feel entitled to ask specifically for something that might inconvenience her partner. She also hasn't had sufficient practice in noticing small things that might help her to feel better because she's been too busy learning to notice small things that will help others. Since she can't ask for what she wants, a woman often hopes the other person will read her mind and give her what she wants without being asked. When things aren't spontaneously given, frustration mounts and she feels resentful. Slowly the pressure builds until the lid blows off. Then she starts attacking rather than asking, pushing for major changes, rather than small, specific and feasible requests. Part of the allure of the other relationship for Diane was that her lover gave her his time and attention without having to be asked. She didn't like the idea of asking Rick for time and attention in small specific ways ("It would mean a lot of me if we could get a sitter and spend the day together Saturday").

Diane's affair enraged Rick, but also made him anxious about losing the relation-ship. He became emotionally prepared to listen. I have seen many couples in my practice for whom some event in their lives (an affair, a heart attack, retirement, one partner sincerely announcing he or she is ready to leave the relationship) opens the ears of the other partner. Enlivened by the crisis, the partners begin to talk and listen to each other. By the time they arrive for the first counseling session, many are already able to report positive changes in the marriage from the talking and listening. Sometimes there has been so much change happening already that the previously estranged partner is concerned, not so much about finding more changes, but in gaining confidence that the current changes can and will continue.

So what is this communication about? What's the goal? Why talk? Harville Hendrix, in his wonderful book *Getting the Love You Want*, suggests that our job in relationships is to discover and give to the other person those things they always wanted but didn't get with their parents. The irony is that we marry people we think have all the positive qualities lacking in our parents, only to find that they also have all the negative qualities. As we stub our toes again and again on the unexpected stones in our partner's personality, we develop negative patterns of communication.

For example, Jean and Mike repeatedly wind up in the same argument over Mike's driving. Jean thinks Mike drives carelessly and puts them both at risk for injury. She reacts to the speed of this driving and to his following other cars too closely. She pleads with him to slow down or back off. He is offended that she challenges his driving, thereby challenging his adequacy and his independence. Mike tells Jean that he knows what he's doing and that she's overly cautious.

What's behind this disagreement is that Jean comes from a family with an alcoholic father whose behavior and moods were quite unpredictable. She grew up living with fear and a deep longing for a sense of security and safety. She also grew up expecting that there was no point in asking for things she wanted. Through counseling, she and Mike came to understand better the root of her fears and Jean was able to put her needs to Mike as a positive request. "Mike, I know that you drive in a way that feels right for you. How you drive is your choice and I can't control it. But I want you to know how important it is for me to feel safe and secure. When you give space to the car in front of you and slow down, I feel secure and cared for and appreciate it very much." The request was delivered at a calm moment and not in the car.

Harville Hendrix suggests an exercise he calls "stretching" to help couples turn their frustrations into positive requests. He asks each person to write down those things their partner does that bother them and write down the desire that lies hidden in each frustration ("I would like to feel safe and relaxed when you're driving"). Then, the couples write specific requests that would help satisfy that desire.

Another reason many couples go wrong is because they don't accept and respect their differences. We have a belief that love should obliterate differences, that compatibility means a shared view of the world. Don Jackson, in his book *The Mirages of Marriage*, says there are a few marriages in which the partners are alike in all aspects of their backgrounds (religion, parents level of income and education, where they were raised, whether their parents were divorced, etc.). In fact, these couples do have a better chance of getting through a long married life together with relatively little conflict. This type of marriage, however, is very much the exception, not the rule. Most couples will have to learn to acknowledge and respect their differences and not try to force the other person to see and do it their way.

It should be noted that differences are not all bad. They have the potential to be good for the marriage and for the family when they are respected. When people have different opinions, it can lead to even better solutions to problems. What's required is not having the same opinions, but having patience and not panicking over the differences in order to allow the solution to emerge. Dog breeders know that too much inbreeding (too much sameness, not enough difference) leads to unhealthy results. Couples should agree to disagree and notice their ways of finding solutions with which both can live.

Perhaps the most common way couples communications fail is through a focus on "problem talk" rather than on "solution talk." Frequently, couples wind up arguing over what the problem is, who has the right view of the problem, what the facts are. They never get around to what their goals are, where they're headed. Couples confuse the means with the end and argue about how to get there, without considering where it is they're going. This is analogous to arguing over whether to fly or drive on the family vacation, arguing the speed of flying versus the economy of driving, without agreeing first on where it is the family wants to go! Once the vision of the Grand Canyon is firmly implanted in everyone's mind, how they get there is a practical but not primary issue.

Many therapists today are learning that couples can resolve problems much more quickly when they spend very little time describing the problem and much more time talking about the solution. When Diane was asked about the times she felt happy with Rick's involvement with the family, she was able to recall times during a recent vacation when he sat at the dinner table and joked with the children and when he spent 15 minutes reading a story to their 3-year-old. These and other experiences Diane could recall turned out to be things Rick was able to do more of, even when not on vacation. Diane felt more hopeful when a few such occasions took place in a week. When Rick heard how much Diane had appreciated those times, he in turn felt optimistic.

Communication itself is not the ultimate goal for couples, it is rather a means to achieve other goals that may not yet be started. So when couples come in saying that they need to communicate better, I ask, "How will that help you? What will you notice different when you're communicating better?" Their specific and positive visions of the present and future are what couples most need to discuss. Although there are many possible strategies for improving communication, here are three in particular I recommend:

1.   Devote 15 minutes a day for a week to listening to your partner. Set aside other thoughts and activities. Simply listen and try to reflect what you hear. "So, Johnny and Jerry were fighting all day and you feel like climbing the walls. That sounds pretty awful." DON'T TRY TO FIX IT! JUST LISTEN! When you see signs of the storm subsiding, you may ask, "Is there anything I can do to help?"

2.   Don't panic! If you're tempted to argue while listening, it's probably because what your spouse is saying makes you anxious, not because you're right. Focus on your breathing instead. Just take some slow, easy breaths. Remember that resolving differences successfully usually involves small, specific and feasible changes, not a complete change in lifestyle and priorities.

3.   Think Solution not Problem. In relationships, unlike medicine, accurate diagnosis is not the key to cure. In fact, that usually just focuses people on the negative. Constructing positive solutions and a positive vision of the future provides hope, energy and satisfaction. Notice things that happen which you'd like to see more of. If you're going to dwell on the past, dwell on something positive that happened and ask for more of it. For more help in constructing solutions, read *Divorce Busting* by Michelle Weiner-Davis.

Learning to talk and listen to each other more positively and effectively takes hard work and commitment. Couples must be patient and remember to express appreciation for any small steps in the right direction. Ultimately, the effort involved can produce a relationship where both people are getting more of what they want individually and what they both hoped for when they were falling in love.

The Sexual Vocabularies of Heterosexual and Homosexual Males and Females for Communicating Erotically with a Sexual Partner

Joel W. Wells, Ph.D.[1]

This study explored what terminology constitutes an erotic or arousing language for male and female, heterosexual and homosexual, and the extent to which that language is used with a sexual partner. Five sexual references were included: male genitalia, female genitalia, lovemaking/coitus, oral-genital contact, and hand-genital contact. Respondents consisted of 120 urban midwestern university students, 30 in each gender and sexual orientation category. Sexual orientation was as powerful a predictor as gender for language that was considered erotic. Lesbians and gay males more often than heterosexual females and males used erotic or arousing vocabulary with a spouse or lover. Gay males more often used slang with a spouse or lover than did heterosexual males and heterosexual females. Implications for sexual arousal based upon communication are discussed.

Key Words: erotic communication; sexual orientation; gender; erotic communication.

Department of Home Economics—Family Studies, 229 Latham Hall, University of Northern Iowa, Cedar Falls, Iowa 50614-0442.

From *Archives of Sexual Behavior*, Vol. 19, No. 2, pp. 139-147. Copyright © 1980 by Plenum Publishing Corporation. Reprinted by permission

Introduction

Previous research has shown that male and female use different terminology to describe sexual behaviors and sexual anatomy in various intimate (Sanders, 1978) and social contexts, including with a spouse or lover (Simkins and Rinck, 1982). MacDougald (1961) first noted that the use of erotic words during sexual intercourse can evoke negative, neutral, or positive reactions in heterosexual arousal. No previous investigation has examined the extent to which vocabulary that is considered erotic or arousing is used with a sexual partner or has included sexual orientation as a variable. Only recently have differences in the use of sexual language in various interpersonal contexts been reported between heterosexuals and homosexuals with results indicating that sexual orientation is a significant variable (Wells, 1989).

Masters and Johnson (1979) suggested that lesbian and gay couples, when compared to heterosexual couples, talk with each other more often about what they want and like sexually. Their findings state that homosexual couples are less performance- or goal-oriented in their sexual interactions as well as less distracted by noises and other people when involved in sex play than are heterosexual couples. In this same research, comparing arousal techniques between homosexual and heterosexual couples, they reported that the former attend more to style of sexual interaction and take longer to give and receive sexual pleasure, i.e., more hugging, caressing, kissing, oral-genital stimulation, and full-body contact. Blumstein and Schwartz (1983) reported that heterosexuals are more constrained than homosexuals by traditional sexual roles. Symons (1979) also argued that lesbian and gay male sexual behavior represents a stereotypically pure form of male and female sexuality in that socialized masculine and feminine sexual behaviors are carried out in the context of a same-sex relationship. Symons suggested that in heterosexual relationships, male and female compromise their true sexual natures.

Because physical sexual arousal techniques have been reported to be different between heterosexuals and homosexuals, even though physiological arousal responses are identical, and because sexual terminology usage differs between male and female as well as between heterosexual and homosexual, the following hypotheses were proposed:

1. Gay males, lesbians, heterosexual males, and heterosexual females will differ on what constitutes erotic or arousing language.

2. Agreement of terms considered erotic or arousing and the use of those terms with a spouse or lover will be greater for lesbians and gay males than for heterosexuals.

3. Verbal sexual communication, use of erotic or arousing words, and the use of slang during sexual interaction will be greater for homosexuals than for heterosexuals.

The purpose of this investigation is to identify sexual terminology that represents erotic or arousing language in intimate relationships for female and male who identify themselves as either homosexual or heterosexual. Further, this study seeks to determine the use and amount of erotic verbal communication in sexual relationships as it relates to gender and sexual orientation.

Method

SUBJECTS

Respondents were 120 urban midwestern undergraduate university students, 96 of whom were enrolled in a human sexuality class and 24 who were members of the gay-lesbian organization on campus. Data were collected in human sexuality courses on a volunteer basis for credit over two semesters with a total of 210 heterosexual males, 225 heterosexual females, 13 lesbians, and 23 gay males responding ($N = 471$) out of a total enrollment of 483 students. Participants clipped a card to the questionnaire with their name on it when returning it. The name card was removed from the questionnaires after credit was recorded for anonymity. Through the campus gay-lesbian organization, 17 more lesbians ($n = 30$) and 21 additional gay males ($n = 44$) participated. Since the lesbian sample was 30, that served as a base number upon which to randomly select respondents from the other three groups. Thus, 30 heterosexual male questionnaires were pulled from the total of 210; 30 heterosexual female questionnaires were pulled from the total of 225; and 30 gay male questionnaires were pulled from the total of 44, so that each of the four groups comprised 30 students. The mean age for each group of 30 was heterosexual males, 22.1; gay males, 22.9; heterosexual females, 21.4; and lesbians, 22.0 years old.

PROCEDURE

Students were asked to self-rate their sexual orientation on the 7-point Kinsey Rating Scale (Kinsey *et al.,* 1948) by using 0 as representing exclusively heterosexual to 6 as representing exclusively homosexual. All 60 heterosexual students self-rated themselves as 0. Lesbians and gay males self-rated their sexual orientation as 5 (17 female and 9 male) or 6 (13 female and 21 male), predominantly homosexual-insignificantly heterosexual and exclusively homosexual, respectively, with a mean of 5.4 for lesbians and 5.7 for gay males.

The questionnaire used was an expanded version of one part of Sanders' (1978) questionnaire, which asked students to write the word they would use with a spouse or lover to indicate male genitalia, female genitalia, and coitus. Oral-genital contact and hand-genital contact were added to the questionnaire in this study. If students would not engage in such a discussion or would rely on nonverbal cues, they were to leave the response area blank. Respondents were also asked to write the word that for them was considered the most erotic or arousing for the same three terms representing sexual behaviors and two terms representing male and female genitalia. If students had never had a spouse or a lover, they were asked to write the word that they expected that they would most likely use for each of the three sexual behaviors and male and female genitalia. Additionally, students were asked to answer three questions about their participation in sexual conversation with a spouse or lover during sexual interaction by using a 10-point scale with 1 interpreted as meaning *never* and 10 as *always*. The three questions were (i) "When I am engaged in lovemaking/coitus, I talk to my sexual partner about what we are doing"; (ii) "When I am engaged in lovemaking/coitus I say 'sexy,' or arousing words to my sexual partner"; and (iii) When I am engaged in lovemaking/coitus, I use slang/four-letter words to talk to my sexual partner."

Three methods of analyzing the data were employed. Rank order by percentage and chi square were used to analyze the word(s) and type of term(s) used with a spouse or lover and considered most erotic or arousing for the three sexual behaviors and male and female genitalia (see Tables 10.1 and 10.2, Hypothesis 1 and 2). *T* tests were used to determine mean differences between heterosexual and homosexual regarding sexual communication. These questions included talk during sexual relations, use of erotic words, and use of slang during sexual relations with a spouse or lover (see Table 10.3, Hypothesis 3).

Results

Analysis revealed that what is considered erotic terminology for male and female and heterosexual and homosexual varied as much for sexual orientation as for gender. Responses for male and female and heterosexual and homosexual in percentages supports Hypothesis 1 (see Table 10.1).

Heterosexual males are more likely than gay males, heterosexual females, or lesbians to consider the term "cunt" as erotic, although "pussy" is the preferred term followed by "vagina." Heterosexual females considered both "vagina" and "pussy" as equally erotic whereas lesbians used "clit" or "clitoris" as the most erotic term. The largest percentage of gay males reported "no term" as erotic or arousing for female genitalia.

Heterosexual females thought "penis" was the most erotic term for male genitalia followed by the term "dick." Heterosexual males used "dick" as their erotic term for male genitalia while gay males and lesbians used "cock."

"Make love" was cited as the most erotic term for lovemaking/coitus for heterosexual males, heterosexual females, and lesbians. Gay males used "fuck" as their most erotic term for lovemaking/coitus followed by "make love."

Table 10.1

Erotic Terminology by Gender and Sexual Orientation in Percentages[a]

	GENDER AND SEXUAL ORIENTATION[B]			
	HETEROSEXUAL		HETEROSEXUAL	
SPECIFIC TERM	MALES	GAY MALES	FEMALES	LESBIANS
Female genitalia				
Vagina	16.7	10.0	33.3	6.7
Clitoris (clit)	13.3	0.0	3.3	46.7
Pussy	30.0	26.7	33.3	30.0
Cunt	23.3	10.0	9.1	0.0
Other	16.7	10.0	16.7	13.3
None	0.0	43.3	10.0	3.3
	$\chi^2(15) = 69.88, p \leq 0.0001$			
Male genitalia				
Penis	20.0	10.0	40.0	20.0
Dick	40.0	13.3	23.3	10.0
Cock	33.3	66.7	10.0	40.0
Other	6.7	10.0	20.0	10.0
None	0.0	0.0	6.7	20.0
	$\chi^2(12) = 39.71, p \leq 0.0001$			
Coitus				
Make love	60.0	36.7	90.0	76.7
Fuck	26.7	53.3	3.3	20.0
Sex	0.0	6.7	3.3	0.0
Screw	6.7	0.0	0.0	0.0
Other	6.7	3.3	3.3	3.3
	$\chi^2(12) = 32.56, p \leq 0.00001$			
Oral-genital contact				
Fellatio/cunnilingus	3.3	0.0	0.0	0.0
Oral sex	16.7	0.0	26.7	0.0
Head	16.7	13.3	3.3	0.0
Blow job	33.3	30.0	6.7	3.3
Suck	3.3	46.7	10.0	46.7
Eat	3.3	3.3	20.0	23.3
Other	23.3	6.7	30.0	23.3
None	0.0	0.0	3.3	3.3
	$\chi^2(21) = 68.73, p \leq 0.00001$			
Hand-genital contact				
Masturbate	20.0	13.3	16.7	10.0
Hand job	23.3	6.7	10.0	23.3
Jack off/Jerk/Beat off	10.0	70.0	0.0	6.7
Fondle/touch/pet	16.7	0.0	43.3	23.3
Stroke	0.0	6.7	10.0	23.3
Other	26.7	3.3	20.0	13.3
None	3.3	0.0	0.0	0.0
	$\chi^2(18) = 80.50, p \leq 0.00001$			

[a]Percentage derived from terms considered erotic out of total terms used.
[b]$N = 30$ in each group.

For oral-genital contact gay males and lesbians preferred "suck" as most erotic. Heterosexual females used "oral sex" as most erotic followed by "eat," whereas heterosexual males reported "blow job" as most erotic. Generally, heterosexuals more than homosexuals considered a wider range of terms as erotic for oral-genital contact.

Gay males listed "jack off," "jerk off," or "beat off" as erotic or arousing terms for hand-genital contact, whereas lesbians considered "pet," "touch," or "stroke" as erotic or arousing terms. Heterosexual females said that "fondle," "pet," and "touch" were the most erotic or arousing. Heterosexual males more often considered "other terms" which are used as euphemisms or indirect expressions for hand-genital contact as erotic or arousing.

Hypothesis 2 was supported. Generally, homosexuals more than heterosexuals used sexual vocabulary with a partner that they agree is erotic or arousing. The only exception in the five categories—male genitalia, female genitalia, lovemaking/coitus, oral-genital contact, and hand-genital contact—is lovemaking/coitus (see Table 10.2).

Though lesbians and gay males talked to their partner during sexual activity more often than heterosexual males and females, a significant difference was not found ($X = 6.20$, heterosexuals; $X = 6.95$, homosexuals, $t = 1.84$, $p \leq 0.06$, Hypothesis 3).

Table 10.2

Percentage of Terms Used Considered Erotic Out of Total Sexual Terms Used With a Spouse/Lover by Sexual Orientation and Gender[a]

SEXUAL ORIENTATION AND GENDER	FEMALE GENITALIA	MALE GENITALIA	COITUS	HAND-GENITAL CONTACT	ORAL-GENITAL CONTACT
Heterosexual males	40.0	36.7	60.0	40.0	40.0
Gay males	30.0[b]	80.8	63.3	70.0	66.7
Heterosexual females	30.0	40.0	66.7	40.0	36.7
Lesbians	50.0	43.3[c]	70.0	60.0	53.3
$\chi^2(3)$ total by column	7.33, $p \leq 0.06$	25.30, $p \leq 0.0001$	0.86, $p \leq 0.83$	12.86, $p \leq 0.005$	11.46, $p \leq 0.009$
Total $\chi^2(12)$			28.79, $p \leq 0.01$		

[a]Percentage derived from terms considered erotic by individuals out of total sexual terms used by individuals with a spouse/lover. $N = 30$ in each group.
[b]Not applicable, 66.7%.
[c]Not applicable, 19.8%.

Table 10.3

T Tests for Verbal Communication With a Spouse/Lover during Coitus/Lovemaking by Sexual Orientation and Gender[a]

VARIABLE	$\overline{X}$[b]	SD	SE	df	t VALUE	p
Use erotic/arousing words						
Female						
Heterosexual	4.90	2.07	0.38			
				58	– 1.58	<0.120
Lesbian	5.83	2.49	0.46			
Male						
Heterosexual	5.07	1.89	0.35			
				58	– 2.13	<0.038
Gay	6.27	2.43	0.44			
Use slang						
Female						
Heterosexual	2.27	1.60	0.29			
				58	– 2.21	<0.031
Lesbian	3.33	2.11	0.39			
Male						
Heterosexual	2.50	1.85	0.34			
				58	– 3.28	<0.002
Gay	4.57	2.91	0.53			

[a]N = 30 in each group.
[b]Mean scores based on a 10-point Likert scale.

Homosexuals generally, gay males particularly, more often than heterosexual respondents used erotic or arousing words during sexual interaction (X = 4.98, heterosexuals; X = 6.05, homosexuals, t = –2.63, $p \leq 0.01$, see Table 10.3, Hypothesis 3). "Gay males and lesbians will make greater use of slang vocabulary as erotic or arousing terminology in their sexual interaction than will heterosexuals" was supported for gay males (X = 2.38, heterosexuals; X = 3.95, homosexuals, t = –3.90, $p \leq 0.0001$, see Table 10.3, Hypothesis 3).

Generally, gay males and lesbians talked with their intimate partner about sexual activity more often than heterosexual females and males did according to the results of this study. Gay males and lesbians also made greater use of erotic or arousing sexual vocabulary and more often used slang words during sexual interaction.

Discussion

There is no universally standard erotic vocabulary for use with a spouse or lover based upon gender or sexual orientation. Rather, gender and sexual orientation are variables that significantly affect the perception of what is considered erotic vocabulary. Homosexuals are significantly more likely to agree on what is erotic and to use such vocabulary with a spouse or lover than are heterosexuals.

Heterosexuals more often than homosexuals use sexual language they do not consider erotic or arousing. Symons (1979) suggested that heterosexuals compromise their true sexual natures in the context of a sexual relationship and thus feel they cannot use what is most erotic or arousing with a partner, possibly because they fear rejection or because of discomfort with such vocabulary. Gay males and lesbians can sexually relate to a same-sex partner in a stereotypically pure form of male and female socialization according to Symons.

Heterosexual male and female appear to show more constraint and adherence to traditional gender roles when it comes to using erotic language with a spouse or lover than gay males and lesbians do with a spouse or lover. Masters and Johnson (1979) proposed that lesbian couples and gay male couples, when compared to heterosexual couples, talk with each other more often about what they want sexually. Although this study did not find a significant difference between homosexuals and heterosexuals in terms of talking with a partner about what they want sexually, results indicate that the differences between these two groups approached significance favoring greater sexual communication among homosexuals.

The greater use of arousing or erotic language with a spouse or lover by gay males and lesbians suggests that if indeed there are barriers to heterosexual erotic communication, heterosexuals may want to break free of stereotypical roles and learn from gay males and lesbians regarding the use of sexually arousing communication. Each partner might give to the other and to themselves what is erotic or arousing in the way of sexual language to enhance their sexual relationship.

References

Blumstein, P. W., and Schwartz, P. (1983). *American Couples: Money, Work and Sex,* Morrow, New York.

Kinsey, A. C., Pomeroy, W. B., and Martin, C. E. (1948). *Sexual Behavior in the Human Male,* W. B. Saunders, Philadelphia.

MacDougald, D. (1961). Language and sex. In Ellis, A., and Arbarbanel, A. (eds.), *Encyclopedia of Sexual Behavior,* Hawthorne, New York, pp. 585-598.

Masters, W. H., and Johnson, V. E. (1979). *Homosexuality in Perspective,* Little, Brown, Boston.

Sanders, J. S. (1978). Male and female vocabularies for communicating with a sexual partner. *J. Sex Educ. Ther. 4*: 15-19.

Simkins, L., and Rinck, C. (1982). Male and female sexual vocabularies in different interpersonal contexts. *J. Sex Res. 18*: 160-172.

Symons, D. (1979). *The Evolution of Human Sexuality,* Oxford University Press, New York.

Wells, J. W. (1989). Sexual language usage in different interpersonal contexts: A comparison of gender and sexual orientation. *Arch. Sex. Behav. 18*: 127-143.

For Better Sex: Less Conflict, More Friendship

CHAPTER 15

USA Today

Men and women have different emotional needs when it comes to revving up their sex lives, a new study says.

For men, the key to improving sex, romance and passion is reducing conflict, those confrontations that raise their blood pressure.

For women, the vital ingredient is increasing friendship, the togetherness they see as just as important at the breakfast table as in the bedroom, says University of Washington-Seattle psychologist John Gottman. Friendship doesn't mean being merely "nice," but rather knowing yourself and your mate at a profound level, he says.

When couples are able to increase friendship and reduce conflict, they are then able to "access their sense of humor and their affection for one another," he says.

For three decades, Gottman has been studying how couples interact. This current project and others, he says, demonstrate that arguing activates a man's "fight or flight" response. He feels "threatened, vigilant," not eager for sex.

If a touchy subject is presented calmly, the level of conflict will be reduced, Gottman says. In stable couples, both spouses express fewer negative and more positive emotions at the start of discussions, his research projects show.

Women need a deep sense of connection and friendship to feel passionate, he says. This type of friendship has three elements:

- Love maps. "This is a road map of your partner's internal world," he says. It means being able to define a mate's "life dreams."

- Fondness and admiration. "This involves respect, affection, small gestures of appreciation. Some partners scan the environment looking for something to criticize rather than something to say thank you for."

- Attempts at connection. "These are jokes, playful comments, bids for attention that test the waters to see if a partner will respond." Responding implies there will be an "emotional connection."

Gottman's research teams have studied more than 2,000 couples in his Seattle "marriage lab." His methods there include conducting extensive interviews and videotaping couples interacting, using various devices to take physical measures such as heart rates as couples discuss troublesome topics.

He also has instructed more than 3,000 couples in various workshop settings. This newest study involved 100 married couples who attended one- or two-day workshops and were contacted for a follow-up study about what worked for them one year later. Some participated in a total of nine sessions of marital therapy to reinforce what was learned in the workshops about conflict, friendship, romance and "a shared sense of meaning," he says.

His findings were presented Thursday to the Smart Marriages conference in Arlington, Va., sponsored by the Coalition for Marriage, Family and Couples Education.

Seeing One's Partner Through Intimacy-Colored Glasses: An Examination of the Process Underlying the Intimacy Goals–Relationship Satisfaction Link

CHAPTER

Catherine A. Sanderson and Sarah M. Evans

Considerable research in both personality psychology and close relationships has shown the importance of intimacy to relationship satisfaction (Berscheid, 1983; Kelley, 1979). Relationship satisfaction is enhanced when individuals have greater emotional involvement in their relationships (Rubin, Hill, Peplau, & Dunkel-Schetter, 1980) and engage in self-disclosure, trust, and interdependence with their partners (Altman & Taylor, 1973; Hendrick, 1981; Levinger & Senn, 1967; Reis & Shaver, 1988). In contrast, relationships with little intimacy are more prone to dissolution (Hendrick, 1981; Hendrick, Hendrick, & Adler, 1988; Hill, Rubin, & Peplau, 1976; Simpson, 1987). Thus, creating intimacy in a relationship plays an important role in satisfaction.

Given the importance of intimacy in creating satisfying and lasting relationships, individuals who are particularly focused on the pursuit of intimacy in their relationships should experience greater satisfaction than those without such a focus. Although the prevailing cultural meaning for dating has emphasized the pursuit of intimacy (e.g., self-disclosure, mutual dependence, and open communication) (see Hazan & Shaver, 1987;

McAdams, 1984), some people choose to pursue goals related to self-exploration and independence within the context of dating relationships (Cantor & Malley, 1991; Clark & Reis, 1988). In fact, research has shown that individuals vary in the extent to which they are focused on and adept at creating intimacy in a relationship (e.g., Berscheid, Snyder, & Omoto, 1989; Cantor, Acker, & Cook-Flannagan, 1992; McAdams, 1984; Prager, 1995; Sanderson & Cantor, 1995, 1997), with those who have secure working models of attachment (Hazan & Shaver, 1987; Simpson, 1990) and successful resolution of identity issues (e.g., Erikson, 1950) being more likely to pursue intimacy goals. Not surprisingly, individuals with intimacy goals do experience greater satisfaction in both dating (Sanderson & Cantor, 1997) and marital relationships (Sanderson & Cantor, in press).

Although prior research demonstrates that the pursuit of intimacy goals is associated with higher levels of relationship satisfaction, little is known about the specific processes underlying this association. This study first examines if those with intimacy goals structure and/or experience their dating relationships in particular ways (e.g., do they engage in intimacy-conducive relationship interactions, have intimacy-focused dating partners, and/or perceive their partners as intimacy focused). Next, we will examine the role of each of these three factors in mediating the link between intimacy goals and relationship satisfaction.

Interactions in Dating Relationships

Considerable research on personal goals has emphasized their role in the structuring and experience of daily life (Cantor, 1994; Gollwitzer, 1993; Mischel, Cantor, & Feldman, 1996; Snyder & Ickes, 1985). Individuals select particular goal-relevant situations in which to spend time; evoke particular actions, strategies, and responses from others; and even manipulate situations to suit their needs (Buss, 1987). For example, Diener and colleagues (Diener, Larsen, & Emmons, 1984) found that extraverts spend more time in social recreation situations, whereas those high in need for order spend more time in typical (as opposed to novel) situations. Similarly, individuals interact within these broadly goal-relevant situations in particular ways (e.g., those high on extraversion may engage in self-disclosure with a variety of others). Individuals therefore are quite adept at structuring and interacting in their daily lives in order to fulfill their goals.

Similarly, individuals with intimacy goals in dating may engage in a variety of patterns of interaction with their dating partner that facilitate intimacy. First, they may spend more time alone with their partner, which allows for communication and companionship and hence may help encourage and strengthen a relationship (Reissman, Aron, & Bergen, 1993). For example, Silbereisen and colleagues (Silbereisen, Noack, & von Eye, 1992) found that adolescents involved in established relationships, who presumably are more interested in self-disclosure and interdependence, select private settings over more public settings when spending time with their partners. Second, individuals with intimacy goals may engage in relationship-enhancing thoughts, such as their feelings about their partner and the positive experiences they have shared (Cate, Koval, Lloyd, & Wilson, 1995; Franzoi, Davis, & Young, 1985). These thoughts may enhance positive feelings about and commitment to both their partner and the relationship. Third, individuals with intimacy goals may be more dependent on their partner and expect their partner to be dependent on them for support, understanding, and resources, which fosters intimacy by enhancing feelings of responsibility to and reliance on the relationship (Fincham & Bradbury, 1990; Kelley, 1979; Sarason, Shearlin, Pierce, & Sarason, 1987). Finally, one of the predominant goals of an intimate relationship is obtaining support and confirmation of self-worth, both of which are fostered through self-disclosure (Hendrick, 1981). In turn, individuals with intimacy goals may share more personal information with their partners (Prager, 1989) and be particularly focused on and adept at eliciting self-disclosure from their partner (Miller, Berg, & Archer, 1983). In sum, we believe that individuals with intimacy goals may engage in distinct types of interactions with their dating partners, including spending more time alone together; engaging in more positive thoughts about their partner; giving and receiving more social support; having greater influence on each other's thoughts, attitudes, and behaviors; and engaging in and receiving more self-disclosure.

Partner Similarity

As described previously, individuals go to considerable lengths to structure their lives in ways that allow for goal fulfillment (Buss, 1987; Diener et al., 1984; Emmons, Diener, & Larsen, 1986; Snyder, 1983). Because an important component of one's dating environment is obviously the other person in the relationship, individuals should have dating partners who will help them fulfill their own goals. For example, research has shown that high self-monitors choose dating partners who are physically attractive and who should thereby facilitate their goal of presenting positively to others (Snyder, Berscheid, & Glick, 1985). Because the goals and plans of each partner are likely to affect the fulfillment of the other person's needs (Miller, Cody, & McLaughlin, 1985; Miller & Read, 1991), individuals should be motivated to have relationship partners who will facilitate their own goal pursuit.

In turn, individuals with intimacy goals may choose and/or create similarly focused partners, who are likely to be best able to help them achieve communion in their relationship. First, an intimacy-focused partner is likely to act in ways to facilitate intimacy (e.g., by providing social support, eliciting self-disclosure, engaging in interdependent activities). Moreover, because creating a truly intimate relationship necessarily requires the co-operation of both partners, an individual with strong intimacy goals needs a similarly oriented partner (Miller, 1990; Miller & Read, 1991). An individual who is trying to fulfill intimacy goals, for example, may experience frustration when his or her partner is primarily focused on independence and self-reliance and lacks the ability or comfort to engage in self-disclosure. We therefore predict that those with strong intimacy goals will be involved with dating partners who share their focus on intimacy.

Partner Perception

Although considerable research has shown the power of personal goals in leading to the structuring and experience of daily life, some recent work in close relationships has focused on the power of perception. For example, Murray and colleagues (Murray, Holmes, & Griffin, 1996a, 1996b) have found that close relationships are more satisfying and likely to persist when individuals hold idealized views about their partners. Moreover, research has shown that the perceived similarity of coping styles between partners is a stronger predictor of satisfaction in both dating and married relationships than the actual similarity of coping styles (Ptacek & Dodge, 1995). The social support literature also suggests that individuals' perceptions of how much social support they receive can be a more important predictor of well-being than actual support received (Brunstein, Dangelmayer, & Schultheiss, 1996; Dunkel-Schetter & Bennett, 1990). Thus, research on close relationships across a variety of domains demonstrates that the mere perception of one's partner's traits and styles plays an important role in creating relationship satisfaction.

Individuals with intimacy goals are likely to see a focus on intimacy as a highly relevant and important feature of their self-concepts and may then project this image onto their partners, regardless of the partners' actual interpersonal attributes. Prior research has shown that individuals project their own traits onto their partners (Murray et al., 1996a) and that such projection may be particularly likely to occur for those who are themselves high in intimacy (Schaefer & Olson, 1981). In fact, empirical work by Ruvolo and Fabin (1999) found that social projection onto one's partner increases with the level of intimacy in the relationship, again suggesting that intimacy-focused individuals will be particularly likely to perceive their partners as sharing their goals. This ability to transform one's perception also may be part of the intimacy-focused individual's repertoire of evocation and manipulation skills. For example, this perception of their partner's goals may lead them to foster intimacy-relevant situations and elicit intimacy-focused behaviors from their partners (regardless of their partner's actual goals) (e.g., Snyder, Tanke, & Berscheid, 1977). We therefore predict that individuals with intimacy goals may be so focused on creating intimacy that they see their worlds, and specifically their partners' goals, through "intimacy-colored glasses."

Mediation Predictions

Several prominent models of relationship functioning have emphasized how individual differences (e.g., in traits, motives, goals) can lead to particular patterns of behavior, which in turn are likely to influence the behavior of one's relationship partner and, over time, to affect relationship quality (Bradbury & Fincham, 1991; Kurdek, 1991; Reis & Shaver, 1988). As described in Reis and Shaver's (1988) model of the intimacy process, intimacy is an "interpersonal, transactional process" (p. 368) in which individuals' own distinct motives, needs, goals, and fears influence how they act toward their partner, which in turn is interpreted and responded to by his or her partner based on their own dispositional tendencies. An individual with approach motives, for example, is likely to engage in affiliative behavior, such as disclosing personal desires and emotions, which their partner will then interpret and respond to based on his or her own needs and goals. Over time, these reciprocal interactions can thus promote intimacy and relationship commitment (or alternatively, if partners' interpretations and reactions are negative, lead to decreases in relationship quality). Similarly, Bradbury and Fincham's (1988) contextual model describes how the distal context of a relationship (e.g., individuals' personality traits, goals) influences the proximal context (e.g., thoughts, behaviors), which in turn affects relational functioning and quality. For example, individuals who are more adept at expressiveness and perspective taking may make beneficial attributions for their partners' behavior, thereby leading to greater relationship satisfaction (Fincham & Bradbury, 1989; Fletcher & Fitness, 1990). These models therefore emphasize the role of individual differences in influencing the structuring of and interaction within close relationships, and ultimately the quality of such relationships.

Based on these prior models of relationship functioning, we propose not only that individuals with strong intimacy goals in dating structure and experience their relationships in distinct ways but also that these patterns of interaction and perception are in turn associated with the quality of these relationships. First, individuals with a strong focus on intimacy in dating may structure their lives in particular ways (e.g., spend time alone with their partner, engage in considerable self-disclosure, provide considerable social support), and these patterns of interaction are likely to facilitate greater intimacy and satisfaction (e.g., Reis & Shaver, 1988). Second, individuals with a strong focus on intimacy may have partners with a similar focus on intimacy, who thereby reciprocate the initial advances (e.g., self-disclosure, social support, etc.), which in turn is again associated with greater relationship quality. Third, individuals with a strong focus on intimacy may see their partners through intimacy-colored glasses and project their own goals onto their partners. This mere perception of intimacy, regardless of its accuracy, may lead them to interpret their partners' behavior in positive (e.g., intimacy-focused) ways and thereby lead to increases in relationship satisfaction. Thus, individuals with a strong focus on intimacy in dating may interact in and experience these relationships in particular ways that enhance relationship quality.

Overview

This study examines the association of intimacy goals and relationship satisfaction in college women. First, we will examine whether intimacy-focused women engage in particular types of interactions within their dating relationship (e.g., spend more time alone together, engage in more positive thoughts about their partner, give and receive more social support, are more influenced by their partner, and engage in and elicit more self-disclosure), have dating partners with intimacy focused goals, and perceive their dating partners as intimacy focused. Next, we will examine the role of each of these three factors (interaction, similarity, perception) in mediating the intimacy goal–relationship satisfaction link.

Method

PARTICIPANTS

The study included 100 University of Massachusetts undergraduate women (M age = 20.04, SD = 1.53). Each participant had been dating her current partner for a mean length of 14.99 months (SD = 14.79).

PROCEDURE

Participants were recruited from the University of Massachusetts undergraduate psychology department. A posting indicated that women in on-campus dating relationships were needed to complete a 30-minute questionnaire about their dating goals and behaviors. Potential participants had to be willing to give their dating partners a brief two-page questionnaire (which included only the intimacy goals and satisfaction measures) to complete and return through the mail. The partner survey was to be mailed within the next 48 hours in exchange for a $2.50 coupon to a local pizza parlor. Participants were run in groups of 5 to 20, in which each participant signed an informed consent form, completed the questionnaire, was debriefed on the theoretical basis of the study, and was given a questionnaire for her dating partner in a self-addressed, stamped envelope. Participants were told that this research was ongoing and hence it was important to not discuss its general focus or their specific responses with others. Moreover, the debriefing focused broadly on how different individuals structured and experienced their relationships in different ways and did not provide specific information about distinct hypotheses. Extra credit points for a psychology class were granted to each woman who participated. Of the 100 participants' partners, 52 completed and returned the partner survey.[1]

MEASURES

Intimacy Dating Goals Scale. To examine participants' orientation toward intimacy in their dating relationships, we used a selection of 9 items from the Social Dating Goals Scale (Sanderson & Cantor, 1995). The original 13-item scale is scored on a 1 to 5 scale (1 = *strongly disagree* to 5 = *strongly agree*) and consists of items assessing individuals' focus on engaging in self-disclosure and dependence in a dating relationship (e.g., "In my dating relationships, I try to share my most intimate thoughts and feelings") as well as their focus on self-exploration and self-reliance (e.g., "In my dating relationships, I try to maintain a strong sense of independence") (= .67).[2] Items assessing self-exploration and self-reliance are reverse-scored prior to summation; hence, higher scores indicate a greater focus on intimacy.[3] The Social Dating Goals Scale meets the standard criteria for determining unidimensionality of a scale (Briggs & Cheek, 1986), namely, high internal consistency, modest mean interitem correlation, and one factor accounting for a substantial portion of the variance, and has been used in a series of studies with adolescent and adult samples (e.g., Karetsky & Sanderson, 2000; Sanderson & Cantor, 1995, 1997; Sanderson et al., 2000; L. T. Volenski, personal communication, March 10, 1995). This scale also was included in the dating partner questionnaire (= .50).

Partner's Perceived Intimacy Dating Goals Scale. Participants also completed the same nine items from the Social Dating Goals Scale based on how they thought their partners would rate the items, thus addressing their perceptions of their partners' goals (e.g., "In our dating relationship, my partner tries to share his most intimate thoughts and feelings") (= .78). These items were again rated on a scale of 1 to 5 (1 = *disagree strongly* to 5 = *agree strongly*).

Patterning of Daily Life – Time Index. An index was developed to determine the amount of time each participant spent in a range of different activities with her dating partner. Participants reported the number of hours they spent doing each activity in the last week. A principal components factor analysis with a varimax rotation was used to determine subscales of this measure. This analysis revealed that a three-factor solution was the best fit of the data. The first subscale includes activities that the participant would do with her dating partner and others (e.g., "The number of hours I spent in the last week relaxing/ socializing with my dating partner and his or my friends"). The second subscale includes activities the participant engaged in with only her dating partner (e.g., "The number of hours I spent in the last week on 'dates' alone with my dating partner"). School-related activities and functions attended with her partner were included in the third subscale (e.g., "The amount of time I spend studying with my dating partner and a group of classmates/friends").

Relationship Thinking Index. The Relationship Thinking Index assesses individuals' thoughts about their close relationships and is composed of three subscales (Cate et al., 1995). The first subscale, partner thinking, consists of four items representing thoughts about one's partner's positivity toward the relationship (e.g., "I think about whether my partner feels the same about me as I do about him") (= .77). The second subscale, positive affect thinking, includes five items assessing positive thoughts about the relationship (e.g., "I reflect on how much I love my partner") (= .85). The third subscale, network thinking, includes four items that represent thoughts about interactions and relationships that surround the dating pair (e.g., "I wonder about how well/poorly I do/ will get along with my partner's family") (= .79). Each of the 13 items is rated on a scale from 1 to 6 (1 = *extremely uncharacteristic* to 6 = *extremely characteristic*). The index is composed of three subscales. Participants obtained a score for each subscale, and higher scores indicate more engagement in that type of thinking.

Strength of influence. The measure of strength of influence was taken directly from the Relationship Closeness Inventory (RCI) created by Berscheid and colleagues (Berscheid et al., 1989). Although the complete scale includes the properties of strength, diversity, and frequency of interaction in a relationship, only the strength subscale was administered in this study because measurements of shared time and activities were obtained through the Patterning Of Daily Life–Time Index. The strength subscale consists of 34 questions examining the extent to which dating partners affect each other's daily decisions, goals, activities, and behaviors (= .90). Participants rated the degree to which they are influenced by their partners in a variety of situations on a scale from 1 to 7 (1 = *disagree strongly* to 7 = *agree strongly*). Items include mundane activities such as "My dating partner influences what I watch on TV" and more meaningful life issues such as "My dating partner influences the basic values that I hold." The appropriate items were reverse-scored and a summed score was obtained to indicate strength of interdependence.

Social Support Index. The Social Support Index of the Quality of Relationships Inventory (Pierce, Sarason, & Sarason, 1991) was used to assess the amount of social support each participant offered to her dating partner. The index is rated on a scale from 1 to 5 (1 = *very slightly or not at all* to 5 = *extremely*) and includes questions such as "To what extent can your dating partner count on you to listen to him when he is very angry with someone else?" and "To what extent can your dating partner turn to you for advice with his problems?" (= .78). This index was then modified to address participants' perceptions of the social support they received in their dating relationships (= .77), again using a scale from 1 to 5 (1 = *very slightly or not at all* to 5 = *extremely*). For example, questions were reworded to the following: "To what extent can you count on your dating partner to listen to you when you are very angry at someone else?" and "To what extent can you turn to your dating partner for advice with your problems?" Higher scores on both scales indicate an increased amount of social support.

Self-Disclosure Scale. A 10-item index (Miller et al., 1983) was used to measure the tendency to disclose to one's dating partner (= .86). The unifactorial index includes such items as "I disclose to my dating partner about my personal habits" and "I disclose to my partner about things I have done that I feel guilty about." This measure is rated on a scale of 1 to 5 (1 = *discuss not at all* to 5 = *discuss fully*), with higher scores indicating a greater tendency to self-disclose.

Opener Scale. The Opener Scale (Miller et al., 1983) examines the tendency to elicit self-disclosure from one's dating partner (= .77). This scale includes items such as "My dating partner trusts me with his secrets" and "I encourage my dating partner to tell me how he is feeling." This index is rated on a scale from 1 to 5 (1 = *disagree strongly* to 5 = *agree strongly*), with higher scores indicating a stronger tendency to elicit self-disclosure from one's dating partner.

Satisfaction Index. The Marital Assessment Questionnaire (Hendrick, 1981) was modified to relate specifically to the perceived quality of the participant's dating relationship (= .88). Items were answered using a scale of 1 to 5 (1 = *disagree strongly* to 5 = *agree strongly*). The questionnaire consists of the following four items: "In general, I am satisfied with my dating relationship," "My dating partner meets my needs," "My dating relationship is better than most," and "I love my dating partner." Higher scores reflect greater relationship satisfaction. Each participant's dating partner answered the same questions in the partner questionnaire (= .76).

Demographic information. Participants provided a variety of demographic information, including age, number of partners dated in the past 2 years, length of longest dating relationship, and length of current dating relationship.[4]

Results

Because prior research as well as our own initial analyses revealed that relationship satisfaction was associated with duration of relationship ($r = .33$, $p < .001$), all analyses controlled for length of relationship. Means and standard deviations for all measures are presented in Table 16.1.

INTIMACY GOALS AND RELATIONSHIP SATISFACTION

First, a hierarchical regression analysis was conducted predicting women's relationship satisfaction from their intimacy goals. This analysis revealed, in line with prior research, that those with intimacy goals experience greater relationship satisfaction ($\beta = .51$, $p = .0001$).[5]

STRUCTURING AND EXPERIENCE OF DAILY LIFE

A series of hierarchical regression analyses were conducted to determine if intimacy-focused individuals report structuring their dating lives in particular ways. Intimacy goals predicted the amount of time participants reported spending alone with their dating partners (see Table 16.2) but not the time they spent with others and their dating partners or at school-related functions with their dating partners. Intimacy goals also predicted the reported frequency of positive affective thinking (e.g., positive thoughts about the relationship) but did not predict the frequency of either partner thinking (e.g., thoughts about their partner's feelings about the relationship) or network thinking (e.g., thoughts about relationships with those around the dating couple). Those with intimacy goals reported having their attitudes and behaviors more influenced by their partner as well as giving more social support to their partner, although there was no association between intimacy goals and amount of support received. Finally, intimacy goals significantly predicted both the participant's reported tendency to self-disclose and to elicit self-disclosure from her partner.

PARTNER SIMILARITY

A hierarchical regression analysis was conducted predicting partner's intimacy goals from one's own intimacy goals. However, this analysis revealed no significant effect of own goals on partner's intimacy goals ($\beta = .13$, ns).

Table 16.1

Means and Standard Deviations for All Measures		
VARIABLE	M	SD
Intimacy goals [a]		
Own	3.63	0.47
Perceived partner	3.35	0.63
Partner	4.19	0.54
Time spent [b]		
Time spent alone with partner	13.59	16.75
Time spent with partner and others	10.12	14.21
Time spent at school-related functions with partner	2.19	2.94
Relationship Thinking [c]		
Positive affect thinking	5.21	0.83
Partner thinking	4.61	1.16
Network thinking	3.93	1.29
Interdependence		
Strength of influence [d]	3.41	0.88
Social support given to partner [e]	4.64	0.43
Social support received from partner [e]	4.44	0.53
Communication		
Amount of self-disclosure [f]	4.09	0.73
Amount of self-disclosure elicited from partner [a]	4.44	0.47
Relationship satisfaction [a]	4.28	0.80

a. Measured on a 1 to 5 scale (1 = strongly disagree to 5 = strongly agree)
b. Measured in hours
c. Measured on a 1 to 6 scale (1 = extremely uncharacteristic to 6 = extremely characteristic)
d. Measured on a 1 to 7 scale (1 = disagree strongly to 7 = agree strongly)
e. Measured on a 1 to 5 scale (1 = very slightly or not at all to 5 = extremely)
f. Measured on a 1 to 5 scale (1 = discuss not at all to 5 = discuss fully)

PARTNER PERCEPTION

Next, a hierarchical regression analysis was conducted predicting women's perceptions of their partner's intimacy goals from their own goals. This analysis indicated that the woman's goals were a significant predictor of her perception of her partner's goals (β = .41, p = .0001). Because individuals' perceptions of their partner's goals were correlated with their partner's actual goals (r = .39, p = .0001), we also conducted this analysis

Table 16.2

Beta Weights Predicting Patterns of Relationship Interaction From Intimacy Goals		
VARIABLE	**BETA WEIGHT**	**p VALUE**
Time spent		
Time spent alone with partner	.29	.01
Time spent with partner and others	.18	—
Time spent at school-related functions with partner	−.01	—
Relationship thinking		
Positive affect thinking	.37	.0001
Partner thinking	−.03	—
Network thinking	.04	—
Interdependence		
Strength of influence	.62	.0001
Social support given to partner	.27	.01
Social support received from partner	.15	—
Communication		
Amount of self-disclosure	.32	.001
Amount of self-disclosure elicited from partner	.27	.01

NOTE: All analyses controlled for length of relationship.

controlling for partner's actual goals. Even with this additional covariate, intimacy goals were still a significant predictor of perceived partner goals (β = .32, p = .009).

MEDIATION ANALYSES

Thus far, we have shown that individuals with intimacy goals report structuring their dating lives in particular ways (e.g., giving more social support, being more influenced in their attitudes and behaviors, spending more time alone with their partner, engaging in and eliciting more self-disclosure, and engaging in more positive affect talk) and believe that their partner shares their focus on intimacy goals in dating. To test if any of these factors is associated with greater satisfaction, we conducted a series of regression analyses to test for mediation. Following Baron and Kenny (1986), mediation is shown if intimacy goals affect patterns of relationship interaction (first regression), intimacy goals affect relationship satisfaction (second regression), and patterns of interaction affect relationship satisfaction when controlling for intimacy goals (third regression). Furthermore, the effect of intimacy goals on relationship satisfaction must be reduced when the interaction variable is included in the equation, with perfect mediation occurring when intimacy goals (the independent variable) have no effect on satisfaction (the dependent variable) when controlling for patterns of interaction (the mediator).

As described previously, intimacy goals are associated with six particular aspects of dating life, thus satisfying the first step in showing mediation, and with relationship satisfaction, thus satisfying the second step in showing mediation. We therefore conducted a series of hierarchical regression analyses testing for the association of each of these aspects of dating interaction with relationship satisfaction, controlling for intimacy goals, to test for the third step in mediation. These analyses revealed significant effects only in the cases of social support given (β = .23, p = .01) and self-disclosure elicited (β = .43, p = .0001). However, in both of these analyses, the effect of intimacy goals was not eliminated but only reduced (social support given: β = .86, p < .0001; self-disclosure elicited: β = .75, p < .0001). Therefore, additional tests were conducted to determine whether the drops in these beta weights were significant using the formula described by Sobel (1982) (see Baron & Kenny, 1986). These analyses revealed that the beta weight for intimacy goals was reduced when self-disclosure elicited was added to the equation (Z = 2.35, p < .02) and that the beta weight for intimacy was reduced when social support given was added to the equation (Z = 1.93, p < .06). These analyses indicate that both reports of self-disclosure elicited and social support given partially mediate the goals–satisfaction association.

Because there was no association between own intimacy goals and partner's goals, partner's goals cannot serve as a mediator of the goals–satisfaction link. However, because intimacy goals were associated with perceptions of partner's goals, we conducted a hierarchical regression analysis testing for the role of perceived partner's intimacy goals in predicting satisfaction (the third step in testing for mediation). Perceived partner goals were a significant predictor of relationship satisfaction, controlling for intimacy goals ($\beta = .46$, $p = .0001$). Because the association of intimacy goals on satisfaction was reduced, but not eliminated, when controlling for perceived partner goals ($\beta = .29$, $p = .003$), an additional test was conducted to determine whether the drop in beta weight was significant. This analysis revealed that the beta weight for intimacy goals was reduced when perceived partner goals was added to the equation ($Z = 3.36$, $p < .0001$), indicating that perceptions of partner's intimacy goals serve as a partial mediator of the goals–satisfaction link.

However, women's perceptions of their partners' goals are correlated with their partners' actual goals, which in turn may account in part for the role of perceptions of one's partners' goals in leading to relationship satisfaction. Therefore, we also examined whether perceived partner goals was a significant predictor of relationship satisfaction controlling for both own goals and partner's actual goals. This analysis still revealed a significant effect of perceptions of partner's goals on satisfaction ($\beta = .54$, $p = .0001$). Once again, because the association of intimacy goals on satisfaction was reduced, but not eliminated, when controlling for perceived partner goals and actual partner goals ($\beta = .21$, $p < .08$), an additional test was conducted to determine whether the drop in beta weight was significant. This analysis revealed that the beta weight for intimacy goals was reduced when both perceived and actual partner goals were added to the equation ($Z = 2.29$, $p < .03$), indicating that perceptions of partner's intimacy goals serve as a partial mediator of the goals–satisfaction link, even controlling for one's partner's actual goals.

Discussion

These findings extend prior research showing that individuals with intimacy goals experience greater satisfaction in dating (Sanderson & Cantor, 1997) and marital relationships (Sanderson & Cantor, in press) by examining three distinct processes that may underlie this association. First, women with intimacy goals do report structuring their dating lives in particular ways. For example, those with intimacy goals report spending more time alone with their partners (although not more time with their partner and others), focusing on positive thoughts about the relationship (although not about their partner's thoughts or about the thoughts of others in the broader social network), providing more social support to their partner, and both engaging in and eliciting more self-disclosure. These findings are all in line with our predictions that women with intimacy goals will behave in distinct ways that should serve to fulfill these goals. Although women with intimacy goals do apparently report engaging in distinct types of relationship interactions (i.e., those presumably fostering intimacy), mediational analyses demonstrated that only two such types of interactions, namely, social support given and self-disclosure elicited, partially mediate the goals–satisfaction link. On the other hand, women with intimacy goals were not particularly likely to have intimacy-focused partners, and having an intimacy-focused partner was not associated with increased satisfaction. Women with intimacy goals do, however, believe their partners share their focus on intimacy, and this perception was an important predictor of relationship satisfaction: Mediational analyses revealed that their perceptions of their dating partner's goals were associated with satisfaction, even controlling for own goals and partner's actual goals.

THE ROLE OF PERCEPTION IN LEADING TO SATISFACTION

Our findings on the importance of perceptions of partner's intimacy goals in predicting relationship satisfaction are in line with those from prior research on the role of perception in leading to satisfaction (Murray et al., 1996a, 1996b; Ptacek & Dodge, 1995). For example, Murray and colleagues (1996a, 1996b) have shown that individuals' idealized perceptions of their dating partners lead to greater satisfaction, and Ptacek and Dodge (1995) found that satisfaction in both dating and married relationships was predicted by the perceived similarity of coping styles between partners. Individuals with intimacy goals may be particularly likely to hold such biased perceptions of their partner's goals (e.g., see their partner through their own intimacy-colored glasses). In fact, Ruvolo and Fabin (1999) demonstrated that the higher the degree of intimacy in the relationship, the more an individual projected their own views onto their partner. Thus, our findings provide additional support for the importance of individuals' perceptions of their partners' traits, styles, and goals in creating relationship satisfaction.

Although these findings indicate that individuals' own intimacy goals predict their perceptions of their partners' goals (e.g., they see their partners through intimacy-colored glasses) and that these perceptions in turn are associated with satisfaction, they do not answer the question of how exactly such perceptions mediate the goals–satisfaction link. First, individuals who perceive that their partner has intimacy-focused goals may act in particular ways to assist their partner in fulfilling these goals, and these efforts to facilitate intimacy in the relationship (e.g., they may themselves engage in more self-disclosure, provide more social support, etc.) may lead to satisfaction. According to this hypothesis, individuals' own behavior (which occurs as a result of their perceptions of their partner's goals) leads them to create opportunities for intimacy in the relationship, which thereby leads to satisfaction. Alternatively, or perhaps in addition to, the perception that one's partner has intimacy goals may lead women to act in particular ways that make their partner more intimacy focused over time (Snyder et al., 1977). In fact, Murray and colleagues (1996b) have found that individuals' perceptions of their partners may actually have the power to become self-fulfilling prophecies (e.g., an individual actually creates the partner he or she envisions by modifying the partner's self-concept). Similarly, intimacy-focused individuals, who perceive their partners as sharing their goals, may be able to create the partners they perceive by shaping and molding their partners' intimacy focus. For example, intimacy-focused individuals may assume their partners are intimacy focused and work to elicit self-disclosure, and over time, as their partners became more and more comfortable with engaging in such behavior, their perceptions of their partners' goals would essentially be realized. Future longitudinal research would contribute to an understanding of the development of intimacy goals by assessing individuals' intimacy goals and their partners' goals at different points in time to gain a better understanding of how each individual's goals influence the other's goals, behavior, and satisfaction.

Finally, although our findings provide some evidence for the role of perceptions of one's partner's intimacy goals in mediating the goals–satisfaction link, these analyses assessed variables at a single time period and therefore cannot demonstrate causality. It is certainly possible, for example, that greater relationship satisfaction leads one to form stronger intimacy goals, structure one's dating relationship in particular ways, and/or perceive one's partner as having intimacy-focused goals (e.g., Snyder, 1983). Future research should examine participants over time (ideally before they have entered a particular dating relationship) to learn how individuals' own goals, patterns of interaction, and satisfaction change and evolve.

LIMITATIONS AND FUTURE RESEARCH

Although this research provides evidence for the role of individuals' perceptions of their partner's goals in mediating the intimacy goals–relationship satisfaction link, there are several limitations that may limit its generalizability. First, only women were included in this study; therefore, it is not clear to what extent these findings would generalize to men. Prior research has shown that the predictors of relationship satisfaction often differ as a function of gender and, typically, that women's satisfaction is more influenced by patterns of relationship interaction than is men's (Acitelli, 1992; Acitelli & Antonucci, 1994; Gaelick, Bodenhausen, & Wyer, 1986; Julien & Markman, 1991). For example, Acitelli (1992) found that wives' satisfaction was positively associated with the amount of relationship talk their husbands engaged in, whereas wives' relationship talk was not associated with husbands' satisfaction. Similarly, the link between marital satisfaction and social support is stronger for women than for men (Acitelli & Antonucci, 1994; Julien & Markman, 1991). Thus, it is not clear whether the patterns we have found between intimacy goals, patterns of interactions, perception of partner's goals, and relationship satisfaction would also be found in men, and future research should certainly examine this issue.

Second, all participants were relatively young and in relatively short relationships; therefore, it is not clear if these findings would generalize to longer and more stable relationships. For example, it may be that women in relatively casual dating relationships do not particularly depend on their partner to facilitate intimacy (e.g., self-disclosure, social support, interdependence) and therefore are able to experience satisfaction merely by believing that their partner is indeed focused on such communion. However, perceptions may not be enough to lead to satisfaction over the long term. Although this is one possibility, findings from a recent study with married couples indicated a similar link between intimacy goals, perception of spouse's intimacy goals, and satisfaction (Sanderson & Cantor, in press).

Third, although we have described our findings as providing evidence that those with intimacy goals structure their lives in particular ways (e.g., time spent, positive affect thinking, social support given, self-disclosure given, and elicited influence), because our study relied exclusively on self-report (albeit by both members of dating couples), we cannot determine the accuracy of such reports. For example, those with strong intimacy goals in dating may see (and describe) themselves as particularly effective at giving social support and eliciting self-disclosure. In fact, considerable research in social cognition has shown that recalling information is a reconstructive process; hence, individuals' cognitive structures and motivations can lead to inaccurate recollections (Fiske & Taylor, 1991; Greenwald & Banaji, 1995). Thus, it is possible that individuals with strong intimacy goals merely believe they structure their lives in particular (and goal-relevant) ways and that these beliefs in turn lead to satisfaction. Although it is likely to be difficult to assess the accuracy of some of these reports (e.g., degree of influence, types of thinking), future research could attempt to examine the accuracy of other measures. For example, research could examine the complete set of measures from both partners to determine whether the perceived amount of self-disclosure elicited and support given by one partner corresponds with the amount of self-disclosure provided and support received from the other partner. Similarly, daily diary or beeper methods might provide evidence about whether those with strong intimacy goals do in fact spend more time alone with their partner.

Finally, although this research examined several possible mediators of the intimacy goals–relationship satisfaction link (e.g., patterns of interaction, partner's actual goals, partner's perceived goals), there are clearly other variables that may serve to mediate this association. For example, those with intimacy goals may be more aware of and focused on their partner's feelings regarding the relationship (Acitelli, 1992) and/or more effective at resolving conflicts constructively (Karetsky & Sanderson, 2000), both of which may lead to increased satisfaction. Individuals with intimacy goals, who are more likely to both engage in and elicit self-disclosure, also may make more accurate and/or positive attributions for their partner's behavior and experience greater relationship satisfaction (Fincham & Bradbury, 1989). Future research should examine these as well as other potential mediators of the intimacy goal–relationship satisfaction link.

Conclusions

These findings extend those of prior research on the association of intimacy goals and relationship satisfaction by exploring three distinct processes that may mediate the goals–satisfaction link and have important implications for research on personality processes as well as on close relationships. In line with prior research on the power of perception in close relationships (Acitelli, Douvan, & Veroff, 1993; Murray et al., 1996a, 1996b; Ptacek & Dodge, 1995), the intimacy goal–relationship satisfaction link was partially mediated by individuals' perceptions of their partners' intimacy goals, even controlling for their partners' actual goals. This research therefore indicates that future work on the role of individual differences factors in predicting relationship satisfaction needs to examine not only the characteristics (e.g., traits, goals, styles) of one individual in the relationship but also the actual and perceived characteristics of their partners. At least for the women in this sample, intimacy (and, in turn, satisfaction) was in the eye of the beholder: Individuals with intimacy goals perceived their partner as sharing these goals, and this perception, in turn, was associated with satisfaction.

Endnotes

1. A series of t tests were conducted to determine if there were any differences between the participants whose partners returned versus did not return their survey. These analyses revealed no differences on length of relationship, $t(94) < 1$, ns, $Ms = 15.95$ versus 13.66 months, for those who did versus did not return their survey. However, those whose partners returned the surveys were somewhat more intimacy goal-focused, $t(98) = 1.91$, $p < .06$, $Ms = 3.40$ versus 3.24, and significantly more satisfied with the relationship, $t(94) = 2.11$, $p < .04$, $Ms = 4.42$ versus 4.08.

2. The original Social Dating Goals Scale was designed to assess individuals' goals in both casual dating relationships (with multiple partners) as well as steady dating relationships (with a single partner). Because in the present study we were specifically interested in examining individuals' goals (and their perceptions of their partners' goals) in their current relationship (and hence we included only participants who were in steady, ongoing relationships), the four items that referred to dating multiple partners were eliminated (e.g., "In my dating relationships I try to date those whom I can count on," "In my dating relationships I try to date those

who make my life more comfortable and stable"). These items were therefore eliminated in all three goals scales (own goals, partners' goals, perceived partners' goals).

3. The decision to include both intimacy-focused and independence focused items in the original Social Dating Goals Scale was made based on the considerable prior research showing that there are two central tendencies that shape personal relationships; namely, the drive toward agency and autonomy versus the drive toward communion and attachment (e.g., Bakan, 1966). We believe that the inclusion of both of these types of goals is particularly important given the focus during late adolescence on the two broad life tasks of independence/identity formation and intimacy (Erikson, 1950). Although some adolescents, such as those with relatively clear ideas of their own personal identity (Orlofsky, 1978), may be ready to focus predominantly on intimacy goals related to sharing, closeness, and trust in their social dating relationships, for those who are still struggling with concerns related to asserting independence from family and experimenting with different identities or "selves" (e.g., Zirkel & Cantor, 1990), social dating may instead provide a critical arena for establishing identity. Correspondingly, the tendency to pursue intimacy goals in dating is positively correlated with interpersonal and ideological ego achievement (Erikson, 1968; Marcia, 1966) and secure attachment (Hazan & Shaver, 1987; Simpson, 1990) and negatively correlated with both interpersonal and ideological ego diffusion and with anxious attachment. For more information about the development and validation of this scale, please see Sanderson and Cantor (1995).

4. The questions on number of dating partners and length of longest dating relationship were asked to replicate prior findings on the association of intimacy goals in dating and patterns of dating. Findings from this sample were in line with those from prior work (e.g., Sanderson & Cantor, 1995) indicating that individuals with stronger intimacy dating goals had longer dating relationships ($r = .33$, $p < .001$) and fewer casual dating partners ($r = -.39$, $p < .0001$).

5. An identical regression analysis conducted only on the male partners also revealed that men with stronger intimacy goals had greater relationship satisfaction, again controlling for length of relationship ($b = .43$, $p < .002$).

References

Acitelli, L. K. (1992). "Gender differences in relationship awareness and marital satisfaction among young married couples." *Personality and Social Psychology Bulletin, 18*, 102-110.

Acitelli, L.K., & Antonucci, T. C. (1994). "Gender differences in the link between marital support and satisfaction in older couples." *Journal of Personality and Social Psychology, 67*, 688-698.

Acitelli, L. K., Douvan, E., & Veroff, J. (1993). "Perceptions of conflict in the first year of marriage: How important are similarity and understanding?" *Journal of Social and Personal Relationships, 10*, 5-19.

Altman, I., & Taylor, D. A. (1973). *Social penetration: The development of interpersonal relationships*. New York: Holt, Rinehart & Winston.

Bakan, D. (1966). *The duality of human existence*. Boston: Beacon.

Baron, R. M., & Kenny, D. A. (1986). "The moderator-mediator variable distinction in social psychological research: Conceptual, strategic, and statistical considerations." *Journal of Personality and Social Psychology, 51*, 1173-1182.

Berscheid, E. (1983). Emotion. In H. H. Kelley, E. Berscheid, A. Christensen, H. Harvey, T. L. Huston, G. Levinger, E. McClintock, L. A. Peplau, & D. Peterson (Eds.), *Close relationships* (pp. 110-168). San Francisco: Freeman.

Berscheid, E., Snyder, M., & Omoto, A. M. (1989). "The relationship closeness inventory: Assessing the closeness of interpersonal relationships." *Journal of Personality and Social Psychology, 57*, 792-807.

Bradbury, T. N., & Fincham, F. D. (1988). "Individual difference variables in close relationships: A contextual model of marriage as an integrative framework." *Journal of Personality and Social Psychology, 54*, 713-721.

Bradbury, T. N., & Fincham, F. D. (1991). "A contextual model for advancing the study of marital interaction." In G. Fletcher & F. Fincham (Eds.), *Cognition in close relationships* (pp. 127-147). Hillsdale, NJ: Lawrence Erlbaum.

Briggs, S. R., & Cheek, J. M. (1986). "The role of factor analysis in the development and evaluation of personality scales." *Journal of Personality, 54*, 106-148.

Brunstein, J. C., Dangelmayer, G., & Schultheiss, O. C. (1996). "Personal goals and social support in close relationships: Effects on relationship mood and marital satisfaction." *Journal of Personality and Social Psychology, 71*, 1006-1019.

Buss, D. M. (1987). "Selection, evocation and manipulation." *Journal of Personality and Social Psychology, 53*, 1214-1221.

Cantor, N. (1994). "Life task problem-solving: Situational affordances and personal needs." *Personality and Social Psychology Bulletin, 20*, 235-243.

Cantor, N., Acker, M., & Cook-Flannagan, C. (1992). "Conflict and preoccupation in the intimacy life task." *Journal of Personality and Social Psychology, 63*, 644-655.

Cantor, N., & Malley, J. (1991). Life tasks, personal needs, and close relationships. In G.J.O. Fletcher & F. D. Fincham (Eds.), *Cognition in close relationships* (pp. 101-125). Hillsdale, NJ: Lawrence Erlbaum.

Cate, R. M., Koval, J., Lloyd, S. A., & Wilson, G. (1995). "Assessment of relationship thinking in dating relationships." *Personal Relationships, 2*, 77-95.

Clark, M. S., & Reis, H. T. (1988). "Interpersonal processes in close relationships." *Annual Review of Psychology, 39*, 609-672.

Diener, E., Larsen, R. J., & Emmons, R. A. (1984). "Person*Situation interactions: Choice of situations and congruence response models." *Journal of Personality and Social Psychology, 47*, 580-592.

Dunkel-Schetter, C., & Bennett, T. L. (1990). Differentiating the cognitive and behavioral aspects of social support. In I. G. Sarason, B. R. Sarason, & G. R. Pierce (Eds.), *Social support: An interactional view* (pp. 267-296). New York: John Wiley.

Emmons, R. A., Diener, E., & Larsen, R. J. (1986). "Choice and avoidance of everyday situations and affect congruence: Two models of reciprocal interactionism." *Journal of Personality and Social Psychology, 51*, 815-826.

Erikson, E. H. (1950). *Childhood and society.* New York: Norton.

Erikson, E. H. (1968). *Identity: Youth and crisis.* New York: Norton.

Fincham, F. D., & Bradbury, T. N. (1989). "The impact of attributions in marriage: An individual difference analysis." *Journal of Social and Personal Relationships, 6*, 69-85.

Fincham, F. D., & Bradbury, T. N. (1990). "Social support in marriage: The role of social cognition." *Journal of Social and Clinical Psychology, 9*, 31-42.

Fiske, S. T., & Taylor, S. E. (1991). *Social cognition* (2nd ed.). New York: Random House.

Fletcher, G., & Fitness, J. (1990). "Occurrent social cognition in close relationship interaction: The role of proximal and distal variables." *Journal of Personality and Social Psychology, 59*, 464-474.

Franzoi, S. L., Davis, M. H., & Young, R. D. (1985). "The effects of private self-consciousness and perspective taking on satisfaction in close relationships." *Journal of Personality and Social Psychology, 48*, 1585-1595.

Gaelick, L., Bodenhausen, G. V., & Wyer, R. S. (1986). "Emotional communication in close relationships." *Journal of Personality and Social Psychology, 49*, 1246-1265.

Gollwitzer, P. (1993). Goal achievement: The role of intentions. In W. Stroebe & M. Hewstone (Eds.), *European review of social psychology* (Vol. 4, pp. 141-185). London: Wiley.

Greenwald, A. G., & Banaji, M. R. (1995). "Implicit social cognition: Attitudes, self-esteem, and stereotypes." *Psychological Review, 102,* 4-27.

Hazan, C., & Shaver, P. R. (1987). "Romantic love conceptualized as an attachment process." *Journal of Personality and Social Psychology, 52,* 511-524.

Hendrick, S. S. (1981). "Self-disclosure and marital satisfaction." *Journal of Personality and Social Psychology, 40,* 1150-1159.

Hendrick, S. S., Hendrick, C., & Adler, N. L. (1988). "Romantic relationships: Love, satisfaction, and staying together." *Journal of Personality and Social Psychology, 54,* 930-988.

Hill, C. T., Rubin, Z., & Peplau, L. A. (1976). "Breakups before marriage: The end of 103 affairs." *Journal of Social Issues, 3,* 147-168.

Julien, D., & Markman, H. J. (1991). "Social support and social networks as determinants of individual and marital outcomes." *Journal of Social and Personal Relationships, 8,* 549-568.

Karetsky, K. H., & Sanderson, C. A. (2000, June). *The influence of social dating goals on coping with conflict in dating relationships.* Paper presented at the 12th Annual Meeting of the American Psychological Society, Miami, FL.

Kelley, H. H. (1979). *Personal relationships: Their structures and processes.* Hillsdale, NJ: Lawrence Erlbaum.

Kurdek, L. (1991). "Correlates of relationship satisfaction in cohabiting gay and lesbian couples: Integration of contextual, investment, and problem-solving models." *Journal of Personality and Social Psychology, 61,* 910-922.

Levinger, G., & Senn, D. J. (1967). "Disclosure of feelings in marriage." *Merril-Palmer Quarterly, 13,* 237-249.

Marcia, J. E. (1966). "Development and validation of ego identity status." *Journal of Personality and Social Psychology, 3,* 551-558.

McAdams, D. P. (1984). Human motives and personal relationships. In V. J. Derlega (Ed.), *Communication, intimacy, and close relationships* (pp. 41-70). Orlando, FL: Academic Press.

Miller, L. C. (1990). "Intimacy and liking: Mutual influence and the role of unique relationships." *Journal of Personality and Social Psychology, 59,* 50-60.

Miller, L. C., Berg, J. H., & Archer, R. L. (1983). "Openers: Individuals who elicit intimate self-disclosure." *Journal of Personality and Social Psychology, 44,* 1234-1244.

Miller, L. C., Cody, M. J., & McLaughlin, M. L. (1985). Situations and goals as fundamental constructs in interpersonal communication research. In M. L. Knapp & G. R. Miller (Eds.), *Handbook of interpersonal communication* (pp. 162-198). Beverly Hills, CA: Sage.

Miller, L. C., & Read, S. J. (1991). On the coherence of mental models of persons and relationships: A knowledge structure approach. In G. O. Fletcher & F. D. Fincham (Eds.), *Cognition in close relationships* (pp. 69-99). Hillsdale, NJ: Lawrence Erlbaum.

Mischel, W., Cantor, N., & Feldman, S. (1996). Principles of self-regulation: The nature of willpower and self-control. In E. T. Higgins & A. W. Kruglanski (Eds.), *Social psychology: Handbook of basic principles* (pp. 329-360). New York: Guilford.

Murray, S. L., Holmes, J. G., & Griffin, D. W. (1996a). "The benefits of positive illusions: Idealization and the construction of satisfaction in close relationships." *Journal of Personality and Social Psychology, 70,* 79-98.

Murray, S. L., Holmes, J. G., & Griffin, D. W. (1996b). "The self-fulfilling nature of positive illusions in romantic relationships: Love is blind, but prescient." *Journal of Personality and Social Psychology, 71,* 1155-1180.

Orlofsky, J. L. (1978). "The relationship between intimacy status and antecedent personality components." *Adolescence, 13,* 419-441.

Pierce, G. R., Sarason, I. G., & Sarason, B. R. (1991). "General and relationship-based perceptions of social support: Are two constructs better than one?" *Journal of Personality and Social Psychology, 61,* 1028-1039.

Prager, K. J. (1989). "Intimacy status and couple communication." *Journal of Social and Personal Relationships, 6,* 435-449.

Prager, K. J. (1995). *The psychology of intimacy.* New York: Guilford.

Ptacek, J. T., & Dodge, K. L. (1995). "Coping strategies and relationship satisfaction in couples." *Personality and Social Psychology Bulletin, 21,* 76-84.

Reis, H. T., & Shaver, P. (1988). Intimacy as an interpersonal process. In S. W. Duck (Ed.), *Handbook of personal relationships* (pp. 367-389). New York: John Wiley.

Reissman, C., Aron, A., & Bergen, M. R. (1993). "Shared activities and marital satisfaction: Causal direction and self-expression versus boredom." *Journal of Social and Personal Relationships, 10,* 243-254.

Rubin, Z., Hill, C. T., Peplau, L. A., & Dunkel-Schetter, C. (1980). "Self-disclosure in dating couples: Sex roles and the ethic of openness." *Journal of Marriage and the Family, 42,* 305-317.

Ruvolo, A. P., & Fabin, L. A. (1999). "Two of a kind: Perceptions of own and partner's attachment characteristics." *Personal Relationships, 6,* 57-79.

Sanderson, C. A., & Cantor, N. (1995). "Social dating goals in late adolescence: Implications for safer sexual activity." *Journal of Personality and Social Psychology, 68,* 1121-1134.

Sanderson, C. A., & Cantor, N. (1997). "Creating satisfaction in steady dating relationships: The role of personal goals and situational affordances." *Journal of Personality and Social Psychology, 73*, 1424-1433.

Sanderson, C. A., & Cantor, N. (in press). The association of intimacy goals and marital satisfaction: A test of four mediational hypotheses. *Personality and Social Psychology Bulletin.*

Sarason, B. R., Shearlin, E. N., Pierce, G. R., & Sarason, I. G. (1987). "Interrelationships between social support measures: Theoretical and practical implications." *Journal of Personality and Social Psychology, 52*, 813-832.

Schaefer, M. T., & Olson, D. H. (1981). "Assessing intimacy: The PAIR inventory." *Journal of Marriage and Family Therapy, 7*, 47-60.

Silbereisen, R. K., Noack, P., & von Eye, A. (1992). "Adolescents' development of romantic friendship and change in favorite leisure contexts." *Journal of Adolescent Research, 7*, 80-93.

Simpson, J. A. (1987). "The dissolution of romantic relationships: Factors involved in relationship stability and emotional distress." *Journal of Personality and Social Psychology, 53*, 683-692.

Simpson, J. A. (1990). "The influence of attachment styles on romantic relationships." *Journal of Personality and Social Psychology, 59*, 971-980.

Snyder, M. (1983). "The influence of individuals on situations: Implications for understanding the links between personality and social behavior." *Journal of Personality, 51*, 497-516.

Snyder, M., Berscheid, E., & Glick, R. P. (1985). "Focusing on the exterior and the interior: Two investigations of the initiation of personal relationships." *Journal of Personality and Social Psychology, 48*, 1427-1439.

Snyder, M., & Ickes, W. (1985). Personality and social behavior. In G. Lindsey & E. Aronson (Eds.), *Handbook of social psychology* (pp. 883-947). New York: Random House.

Snyder, M., Tanke, E. D., & Berscheid, E. (1977). "Social perception and interpersonal behavior: On the self-fulfilling nature of social stereotypes." *Journal of Personality and Social Psychology, 35*, 656-666.

Sobel, M. E. (1982). Asymptotic confidence intervals for indirect effects in structural equations models. In S. Leinhart (Ed.), *Sociological methodology 1982* (pp. 290-312). San Francisco: Jossey-Bass.

Zirkel, S., & Cantor, N. (1990). "Personal construal of a life task: Those who struggle for independence." *Journal of Personality and Social Psychology, 58*, 172-185.

The Science of a Good Marriage

17

CHAPTER

Barbara Kantrowitz and Pat Wingert

Psychology is unlocking the secrets of happy couples.

The myth of marriage goes like this: somewhere out there is the perfect soul mate, the yin that meshes easily and effortlessly with your yang. And then there is the reality of marriage, which, as any spouse knows, is not unlike what Thomas Edison once said about genius: 1 percent inspiration and 99 percent perspiration. That sweaty part, the hard work of keeping a marriage healthy and strong, fascinates John Gottman. He's a psychologist at the University of Washington, and he has spent more than two decades trying to unravel the bewildering complex of emotions that binds two humans together for a year, a decade or even (if you're lucky) a lifetime.

Gottman, 56, comes to this endeavor with the best of qualifications: he's got the spirit of a scientist and the soul of a romantic. A survivor of one divorce, he's now happily married to fellow psychologist Julie Schwartz Gottman (they run couples workshops together). His daunting task is to quantify such intangibles as joy, contempt and tension. Ground zero for this research is the Family Research Laboratory on the Seattle campus (nicknamed the Love Lab). It consists of a series of nondescript offices equipped with video cameras and pulse, sweat and movement monitors to read the hearts and minds of hundreds of couples who have volunteered to be guinea pigs in longitudinal studies of the marital relationship. These volunteers have opened up their lives to the researchers, dissecting everything from the frequency of sex to who takes out the garbage. The results form the basis of Gottman's new book, "The Seven Principles for Making Marriage Work," which he hopes will give spouses a scientific road map to happiness.

Among his unexpected conclusions: anger is not the most destructive emotion in a marriage, since both happy and miserable couples fight. Many popular therapies aim at defusing anger between spouses, but Gottman found that the real demons (he calls them "the Four Horsemen of the Apocalypse") are criticism, contempt, defensiveness and stonewalling. His research shows that the best way to keep these demons at bay is for couples to develop a "love map" of their spouse's dreams and fears. The happy couples all had such a deep understanding of their partner's psyche that they could navigate roadblocks without creating emotional gridlock.

Gottman's research also contradicts the Mars-Venus school of relationships, which holds that men and women come from two very different emotional worlds. According to his studies, gender differences may contribute to marital problems, but they don't cause them. Equal percentages of both men and women he interviewed said that the quality of the spousal friendship is the most important factor in marital satisfaction.

Gottman says he can predict, with more than 90 percent accuracy, which couples are likely to end up in divorce court. The first seven years are especially precarious; the average time for a divorce in this group is 5.2 years. The next danger point comes around 16 to 20 years into the marriage, with an average of 16.4 years. He describes one couple he first met as newlyweds: even then they began every discussion of their problems with sarcasm or criticism, what Gottman calls a "harsh start-up." Although they professed to be in love and committed to the relationship, Gottman correctly predicted that they were in trouble. Four years later they were headed for divorce, he says.

An unequal balance of power is also deadly to a marriage. Gottman found that a husband who doesn't share power with his wife has a much higher risk of damaging the relationship. Why are men singled out? Gottman says his data show that most wives, even those in unstable marriages, are likely to accept their husband's influence. It's the men who need to shape up, he says. The changes can be simple, like turning off the football game when she needs to talk. Gottman says the gesture proves he values "us" over "me."

Gottman's research is built on the work of many other scientists who have focused on emotion and human interaction. Early studies of marriage relied heavily on questionnaires filled out by couples, but these were often inaccurate. In the 1970s several psychology labs began using direct observation of couples to study marriage. A big boon was a relatively new tool for psychologists: videotape. Having a visual record that could be endlessly replayed made it much easier to study the emotional flow between spouses. In 1978 researchers Paul Ekman and Wallace Freisen devised a coding system for the human face that eventually provided another way to measure interchange between spouses.

Although early studies focused on couples in trouble, Gottman thought it was also important to study couples whose marriages work; he thinks they're the real experts. The Love Lab volunteers are interviewed about the history of their marriage. They then talk in front of the cameras about subjects that cause conflict between them. One couple Gottman describes in the book, Tim and Kara, argued constantly about his friend Buddy, who often wound up spending the night on Tim and Kara's couch. The researchers take scenes like this and break down every second of interaction to create a statistical pattern of good and bad moments. How many times did she roll her eyes (a sign of contempt) when he spoke? How often did he fidget (indicating tension or stress)? The frequency of negative and positive expressions, combined with the data collected by the heart, sweat and other monitors, provides a multidimensional view of the relationship. (Tim and Kara ultimately decided Buddy could stay, only not as often.)

Gottman and other researchers see their work as a matter of public health. The average couple who seek help have been having problems for six years—long enough to have done serious damage to their relationship. That delay, Gottman says, is as dangerous as putting off regular mammograms. The United States has one of the highest divorce rates in the industrialized world, and studies have shown a direct correlation between marriage and well-being. Happily married people are healthier; even their immune systems work better than those of people who are unhappily married or divorced. Kids suffer as well; if their parents split, they're more likely to have emotional or school problems.

But going to a marriage counselor won't necessarily help. "Therapy is at an impasse," Gottman says, "because it is not based on solid empirical knowledge of what real couples do to keep their marriages happy and stable." In a 1995 Consumer Reports survey, marriage therapy ranked at the bottom of a poll of patient satisfaction with various psychotherapies. The magazine said part of the problem was that "almost anyone can hang out a shingle as a marriage counselor." Even credentialed therapists may use approaches that have no basis in research. Several recent studies have shown that many current treatments produce few long-term benefits for couples who seek help.

One example: the process called "active listening." It was originally used by therapists to objectively summarize the complaints of a patient and validate the way the patient is feeling. ("So, I'm hearing that you think your father always liked your sister better and you're hurt by that.") In recent years this technique has been modified for marital therapy— ineffectively, Gottman says. Even highly trained therapists would have a hard time stepping back in the middle of a fight and saying, "So, I'm hearing that you think I'm a fat, lazy slob."

Happily married couples have a very different way of relating to each other during disputes, Gottman found. The partners make frequent "repair attempts," reaching out to each other in an effort to prevent negativity from getting out of control in the midst of conflict. Humor is often part of a successful repair attempt. In his book, Gottman describes one couple arguing about the kind of car to buy (she favors a minivan; he wants a snazzier Jeep). In the midst of yelling, the wife suddenly puts her hand on her hip and sticks out her tongue—mimicking their 4-year-old son. They both start laughing, and the tension is defused.

In happy unions, couples build what Gottman calls a "sound marital house" by working together and appreciating the best in each other. They learn to cope with the two kinds of problems that are part of every marriage: solvable conflicts and perpetual problems that may represent underlying conflicts and that can lead to emotional gridlock. Gottman says 69 percent of marital conflicts fall into the latter category. Happy spouses deal with these issues in a way that strengthens the marriage. One couple Gottman studied argued constantly about order in their household (she demanded neatness, and he couldn't care less). Over the years they managed to accommodate their differences, acknowledging that their affection for each other was more important than newspapers piled up in the corner of the living room.

As psychologists learn more about marriage, they have begun devising new approaches to therapy. Philip Cowan and Carolyn Pape-Cowan, a husband-and-wife team (married for 41 years) at the University of California, Berkeley, are looking at one of the most critical periods in a marriage: the birth of a first child. (Two thirds of couples experience a "precipitous drop" in marital satisfaction at this point, researchers say.) "Trying to take two people's dreams of a perfect family and make them one is quite a trick," Pape-Cowan says. The happiest couples were those who looked on their spouses as partners with whom they shared household and child-care duties. The Cowans say one way to help spouses get through the transition to parenting would be ongoing group sessions with other young families to provide the kind of support people used to get from their communities and extended families.

Two other researchers—Neil Jacobson at the University of Washington and Andrew Christensen at UCLA—have developed what they call "acceptance therapy" after studying the interactions of couples in conflict. The goal of their therapy is to help people learn to live with aspects of their spouse's characters that simply can't be changed. "People can love each other not just for what they have in common but for things that make them complementary," says Jacobson. "When we looked at a clinical sample of what predicted failure in traditional behavior therapy, what we came upon again and again was an inability to accept differences."

Despite all these advances in marital therapy, researchers still say they can't save all marriages—and in fact there are some that shouldn't be saved. Patterns of physical abuse, for example, are extremely difficult to alter, Gottman says. And there are cases where the differences between the spouses are so profound and longstanding that even the best therapy is futile. Gottman says one quick way to test whether a couple still has a chance is to ask what initially attracted them to each other. If they can recall those magic first moments (and smile when they talk about them), all is not lost. "We can still fan the embers," says Gottman. For all the rest of us, there's hope.

Know Your Spouse

Test the strength of your marriage in this relationship quiz prepared especially for NEWSWEEK by John Gottman.

		TRUE/FALSE
1.	I can name my partner's best friends	
2.	I can tell you what stresses my partner is currently facing	
3.	I know the names of some of the people who have been irritating my partner lately	
4.	I can tell you some of my partner's life dreams	
5.	I can tell you about my partner's basic philosophy of life	
6.	I can list the relatives my partner likes the least	
7.	I feel that my partner knows me pretty well	
8.	When we are apart, I often think fondly of my partner	
9.	I often touch or kiss my partner affectionately	
10.	My partner really respects me	
11.	There is fire and passion in this relationship	
12.	Romance is definitely still a part of our relationship	
13.	My partner appreciates the things I do in this relationship	
14.	My partner generally likes my personality	
15.	Our sex life is mostly satisfying	
16.	At the end of the day my partner is glad to see me	
17.	My partner is one of my best friends	
18.	We just love talking to each other	
19.	There is lots of give and take (both people have influence) in our discussions	
20.	My partner listens respectfully, even when we disagree	
21.	My partner is usually a great help as a problem solver	
22.	We generally mesh well on basic values and goals in life	

Scoring: Give yourself one point for each "True" answer.

Above 12: You have a lot of strength in your relationship. Congratulations.

Below 12: Your relationship could stand some improvement and could probably benefit from some work on the basics, such as improving communication.

Facing Your Problems

In the lab, the way a married couple fights can often tell psychologists more than what they fight about. The expressions and underlying emotions displayed during a conflict may reveal the strength or weakness of the marriage. During a couple's 15-minute conversation—on a topic known to be a sore point—researchers at the University of Washington measure physiological responses (below) and facial expressions, which can reveal true feelings even when words don't. Videotapes also show how long the partners' emotional responses last—even the happiest of couples has fleeting moments of bad feeling, but if the negative indicators tend to endure, it can signal a marriage in trouble.

Surprise: A big smile, with popping eyes, indicates a positive surprise. Something unexpected but unpleasant yields the eye-pop only. Either way, a short-lived state.

Interest: A calm voice and positive body language—leaning forward, for example—signal the genuine article. It's a real desire to hear a partner's opinion, not an attempt to influence.

Anger: The tone is cold or loud, the wording staccato. But honest anger, an internal state, is different from contempt, directed at the spouse. A fake smile, without raised cheeks, may mask anger.

Domineering: A "low and slow" voice often signals that one partner is trying to force the other to his or her view. Ranges from lawyerly cross-examination to blatant threats.

Fear: Outright fear is rare; a lower-grade version—tension—is more common. And a wife's tension, if pronounced, can be a predictor for divorce down the road.

Sadness: Passivity and sulking can look like stonewalling or disengaging from a fight, but sad people maintain more eye contact than stonewallers.

Contempt: If prolonged, this expression is a red alert. Especially when accompanied by sarcasm and insults, it suggests a marriage in serious trouble.

Great Expectations

Polly Sherman

CHAPTER

Q: How do you turn a good relationship sour?

A: Pursue your inalienable right to happiness, hot sex, true love and that soul mate who must be out there somewhere.

Marriage is dead! The twin vises of church and law have relaxed their grip on matrimony. We've been liberated from the grim obligations to stay in a poisonous or abusive marriage for the sake of the kids or for appearances. The divorce rate has stayed constant at nearly 50 percent for the last two decades. The ease with which we enter and dissolve unions makes marriage seem life a prime-time spectator sport, whether it's Britney Spears in Vegas or bimbos chasing after the Bachelor.

Long live the new marriage! We once prized the institution for the practical pairing of a cash-producing father and a home-building mother. Now we want it all—a partner who reflects our taste and status, who sees us for who we are, who loves us for all the "right" reasons, who helps us become the person we want to be. We've done away with a rigid social order, adopting instead an even more onerous obligation: the mandate to find a perfect match. Anything short of this ideal prompts us to ask: Is this all there is? Am I as happy as I should be? Could there be somebody out there who's better for me? As often as not, we answer yes to that last question and fall victim to our own great expectations.

That somebody is, of course, our soul mate, the man or woman who will counter our weaknesses, amplify our strengths and provide the unflagging support and respect that is the essence of a contemporary relationship. The reality is that few marriages or partnerships consistently live up to this ideal. The result is a commitment limbo, in which we care deeply for our partner but keep one stealthy foot out the door of our hearts. In so doing, we subject the relationship to constant review: Would I be happier, smarter, a better person with someone else? It's a painful modern quandary. "Nothing has produced more unhappiness than the concept of the soul mate," says Atlanta psychiatrist Frank Pittman.

Consider Jeremy, a social worker who married a businesswoman in his early twenties. He met another woman, a psychologist, at age 29, and after two agonizing years, left his wife for her. But it didn't work out—after four years of cohabitation, and her escalating pleas to marry, he walked out on her, as well. Jeremy now realizes that the relationship with his wife was solid and workable but thinks he couldn't have seen that 10 years ago, when he left her. "There was always someone better around the corner—and the safety and security of marriage morphed into boredom and stasis. The allure of willing and exciting females was too hard to resist," he admits. Now 42 and still single, Jeremy acknowledges, "I hurt others, and I hurt myself."

Like Jeremy, many of us either dodge the decision to commit or commit without fully relinquishing the right to keep looking—opting for an arrangement psychotherapist Terrence Real terms "stable ambiguity."

"You park on the border of the relationship, so you're in it but not of it," he says. There are a million ways to do that: You can be in a relationship but not be sure it's really the right one, have an eye open for a better deal or something on the side, choose someone impossible or far away.

Yet commitment and marriage offer real physical and financial rewards. Touting the benefits of marriage may sound like conservative policy rhetoric, but nonpartisan sociological research backs it up: Committed partners have it all over singles, at least on average. Married people are more financially stable, according to Linda Waite, a sociologist at the University of Chicago and a coauthor of *The Case for Marriage: Why Married People are Happier, Healthier and Better Off.* Both married men and married women have more assets on average than singles; for women, the differential is huge.

The benefits go beyond the piggy bank. Married people, particularly men, tend to live longer than people who aren't married. Couples also live better: When people expect to stay together, says Waite, they pool their resources, increasing their individual standard of living. They also pool their expertise—in cooking, say, or financial management. In general, women improve men's health by putting a stop to stupid bachelor tricks and bugging their husbands to exercise and eat their vegetables. Plus, people who aren't comparing their partners to someone else in bed have less trouble performing and are more emotionally satisfied with sex. The relationship doesn't have to be wonderful for life to get better, says Waite: The statistics hold true for mediocre marriages as well as for passionate ones.

The pragmatic benefits of partnership used to be foremost in our minds. The idea of marriage as a vehicle for self-fulfillment and happiness is relatively new, says Paul Amato, professor of sociology, demography and family studies at Penn State University. Surveys of high school and college students 50 or 60 years ago found that most wanted to get married in order to have children or own a home. Now, most report that they plan to get married for love. This increased emphasis on emotional fulfillment within marriage leaves couples ill-prepared for the realities they will probably face.

Because the early phase of a relationship is marked by excitement and idealization, "many romantic, passionate couples expect to have that excitement forever," says Barry McCarthy, a clinical psychologist and coauthor—with his wife, Emily McCarthy—of *Getting It Right the First Time: How to Build a Healthy Marriage.* Longing for the charged energy of the early days, people look elsewhere or split up.

Flagging passion is often interpreted as the death knell of a relationship. You begin to wonder whether you're really right for each other after all. You're comfortable together, but you don't really connect the way you used to. Wouldn't it be more honest—and braver—to just admit that it's not working and call it off? "People are made to feel that remaining in a marriage that doesn't make you blissfully happy is an act of existential cowardice," says Joshua.

Coleman, a San Francisco psychologist, says that the constant cultural pressure to have it all—a great sex life, a wonderful family—has made people ashamed of their less-than-perfect relationships and question whether such unions are worth hanging on to. Feelings of dissatisfaction or disappointment are natural, but they can seem intolerable when standards are sky-high. "It's a recent historical event that people expect to get so much from individual partners," says Coleman, author of Imperfect Harmony, in which he advises couples in lackluster marriages to stick it out—especially if they have kids. "There's an enormous amount of pressure on marriages to live up to an unrealistic ideal."

Michaela, 28, was drawn to Bernardo, 30, in part because of their differences: She'd grown up in European boarding schools, he fought his way out of a New York City ghetto. "Our backgrounds made us more interesting to each other," says Michaela. "I was a spoiled brat, and he'd been supporting himself from the age of 14, which I admired." Their first two years of marriage were rewarding, but their fights took a toll. "I felt that because he hadn't grown up in a normal family, he didn't grasp basic issues of courtesy and accountability," says Michaela. They were temperamental opposites: He was a screamer, and she was a sulker. She recalls, "After we fought, I needed to be drawn out of my corner, but he took that to mean that I was a cold bitch." Michaela reluctantly concluded that the two were incompatible.

In fact, argue psychologists and marital advocates, there's no such thing as true compatibility.

"Marriage is a disagreement machine," says Diane Sollee, founder of the Coalition for Marriage, Family and Couples Education. "All couples disagree about all the same things. We have a highly romanticized notion that if we were with the right person, we wouldn't fight." Discord springs eternal over money, kids, sex and leisure time, but psychologist John Gottman has shown that long-term, happily married couples disagree about these things just as much as couples who divorce.

"There is a mythology of 'the wrong person,'" agrees Pittman. "All marriages are incompatible. All marriages are between people from different families, people who have a different view of things. The magic is to develop binocular vision, to see life through your partner's eyes as well as through your own."

The realization that we're not going to get everything we want from a partner is not just sobering, it's downright miserable. But it is also a necessary step in building a mature relationship, according to Real, who has written about the subject in *How Can I Get Through to You: Closing the Intimacy Gap Between Men and Women*. "The paradox of intimacy is that our ability to stay close rests on our ability to tolerate solitude inside a relationship," he says. "A central aspect of grown-up love is grief. All of us long for—and think we deserve—perfection."

We can hardly be blamed for striving for bliss and self-fulfillment in our romantic lives—our inalienable right to the pursuit of happiness is guaranteed in the first blueprint of American society.

This same respect for our own needs spurred the divorce-law reforms of the 1960s and 1970s. During that era, "The culture shifted to emphasize individual satisfaction, and marriage was part of that," explains Paul Amato, who has followed more than 2,000 families for 20 years in a long-term study of marriage and divorce. Amato says that this shift did some good by freeing people from abusive and intolerable marriages. But it had an unintended side effect: encouraging people to abandon relationships that may be worth salvaging.

In a society hell-bent on individual achievement and autonomy, working on a difficult relationship may get short shrift, says psychiatrist Peter Kramer, author of *Should You Leave?*

"So much of what we learn has to do with the self, the ego, rather than giving over the self to things like a relationship," Kramer says. In our competitive world, we're rewarded for our individual achievements rather than for how we help others. We value independence over cooperation, and sacrifices for values like loyalty and continuity seem foolish. "I think we get the divorce rate that we deserve as a culture."

The steadfast focus on our own potential may turn a partner into an accessory in the quest for self actualization, says Maggie Robbins, a therapist in New York City. "We think that this person should reflect the beauty and perfection that is the inner me—or, more often, that this person should compensate for the yuckiness and mess that is the inner me," says Robbins. "This is what makes you tell your wife, 'Lose some weight—you're making me look bad,' not 'Lose some weight, you're at risk for diabetes.'"

Michaela was consistently embarrassed by Bernardo's behavior when they were among friends. "He'd become sullen and withdrawn—he had a shifty way of looking off to the side when he didn't want to talk. I felt like it reflected badly on me," she admits. Michaela left him and is now dating a wealthy entrepreneur. "I just thought there had to be someone else out there for me."

The urge to find a soul mate is not fueled just by notions of romantic manifest destiny. Trends in the workforce and in the media create a sense of limitless romantic possibility. According to Scott South, a demographer at SUNY-Albany, proximity to potential partners has a powerful effect on relationships. South and his colleagues found higher divorce rates among people living in communities or working in professions where they encounter lots of potential partners—people who match them in age, race and education level. "These results hold true not just for unhappy marriages but also for happy ones," says South.

The temptations aren't always living, breathing people. According to research by psychologists Sara Gutierres and Douglas Kenrick, both of Arizona State University, we find reasonably attractive people less appealing when we've just seen a hunk or a hottie— and we're bombarded daily by images of gorgeous models and actors. When we watch *Lord of the Rings*, Viggo Mortensen's kingly mien and Liv Tyler's elfin charm can make our husbands and wives look all too schlumpy.

Kramer sees a similar pull in the narratives that surround us. "The number of stories that tell us about other lives we could lead—in magazine articles, television shows, books— has increased enormously. We have an enormous reservoir of possibilities," says Framer.

And these possibilities can drive us to despair. Too many choices have been shown to stymie consumers, and an array of alternative mates is no exception. In an era when marriages were difficult to dissolve, couples rated their marriages as more satisfying than do today's couples, for whom divorce is a clear option, according to the National Opinion Research Center at the University of Chicago.

While we expect marriage to be "happily ever after," the truth is that for most people, neither marriage nor divorce seem to have a decisive impact on happiness. Although Waite's research shows that married people are happier than their single counterparts, other studies have found that after a couple years of marriage, people are just about as happy (or unhappy) as they were before settling down. And assuming that marriage will automatically provide contentment is itself a surefire recipe for misery.

"Marriage is not supposed to make you happy. It is supposed to make you married," says Pittman. "When you are all the way in your marriage, you are free to do useful things, become a better person." A committed relationship allows you to drop pretenses and seductions, expose your weaknesses, be yourself—and know that you will be loved, warts and all. "A real relationship is the collision of my humanity and yours, in all its joy and limitations," says Real. "How partners handle that collision is what determines the quality of their relationship."

Such a down-to-earth view of marriage is hardly romantic, but that doesn't mean it's not profound: An authentic relationship with another person, says Pittman, is "one of the first steps toward connecting with the human condition—which is necessary if you're going to become fulfilled as a human being." If we accept these humble terms, the quest for a soul mate might just be a noble pursuit after all.

Part

Relationship Decisions

The New Trophy Wife

Deborah Siegel

Pete Beeman, a 36-year-old sculptor, met Page Fortna, 34, on New Year's Eve 1997, while she was studying for a doctorate in political science. "I was totally impressed that she was getting a Ph.D.," recalls Beeman. "She has a powerhouse background that speaks of personal drive and dedication. It was attractive, not in a sexual way, but in a necessary way. I am not interested in someone who doesn't have as much to offer me as I have to offer her."

Massimo Tassan-Solet met Karin Dauch at an Internet merger party in 2000. She introduced herself to the derivatives trader, now 36, by announcing, "Hi, I'm Karin, and I have to go now." "She was strong and unconventional in her approach, but she did it with humor," recalls Tassan-Solet of Dauch, who at age 29 owns doubleKappa, a Web design and branding company. "I don't look at people as a list of what they've done," says Tassan-Solet. "But what she's done is remarkable."

Beeman and Tassan-Solet aren't the only newlyweds who are proud of their wives' CVs. New trends in the mating game—marrying someone like yourself—plus an unstable economy breathe new life into the term "peer marriage." In previous generations, successful doctors, lawyers and bankers sought wives who looked good, were well-bred and made a mean Stroganoff to boot. Now, more and more alpha males are looking for something else from the A-list: accomplishment.

According to a recent Match.com poll, 48 percent of men (and an equal percentage of women) report dating partners who draw the same income they do. Twenty percent of men report dating women who earn more. Jim Pak, 34, was introduced to Kristin Ketner, 38, a Harvard MBA and a hedge fund manager, through a mutual friend, who warned

---

him not to be intimidated by her credentials. She was a research analyst for Goldman Sachs; he was unemployed and playing a lot of golf. "In certain regards, she outshines me," says Pak of his wife. "She's more accomplished academically. People may be more impressed with her than with me." (Pak is now chief financial officer at an electronic stock trading services group.)

Men's attraction to professionally achieving mates is one piece of a much larger story. "We're experiencing a historic change in the things people want out of marriage, the reasons they enter into it and stay in it," says historian Stephanie Coontz of Evergreen State College in Olympia, Washington. Men in their 20s and 30s embarking on first marriages are relieved to no longer be the sole breadwinner and decision-maker, a burden many watched their fathers shoulder. "These men are truly redefining masculinity," says Terrence Real, a psychologist and author of *How Can I Get Through to You? Closing the Intimacy Gap Between Men and Women.* And the pursuit of a high-achiever is not solely the province of youth. Status-conscious tycoons want to have second marriages—and affairs—with alpha women. "Older men now want the most impressive achiever in the office. In the eyes of a man's peers, the woman with the career and degrees counts for more than Miss America," says Frank Pittman, psychiatrist to Atlanta's elite. "Status is attached to a woman who is successful, not to a woman with a perfectly pear-shaped ass."

Common wisdom holds that men are socially programmed and biologically compelled to select women based on beauty and youth, physical traits that signal reproductive health. But many men today date "across" and, increasingly, "up" the axes of education and achievement, with less regard for age, or for the notorious "arm candy" factor.

"There's a higher degree of parity today between marital partners," observes Pak. "Men want a wife who reflects well in every aspect." In some circles, more eyebrows are raised when a guy marries a woman who doesn't match him in education or professional status. Says David, a single 33-year-old assistant professor at a prestigious university who routinely filters online dating ads using the criterion of education: "If I were with someone who wasn't of comparable intelligence, energy and drive, there'd be those who thought I'd wimped out and chosen a relationship where I could call the shots and be the all-powerful center."

"Showing up with a stacked bubblehead is like conspicuous consumption," agrees Real. "It's embarrassing to flag yourself as not interested in a real relationship."

But is a woman's success sexy?

"Absolutely," says David. "And the absence of an attempt to do something interesting or difficult is a turnoff." Henry Kissinger may have been right: Power is the ultimate aphrodisiac.

Rise of the Power Bride

When Scott South, a sociologist at the University at Albany, State University of New York, examined the characteristics most desirable to black and white men ages 19 to 35, he found that a woman's ability to hold a steady job mattered more than her age, previous marriages, maternal status, religion or race. Men were more willing to marry women with more, rather than less, education than they themselves had. A wise move, since women today eclipse men in the rates at which they attain bachelor's and master's degrees, and the number of women pursuing higher education continues to steadily climb.

Many of today's grooms believe that through positive or negative example, their own moms set the stage for a high-octane wife. After his parents separated when he was 12, Jim Pak watched his mother raise three kids while pursuing an advanced degree in art history. "That kind of role model helps you not be intimidated by highly motivated, successful women," he says. Others view their mothers' lives as cautionary tales. "My mom was very unhappy that she had little energy for anything other than raising her four kids," says a groom who recently married a woman who works in finance. "I wouldn't want to marry someone who felt that unfulfilled."

"Our generation is highly cognizant of the divorce rate," adds Pak. "We learned from our parents' mistakes."

But it's not always easy. Charting a marital course markedly different from that of one's parents means there's no role model to consult. And today's alpha woman expects more of a domestic partnership—and an emotional connection—than her husband may have seen growing up. "Women are demanding more emotionally because logistically they don't have to get married," says Real. "They want guys to be articulate and open about their feelings." The trouble, finds Real, is that "most men today are not trained to do those things."

A solution to this impasse, says Barry McCarthy, a psychologist in Washington, D.C., who works with many high-achieving couples, is for spouses to communicate their expectations from the get-go: "It's great that the man is no longer the success object and the woman is no longer the sex object. But when people organize their lives differently from their cultures or families of origin, they have to make it work practically and emotionally. You have to negotiate before [marriage] how you're going to deal with the core issues of sex, money and kids."

The Unromantic Bottom Line

There's another pragmatic reason men prize new high-earning brides. Our romantic ideals are always grounded in economic realities, from the Victorian marriage model to the 1980s masters of the universe for whom a standard-issue trophy wife was a badge of honor. Today's bearish market calls for couples to act as an economic unit. Families with two breadwinners have been in the majority since 1998, and single twentysomethings' and thirtysomethings' desire for a two-income merger has intensified in the shadow of the recession. Women still earn less than men (78 cents to the male dollar) and seriously lag in the highest-paying sectors, like engineering, investment banking and high tech. But wives have been catching up to or surpassing their husbands since the 1980s, particularly among the well-off. (Of wives who earn more than $100,000, one in three is now married to a husband earning less.)

"It used to be that men were a good catch because they were high earners. It now looks like this applies to women, too," says University of Wisconsin economist Maria Cancian, who recently teamed up with Megan Sweeney, a University of California, Los Angeles sociologist, to study the increased importance of wives' wages.

How openly embraced is the prospect of a female breadwinner? According to Pak, a 30-year-old today is much less likely than his father to correlate his self-worth with his ability to provide for a family. Pak's wife, Ketner, believes that men who are comfortable with themselves will factor a potential bride's income into the marital calculus, as women have long done. Says Page Fortna, "Men think, 'If we combined our two incomes, how would we do?' But I wouldn't say it's flipped [to the point where] men say, 'I won't have to work, I'll just live off her.'"

Real is more emphatic: "Men aren't just OK with it. They're relieved." Men have long considered traditional marital roles "anemic and constricting," according to Real, and no longer being the sole breadwinner is a loosening of the straitjacket. Not to mention the improved standard of living. "These guys aren't worried about their male ego in relation to their wife's income," says Real. "They just want to plan a nice vacation together."

If financial straits make alpha women hot commodities for younger men, then financial and social status make these same women desirable to older men seeking a mistress or second wife. "Men have always chosen women who make them feel heroic," states Pittman. "It used to be sufficient to be the hero in your wife's and children's eyes. But when narcissistic men feel they've undermarried and their kids are grown, the real audience becomes your peers, the guys who are eating their hearts out because you've just married a former stripper turned circuit court judge."

Powerful men seek powerful wives, and in an era in which power is increasingly equated with intellectual capital, that translates into wives who match or perhaps even exceed their husbands in educational and professional status. (Think Candace Carpenter, founder of iVillage and second wife of Random House president and CEO Peter Olson.)

If men in first marriages are relieved to be outearned by spouse or partner, some older men are positively "proud" of this fact, finds Pittman, who also notes a spike in the number of thirtysomething and fortysomething men pursuing older, successful women. But when it comes to second wives, some things never change. Whether she's a 27-year-old secretary or a 47-year-old corporate vice president, the second wife will likely not be as beneficial a partner as was the first, says Pittman. "The woman who has seen a man get started and develop is more useful than the woman for whom he always has to perform, who may bring out the worst in him."

Alpha-alpha first and second marriages make sense against the backdrop of a shifting pecking order in the nation's governing class. As author David Brooks has noted, changes in the prestige factor among couples whose wedding announcements make The New York Times bear this out. "Pedigreed elite used to be based on noble birth and breeding," writes Brooks in *Bobos in Paradise: The New Upper Class and How They Got There*. "Now it's genius that enables you to join the elect."

A Confidence Gap

If high-aiming women are more marriage-eligible than ever, why don't they seem to know it? When a Match.com poll asked marriage-minded men whether they were reluctant to seek out career women as partners, 62 percent said no. But 74 percent of the women surveyed think men are intimidated by women with high-powered careers. "Women have an asset they perceive as a liability," says Pepper Schwartz, author of *Love Between Equals: How Peer Marriage Really Works* and professor of sociology at the University of Washington. "Young men see these women growing up: She's your doctor, your teacher, your professor. These models can be quite erotic."

So why, then, the confidence gap? Men may be more intimidated by high-powered women than they're willing to admit. And high-achieving women, who tend to marry later, are used to being told that success causes their marrying and childbearing stock to plummet. Sylvia Ann Hewlett, author of *Creating a Life: Professional Women and the Quest for Children*, made headlines in 2002 by recycling the claim that the more a woman achieves in the workplace, the less likely she is to marry or to have kids. The book triggered a panic reminiscent of Newsweek's highly publicized 1986 report that a 40-year-old woman was more likely to be attacked by terrorists than to marry. That "finding" turned out to be a tale as tall as the heels on single icon Carrie Bradshaw's Manolo Blahniks, and

Hewlett's conclusions, based on a small sample of highly elite women, are equally suspect when applied to professionally ambitious women at large.

When Heather Boushey of the Center for Economic Policy Research in Washington, D.C., crunched numbers on 33.6 million American women (gleaned from the 2000 and 2001 Current Population Survey), she found that women between the ages of 28 and 35 who work full time and earn more than $55,000 per year or have a graduate or professional degree are just as likely to be successfully married as other women who work full time. They're just finding love slightly later. While American women marry on average at age 25, college graduates marry at 27. Those with masters or professional degrees wed on average at age 30.

Pop-psych punditry about fragile male egos may cloud the real problem inherent in many alpha-alpha marriages. Psychologists agree that difficulties most often arise not because a man feels emasculated by his wife's star power ("No one can emasculate you except you," avows Pak), but because the woman grows disappointed with her partner.

"If a woman is powerful, smart and ambitious, her expectations for her husband, and for the relationship, rise," says Nando Pelusi, a New York City psychologist who has counseled plenty of alpha-alpha pairings. McCarthy says it's the primary reason that middle-class marriages fail in the first five years: The woman feels her spouse is not keeping his end of the pact.

And when women feel that their husbands aren't reaching their earning or emoting potential, men may decide they've gotten more than they bargained for. "Men truly want brighter, more articulate, aggressive women. They want to be seen in the world with them. But they also want these women to leave some of it at the doorstep," says Real. "These guys love their wives. They just haven't figured out what to do when that strength is channeled toward them."

Real is quick to add that most wouldn't have it any other way. "I must have said it a thousand times," he quips: "'Mr. Jones, you wouldn't be happy with the kind of woman who would put up with you.'"

True to form, most alpha males take pride in the bumps. "If I can sustain a relationship with a real, serious, powerful, happening gal, it means that I'm more real, serious and happening," says Beeman.

"Being involved with these women is like driving a Ferrari," says Pelusi. "It can be uncomfortable and dangerous, but it's ultimately more rewarding than owning a Ford Taurus, which is safe but boring."

Why Women Have to Work

Amelia Warren Tyagi

Why are today's mothers working so hard, putting in long hours at home and at the office? For the money.

Oh, sure, those ladies who took their grandmothers' advice and married a doctor, a lawyer or an Enron executive may show up for work to "fulfill themselves" or to "expand their horizons." But for most women who, like me, came of age in the '90s, it comes down to dollars and cents, and the calculation is brutal.

In one column sits that big-eyed slobbery youngster, and a mother's heart beating to be there so she can give him everything. And in the other column sits the mother's heart...beating to give him everything.

Because in most of the U.S. it is no longer possible to support a middle-class family on Dad's income alone. This isn't a question of having enough cash to buy Game Boys and exotic trips. It is a question of having enough to buy the basics.

Like a home. Anyone who hasn't been hiding under a rock in Montana knows that it costs more to purchase a house than it used to. But what many do not realize is that this increase has become a family problem, with mothers caught in the cross hairs. Over the past generation, home prices have risen twice as fast for couples with young children as for those without kids. Why? Confidence in the public schools has dwindled, leaving millions of families to conclude that the only way to ensure Junior a slot in a safe, quality school is to snatch up a home in a good school district. In most cities that means paying more for the family home. Since the mid-'70s, the amount of the average family budget earmarked for the mortgage has increased a whopping 69% (adjusted for inflation). At the same time, the average father's income increased less than 1%. How to make up the difference? With Mom's paycheck, of course.

These moms aren't marching to the office so they can get into brand-new McMansions. In fact, the average family today lives in a house that is older than the one Mom and Dad grew up in, and scarcely half a room bigger. The average couple with young children now shells out more than $127,000 for a home, up from $72,000 (adjusted for inflation) less than 20 years ago.

Then there is preschool. No longer an optional "Mother's Day Out" enterprise, preschool is widely viewed as a prerequisite for elementary school. But that prerequisite isn't offered at most public schools, which means that any mother who wants her kids to have access to this "essential start to early education," as the experts call it, has to come up with cold, hard cash. A full-time preschool program can cost over $5,000 a year—more than a year's tuition at most state universities! Add the cost of health insurance (for those lucky enough to have it) and the eventual price of sending a kid to college (double—when adjusted for inflation—what it was a generation ago), and most middle-class moms find they have no choice but to get a job if they want to make ends meet.

To be sure, there are plenty of mothers who scrimp and save and find a way to stay home (at least for a few years). But there are plenty more who decide that the cost is just too high, and the choice of whether to stay home is no choice at all.

Men Want Change Too

Michael Elliot

We were young; we were smart; we were looking forward to the world of work. And when we graduated from Oxford University in the early 1970s, my wife and I (we've been together 33 years) thought we'd have it all. We'd both have successful, satisfying careers. We'd have enough free time to travel the world and do fun stuff (you should have seen the shirts and dresses she used to make). We'd share in our kids' upbringing and divide the chores. We were convinced that the world of stay-at-home moms and job-trapped dads had ended, oh, sometime around 1969.

We were wrong, of course. In her 30s, my wife gave up a high-powered career as a government official to have children. Consciously trying to balance work and family, she took part-time jobs that in some cases were enjoyable but that never gave her the recognition or professional advancement that you get if you're in full-time employment. Meanwhile—first for fun, later because the extra income helped—I allowed work to take over my life, spending nights and weekends working on books or TV films. I've spent nothing close to the time I wanted to with my two daughters. Granted, there should be some rule against well-paid journalists complaining about their lot in life, so let the record show that I love my work and that my children are charming, healthy teenagers. But the three-way balance among work, family and the nonjob, nonkid stuff that provides much of the spice of life—what ever happened to my tennis game or the trip to Machu Picchu?—is nothing like what my wife and I imagined it would be. It's not just women who are disappointed that modern life has not accommodated their various needs. So are millions of baby-boomer men who wanted their marriage to be a genuine partnership of equals.

Why did we get it so wrong? We weren't all smoking something—O.K., some of us were—and we weren't unutterably naive. But we left college at a very specific moment in time. We were the beneficiaries of eight decades of astonishing technological change, and we subconsciously thought it would continue. But a long wave of improvement in every-day life came to an end in the 1970s. Look around your home; you will not see a significant labor-saving device invented since the 1960s. Nothing has happened since then to make feeding the kids, washing their clothes or cleaning the home easier. Think about the time you spend schlepping around; note that New Yorkers travel in the same way and at much the same speed as they did in the 1930s.

The most significant technological development of the past 30 years has been a collapse in the price of a unit of information. That, it turns out, has been disastrous for the work-life balance. Information is now ubiquitous. Home life is no easier than it was, but work has invaded the domestic space—which is what my daughters mean when they scream at me to stop answering e-mail in the evening. The incessant demands of an al-ways-on, 24/7 world of free information have made some middle-aged women who would like to go back to work consider whether the benefits are worth the hassle. But so long as they stay out of the labor market, their husbands are trapped in it—otherwise family incomes would fall. Hence that familiar social phenomenon: a married couple in their 50s in which the wife is resentful because she does too little paid work and the husband is resentful because he does too much.

Thirty years ago, we dreamed of something different. Pity it didn't work out.

Redefining Our Relationships: Guidelines for Responsible Open Relationships

22

CHAPTER

Wendy-O Matik

Introduction

"The most vital right is the right to love and be loved." Emma Goldman

"Our belief is that the human capacity for sex and love and intimacy is far greater than most people think—possibly infinite—and that having a lot of satisfying connections simply makes it possible for you to have a lot more." Easton and Liszt, *The Ethical Slut: A Guide to Infinite Sexual Possibilities*

I'm an activist of the heart. I have always felt as if I have an enormous capacity to love everyone—the homeless guy down the street, the little old lady next door, someone I just had a five-hour mind-blowing conversation with, and then, of course, my friends, lovers, and family. When I finally admitted to myself—without guilt—that I have a human right and obligation to myself to love as many people as I want or need, then I became aware of how a monogamous relationship, outlined by conventional social norms, was never going to work for me. I would never be able to conform. Radical love, or the freedom to love as many as you desire, has become a way of life. This is part of why I have taken on the challenge of redefining all of my significant relationships based on my values and lifestyle. An open relationship is a radically different, redefined relationship outside the status quo, where partners encourage non-restrictive paths of love while remaining seriously committed to their partner(s), friends, and lovers. Open relationships, in theory, seek a non-hierarchical form of love.

I was initially inspired to write this book based on a healthy, responsible, thirteen-year open relationship, as well as a lot of encouragement from friends. Despite the ending of that relationship, we spent a great deal of time negotiating what our relationship could be, or could have the potential to be, if we put our creative hearts and minds into it. We laid down a foundation of trust based on mutually agreed upon rules that helped us to grow and evolve as a couple. We have shared lovers, supported each other in having outside lovers, as well as supported our friends to forge relationships that better suited their lifestyles, particularly in the late 80's and early 90's when many of us had no real role models to follow.

I'll be the last one to advocate one type of relationship over another, monogamy versus non-monogamy. What I am most interested in is planting the seeds of autonomy. We have choices. We have options. Just because monogamy is the popular prescribed relationship model doesn't mean it's right for everyone. There simply cannot be just one formula for all when our needs and desires are so unique and varied. Carve out your own lifestyle. Imagine your own ideal relationship. Radicalize your life and challenge yourself to have deep, meaningful relationships with anyone who you feel is important to you—including your parents, siblings, friends, lovers, pen pals, and neighbors. If you define "open" to include cuddling, kissing, and heartfelt communication, then work that into your life. If open means sexual liberation, then be honest with yourself and the ones you love, and take the responsible steps to achieve this. Love is a revolution that starts in the privacy of your home and touches everyone you love and come in contact with.

I am advocating responsible relationships that are entrenched in the principles of honesty, communication, and consent. All relationships have certain guidelines that are agreed upon. When you go outside the mutually agreed upon rules, then you betray yourself and your loved ones. That's cheating, and people get hurt. This is how jealousy gets flared and how couples start lying when they're not being honest about their true desires. This is the grey area of intimacy through which many people find difficulty navigating. We all have natural tendencies to feel desire, to flirt, to fantasize—this is a healthy part of being human. It's when we deny these urges and suppress them that we run into trouble. In an ideal relationship of any kind, I would imagine that having an open and honest discussion about these fantasies would be a healthy place to start. In many ways, I wrote my book precisely for the people who don't want to scare away their partner with their desires to open up the relationship, and particularly for those who want to make a commitment to avoiding stagnation, instilling honesty, giving voice to their true desires, dedicating themselves to creative options, and supporting one another in their pursuit of the personal freedom to love many people.

The societal and cultural reality for most of us is that we are a far cry from sexual equality in this day and age. Men, straight or gay, have benefited from the luxury of sexual liberation without so much as their moral values being scrutinized by society. Women, whether straight or queer, have no such freedom. Labels such as slut or "nympho" continue to plague women who seek sexual autonomy. These stereotypes and misconceptions are perpetuated in the media, government, education, religious institutions, and even within the women's movement. We still have a long way to go before we can dismantle these derogatory perceptions and liberate ourselves from the social constraints that have been imposed upon us since birth. The first place to start is with one's self, confronting your own self-imposed guilt and your fears of stepping outside the standards of societal norms. It starts with freeing your mind, body, and heart to love openly despite judgment.

It is my hope that this book reflects both the struggle inherent in living an alternative lifestyle as well as the work that still needs to be done before there is greater social acceptance. I write from one woman's experience and fight for autonomy. Part of my awareness and radicalization as a woman, under institutionalized patriarchy, is this struggle to break free of male concepts of a relationship, male domination of sexuality, male control over my freedom to live how I want, love who I want, and how many I want. I believe that we have a responsibility to challenge this patriarchal and hierarchal notion of a relationship and redefine something more empowering and more fulfilling for ourselves. But ultimately you have the right to love and live as you see fit, based on your ideals and values, while keeping respect and integrity at the core.

Our patriarchal culture defines a relationship by a hierarchical paradigm, by this I mean something comparable to a pyramid analogy, whereby the your sexual partner is at the top of the mountain for love and devotion and everyone else—family, friends, and ex-partners—is conveniently at the bottom. I believe that the nature of this model is part of what perpetuates unhealthy co-dependency and unsatisfying relationships for many people and also contributes to infidelity for the partner who cannot conform to a single-partner love arrangement. Imagine if we could design our own relationship model based on our deepest desires and core values?

It's not easy to be an activist in your own "backyard," in your own personal life and relationships. Even the most adventurous and most open-minded will struggle with their own imbedded stereotypes. It's not a simple task to open a discussion up with your partner or lovers about how patriarchy affects you in bed, between the sheets. Most of us find it challenging to grapple with our own insecurities, jealousy, and possessiveness. Often we don't even have the safe space to discuss these topics openly. Non-monogamy takes a lot of work, commitment, and emotional maturity, and it is often easier to conform, rather than face all your fears and deal with the criticism and misunderstandings from others who may not support or understand you. The bottom line is that you have choices. If you don't honor these choices and the inherent responsibility that comes with them, than you'll never know the true potential of your heart.

Since the beginning of time, indigenous people have lived in alternative extended family structures for their survival and inherent harmony. Today, there are people all over the world who are reinventing the structure of their relationships to include multiple partnerships, multiple lovers (platonic and romantic), and extended family arrangements. If it really does take a village to raise a child, then how can we foster new relationship models that are inclusive of multiple partnerships whereby friends, family, loved ones, acquaintances, and your community are included into our vision of an ideal society for the future? Our survival on this planet may depend on it.

Why an Alternative Relationship?

> "Multipartner relationships is seen as this alternative. It combines traditional concepts of commitment, love and "a lifelong intention to support each other in whatever ways seem appropriate" with the more controversial idea of sexually relating to more than one person at the same time with all partners fully aware of this." (Lano & Parry, *Breaking the Barriers to Desire: New Approaches to Multiple Relationships*)

I have spent the greater part of my life coming to grips with the fact that I am unable to be monogamous, unable to restrain my heart from loving other people, unable to keep my desires under lock and key. Concepts like "cheating," "betrayal" and "faithfulness to one and only one person" continue to confuse me. I have always enjoyed different people for different reasons. As a woman who fiercely guards her freedom, I can't imagine being limited by a monogamous relationship where one person must try to fulfill all my needs and desires.

A great concern for many bisexual and pansexual people is the inherent limiting nature of monogamy. I love both men and women. It will always be difficult for me to make a choice between the sexes. My relationships with all genders are complex and varied, and that is precisely why I enjoy the intimate companionship of all. Most bisexuals might agree that the beauty of sculpting a relationship that can accommodate our desires for many is as important and necessary as our freedom to choose who our friendships are.

By redefining my relationship, I have come to learn so much about myself and the nature of a long-term, sustainable partnership. I have learned that in reality, I can't depend on one person to be my sole provider of everything I have ever desired in life. No one can be all those things, that's why we have friends and family and that's why we foster nurturing relationships with other people. Other friends and relationships can alleviate the pressure imposed on a partner to meet all our needs. Expecting my partner to provide all these things is unfair and unrealistic—it sets one up for disappointment when a partner can't meet one's expectations.

I strongly believe that open relationships reduce the hazards that accompany unhealthy co-dependency. Open relationships challenge us to confront our jealousy and possessiveness. Committing to a relationship not mapped out by our parents or society or Hollywood's version means tearing down the very foundation of status quo and conformity. It means redefining and rebuilding your own version of an alternative relationship based on your needs and desires.

Put together your own vision of an ideal relationship, re-sculpt your own belief system, redefine the potential of a friendship, imagine a thousand ways to make love to yourself, to the planet, and to anyone you care about. And while you're at it, re-invent your gender and sexual preferences—be gay, straight, bisexual, transgender or all of the above.

Radicalize your relationship by imagining your wildest ideal partnership together. Avoid stagnancy by challenging your old familiar routine and re-inventing new levels of commitment. Face your true desires in life by asking yourself what you really want from your connections, and then make those desires clear to all those involved, from friends to lovers to partners. Have you ever dreamed of a live-in partner or maybe two? Do you prefer to live alone and have several outside, meaningful relationships where you work out a fair system to spend time with all of them at different times, like you manage to do with your friends? It can be done. If you are skeptical and doubtful that non-monogamy can work, then it won't work. If you believe in the freedom of desires and have the determination to pursue your heart, then anything is possible. All partners or lovers must agree on this as a mutual goal for this to work.

An open relationship allows you to be a better lover to yourself as well as to others. It opens your perception and helps you to cope with the reality of human nature, which is to seek out love, to give love, and to receive love over and over again in its many forms and many faces.

One man writes, "I would like to hear more discussions on the idea that one person cannot fulfill all our needs—it's one of the strongest arguments for non-monogamy for me. There are real virtues and benefits of non-monogamy (not just the logistics of how to do it), such as the personal growth one experiences by letting go of jealousy, knowing that your lover or partner is a freer person because of your understanding, and the fact that all involved have an opportunity to get to know, love, and experience different people."

Intimacy

"Love for another does not diminish or alter our love for existing partners. It enhances it. More partners allow us to experience ourselves in different ways and fulfill more of our potentials. We become more integrated and are less likely to resent monogamous partners because of unmet needs." Paul King, *Polyamory: Ethical Non-Monogamy*

The widely acclaimed "bible" among many non-monogamists is *The Ethical Slut: A Guide to Infinite Sexual Possibilities* (Easton and Liszt 1997). I found this book to be a helpful guide in understanding the sexual component in ourselves and in our relationships, managing multiple partners or lovers, handling jealousy, and conflict resolution. For the purposes of my book, I have intentionally de-emphasized the topic of sex, intercourse, or the sexual component of open relationships. My reasons for this are complex and would require another book to make my philosophy on physical love comprehensible. But in a nutshell, I am asking people to re-invent their common notions of sex, to go beyond the limits of intercourse equating to sex, beyond the physical, expanding one's mind and heart to the enormous and mysterious gray area of intimacy.

Have you ever gotten into one of those mind-blowing, heart-expansive discussions with someone, felt your body temperature rise, experienced the exchange of a truly passionate and intimate dialogue and when it was over, you felt as if you had made love to that person? You feel somehow changed, receptive, and bursting with a kind of love for that person that you may not have felt before. Have you ever felt as though you just had "sex" after a romantically succulent meal with someone? Has a hug or a long awaited embrace ever felt like you were falling in-love? Have you ever imagined yourself exchanging a kiss that was better than sex, that somehow could convey all the love that you feel in a single ignited moment?

This is the gray area of intimacy that I am trying to scratch the surface of. To give love is a personal and revolutionary act for me. Everyone I love as a friend or a lover or a sister or a grandmother embodies a form of daily activism in my life. Every love letter, every hug, every tender kiss, every flower picked, every consoling talk is my heart acting out all the love and kindness that overfills me. I have other outlets—gardening, motorcycle riding, cooking, sewing, poetry, spoken word, playing my bass, exchanging letters and so on—but my deeper connections with special people give me such an untouchable high and satisfaction. *This* is why I practice and believe in open relationships. It's not their sexual validation that I'm searching for, but the mere act of giving, sharing, growing, inspiring, and loving creatively. I almost feel like I could not go on with life without these connections.

My point is that an open relationship cannot be reduced to sex alone. There are more than a thousand ways to make love, to re-create intimacy in your every day life, to suck the juices from a piece of fruit and to feel full for the first time. Being in an open relationship means you have the revolutionary opportunity to have guilt-free sex with life, with yourself, with your soul. Expand your notions of eroticism, re-discover verbal affection, invent a new way to hug that truly expresses how much you feel for that person, massage every inch of your lover's body without making sex the goal. Redefine for yourself what it means to make love and to be intimate. I define "making love" as being loving, anything and everything that you put your heart into, including intercourse, a hand shake, kissing, a love letter, a peace offering, S&M, art, music, masturbation, fetishes, fantasies, a phone call, a warm embrace, whatever pleases you, whatever feels good, the sky is the limit. I dare you to count the ways you can single-handedly make love to the planet or yourself or your best friend or your new lover.

Above all else, exercise being vulnerable with partners, friends, lovers and family members. Open up that under-worked heart of yours and tell someone you love how much he or she means to you, give them a compliment, stroke their ego, reveal something tender and real about yourself. The odds are that it may not be returned by the one desired individual that you have chosen to open up to, but it doesn't mean that it won't come around in another way, by a different means. To give without expecting something in return is the ultimate gift of love, but it takes practice. Strive to be intimate and loving every day.

Make it up as you go along. This is the beauty of re-inventing your own relationship. The benefits of multiple partners or lovers or friends means you get to experience the different parts of yourself with different people. Re-examine such concepts as betrayal, cheating or unfaithfulness and ask yourself if these still apply to your relationships, how and why. Practice being faithful to all your lovers by respecting them, honoring your commitments, and being a good friend to all. It shouldn't surprise you how filled our heads are with Hollywood's preconceived notions of honor and loyalty. It shouldn't surprise you how indoctrinated we all are in patriarchal concepts of possessiveness. If these institutions are not exposed for the tools of inequality that they are, then we will continue to blindly perpetuate them.

Misconceptions

> "Monogamous marriage as we know it today is based on patterns established in Biblical times governing men's ownership of women. In Biblical days, the law prescribed that women be stoned to death for taking a lover, but men were allowed as many secondary wives or concubines as they could afford."
> Dr. Deborah M. Anapol, *Polyamory: The New Love Without Limits*

Open relationships are not just about open sex. This seems like an obvious statement to most people who practice radically different relationships, but there are many people who misunderstand what you mean by "open." There are a thousand or more ways to be loving with someone—sex is the easy part. It's being creative enough to actively commit to being a loving person on a multitude of levels, such as cuddling, holding, listening, love letters, the exchange of inspiration and so on, that separates you from the norm. An open relationship has less to do with sex and everything to do with consent, honesty, consequences, dispelling of feelings of possessiveness, being supportive and communicative. Be aware of your own stereotypes of what an open relationship means. You are free to define your relationship any way your heart desires, so long as personal respect and integrity are at the core.

Open relationships are a way of life. It is a form of multi-partnerships, which encompasses economic, political, social and philosophical alternatives to every day life. Non-monogamy does not equate to marathon sex or a game by which the person with the most sexual partners wins. Responsible non-monogamy is an expression of the true desires of your heart and a calling in your soul.

Another misconception for those new to open relationships is the issue of commitment. Responsible open relationships require the truest adherence to commitment to the future of any and all relationships. Non-monogamous individuals are not necessarily "swingers" looking for an easy lay or sex without strings. In fact, open relationships do not function at all without all parties involved making a commitment to honesty, communication, patience, and hard work. Non-monogamous partners are simply willing to engage in deeply committed, deeply serious relationships with more than one person, such as a partner, friend, lover, pen pal.

An equally disheartening misconception is the old adage, "intimacy or sex will ruin the friendship." This is certainly true if you haven't established a good foundation of trust and communication with this friend or if you never really had a commitment to the friendship in the first place. Every lover for me has always been my friend first. If you are seeking something shallow and a one-night-stand, then that is just what you'll get. If you set out to communicate and understand your expectations (reasonable and otherwise) with your friends, then you may be surprised by the potential of a friendship to evolve into something more intimate, more sexual, or more emotionally bonding. Keep in mind that sex is only one of a million ways to express love. But underlying all motives and ulterior pursuits, there must be a firm commitment to simply being friends. The new adage should be: Intimacy with a friend means never having to break up because you know that you're still friends the next day.

Alternative relationships are not easy or simple. It requires rigorous communication skills and a constant re-working and re-adjusting to manage these growing and evolving connections. It demands attentive reassurance, a kind of blind faith in Love, and an ability to learn in the face of tremendous challenge. It is a constant struggle to overcome jealousy and to work through the embedded socialization process that can predetermine or affect our perceptions of what we feel and how we feel.

These are not simple concepts to understand, let alone fully come to grips with in the early stages of an open relationship. Alternative relationships allow you the right to make ethical decisions for yourself, based on what is ultimately right for you. What you do with your life and your body and your heart is your own personal choice. Yet, even as you are free to make those choices, you must also be constantly aware of your effect on others. Your choices do affect your partner and your lovers, and this is no small juggling act.

Guidelines

When you respect mutually agreed upon boundaries, you build upon the foundation of lasting trust, which is the key ingredient in an open relationship. This list is only meant to be a helpful beginning for the do's and don'ts of alternative relationships for establishing and maintaining trust. Every couple must decide for themselves their own guidelines in the beginning, in order to avoid later issues of distrust and hurt feelings. Every friend, lover, or partner will have different ideas on how to establish personal boundaries, so approach this section as a work in progress.

- **Practice Safe Sex:** Be responsible for your body and the bodies you come in contact with; our lives depend on it.

- **Respect Space Boundaries:** Discuss with your partner what is acceptable and respectful physical contact with outside lovers if you live in the same house or if you are sharing space with your partner. Talk about comfortable intimate or physical contact boundaries for the occasions when partners and lovers are in the same space, such as social gatherings or public places. For example, when your partner and your lover are at the same party, it may be perfectly acceptable to hug and hang out with both of them, but be considerate of how your actions and overt displays of affection may make either of them feel uncomfortable.

Designate neutral territory and safe or sacred space that you both agree upon. For example, consider places that are off limits to outside lovers for sex, such as your partner's bed, house, or car.

- **The "24-Hour" Rule:** This rule came into effect when my partner and I agreed that you couldn't possibly know someone very well in less than 24 hours. We both agreed that there were far too many issues to discuss and to come to terms with before leaping in the sack with someone you don't know very well. I recommend that you take your time before getting too intimate with someone new without having sufficient time to get to know one another and to fully explain your "open" relationship parameters. It is only fair to be honest with a new lover from the get-go and to not mislead them into falsely believing that your relationship is almost over and they are next in line, or that you are looking to replace your relationship. It is only fair that a new lover have time (days, maybe weeks) to decide if they even want to get involved with you.

- **Honesty:** This goes for all new lovers about your relationship situation as well as with your partner. Honesty should not be confused with brutal insensitivity. For example, "I'm sorry I didn't get your call; I didn't have my pager on me" as opposed to "my pager was in my pants which were on the floor as I was fucking so and so." There are loving ways to communicate what you choose to do with your life without being insensitive to your partner's feelings and insecurities. Ultimately, we are sensitive creatures, so it is important to pay attention to the words you choose, the people you spend time with, and the decisions you make.

  No lies. Don't hide other friendships, lovers, or partners. You might not tell them all the details of every relationship, but never hide where you go, whom you're with, or when you'll be back. Once you start down that path of lies, you only dig yourself into deeper mistrust in the future.

- **Reassurance and Communication:** All partners, lovers, friends, and casual cuddle buddies deserve reassurance and communication time. Exercise the active listener in you. What bothers you or seems like a concern should be communicated before it festers into something buried with resentment and insecurities. Don't hold things on people. Keep your connections clean. Learn how to ask for reassurance. Don't expect someone else to read your mind. Set aside special time for your needs or concerns to be addressed. The ten minutes before they are out the door for work should not be the designated time to have that heartfelt talk. Put aside quality time to respond to hurt feelings, practice compassionate listening, be loving, resist getting defensive, extend comfort and reassurance, and be willing to hold space for their pain. Discuss with your partner what is comfortable to do with others and what you may want to reserve to do with each other. Never invalidate the feelings of a loved one.

Whenever conceivably possible, take your time, make wise choices, not hormone-crazed ones. Talk about risk factors, sexual history, sexually transmitted diseases, prior rape or abuse issues, sexual restrictions, what you can and can't handle physically or emotionally, and what issues trigger your insecurities and fears. If you don't like one-night-stands, be clear about this. Sex is not about conquest. Be up-front from the start. Granted, none of us admit full disclosure of our situation to someone we've only had a ten-minute conversation or flirtation with. Designate an appropriate time to have "the talk." New lovers have a right to know if you're "available," and what this availability entails, restricts, or permits. It is important to be clear about intentions, motivations, and what you want out of this newly forming connection.

Timing is everything! Find a time when you and your lover are both available to talk and are in a good mood. The time to have that talk is not when you're stressed out, or at a party, or you've just made love.

Learn to make love through communication. Take the time to improve your verbal and written skills. It will surprise you how powerful words can touch, stroke, caress, and fondle without ever making physical contact.

- **Drugs and Alcohol:** Critical decisions regarding sexual intimacy with a new lover are best made with a clear mind and an open heart, not a swirling, soggy brain. Think about how many sloppy decisions you've made under the influence. Ask yourself how it would feel if your partner made intimacy decisions under the same circumstances.

- **Motives:** Pursue friendship and love first. A large part of what makes open relationships work, in my opinion, is that you know in your heart that all relationships are, first and foremost, in the pursuit of friendship and loving connections. Personal motives and hormones need to be kept in check, especially if you are a very sexual person or a big flirt or you crave constant physical contact with others.

- **Privacy:** Never brag about other private, intimate connections to your partner or other lovers. Your experiences with other lovers and your partner are Private. Not every partner or lover wants to hear or can handle emotionally the details of your affairs. What you share and don't share about the physical attraction or the sexual content of your relationships is something you and your partner or lovers should discuss beforehand.

- **The Bed-Hopping Rule:** Try to avoid bed-hopping, emotionally and physically, between lovers and your partner. Make sure you have had ample time to process your emotions, wade through feelings, and then move forward in other directions. Bed-hopping can create emotional confusion. At the risk of sounding obvious, take a shower between lovers, wash your mind and body of another sacred place and person. Write a love letter, go for a walk and clear your thoughts before returning to the home (or bed-side) of your partner's embrace. It is the thoughtful gesture that they deserve and truthfully, you want to be fully present when you are with someone you love.

- **Revise and Redefine All Boundaries Regularly:** Frequently review your boundaries, add new ones, modify old ones. Partners, friends, and lovers must commit to discussing regularly whether these boundaries are working or if new ones need to be added or altered. As relationships evolve so do our needs—our boundaries should reflect this evolution. If you believe in the impossible, then the world is your banquet. Don't be defeated by what countless others seem to think. Make your own choices.

- **Treat Others as You Wish to be Treated.**

- **Leave a Note:** At the risk of sounding trite, if you live with your partner, always leave a note or call and leave a message when you anticipate that you might not come home at night. We are creatures of habit; if our partner doesn't come home, we will worry. Spare your partner the emotional crisis of wondering if you are alive and call, regardless of the time. With practice, it becomes second nature, and you will be relieved in the long run to know that they are o.k. Always leave a number where your partner can reach you, especially if you live together. You have a responsibility to your live-in partner. This means a commitment to your future together. If you take this seriously, then leaving them a number gives them permission to reach you in case of an emergency or for reassurance or something truly important. Ultimately, you want to be available to your partner for anything of importance.

- **Never Act Out of Anger:** Never act out against a partner or lover in anger or vengeance by sleeping with someone else.

- **Sharing:** If you are both attracted to the same person, either share or find a comfortable way to keep it separate without making anyone choose. Make a firm commitment to not letting this come between you and your partner.

- **Cuddle Companions:** There is no such thing as too many cuddle buddies.

- **Sex, Sexual Contact, and Consensual Intimacy:** All sexual experiences are sacred. Find the right time to discuss your boundaries around all aspects of sexual conduct, be it as innocent as hugging and kissing to intercourse and oral sex. There may be things you only do with your partner and not your lovers, or the other way around. Decide what experiences may not be shared for now, discuss what is reasonable to ask of a partner, and what will take more time to adjust to.

> A bisexual woman writes, "My boyfriend still has issues with me being sexual with other guys. We don't want to end our relationship over this one issue, so I have agreed to only be sexual with women. I can still snuggle, kiss and be as affectionate as I would like to with men, but I understand that he is still trying to battle his jealousy for now. We will come back to this issue some time down the line and reassess how it's working out. The process of redefining boundaries and re-examining our relationship is an ongoing discussion for us."

I am a firm believer in the right to love anyone, anywhere, anytime, anyhow, but even loving connections have boundaries on intimacy. These "red flag" instances include intimacy or sexual contact with close friends or acquaintances of your partner or other lovers. Under these scenarios, be cautious—even a casual step in this direction can cause undue stress, misunderstanding, and severe (even irreparable) damage between you and your partner. Set boundaries around certain people that you and your partner feel would jeopardize your relationship. My partner and I try, whenever possible, to not get involved with overly jealous people because we have dealt with the drama that comes along with it. Some couples may need boundaries around, for example, band members or best friends or family members.

The heart may think it knows best, but I highly recommend communication and prior consent from your partner before acting out your desires with someone new. This is the time for patience and really thinking through your desires. Always consider the consequences of your actions. Ask yourself how you would feel if your partner got together with your best friend. And maybe it would hurt at first, maybe it would feel awkward the first couple of times you hung out with your best friend, maybe you would feel threatened that your partner and best friend would talk about you, maybe you secretly envy your partner's choice in lovers, or maybe the extended family ties of love and connectedness would bring everyone closer together in some unfathomable and magical way.

- **You Belong to Yourself:** No one can own another person. You are not sexual property to be fenced in, controlled, or monitored. No one can hold another person's body or love under lock and key. The ultimate goal of an open relationship is to love without possessing another person.

    A woman writes, "I may not approve of my partner's choices, which I'll let him know, but he's free to do what he wants with or without my permission. I view this as another way that we wield power over others. If it's someone I object to, my partner has agreed to take that into consideration but ultimately I have to trust him to make his own choices for his own reasons."

- **Rivals are Not Allowed:**

    As one friend suggests, "It is important not to get involved in situations where two people may be pitted against each other. Anyone who cannot accept the place of my primary partner as Primary in my life should be dealt with caution. This may mean avoiding becoming too involved with someone who could challenge my feelings for my partner or someone who cannot accept the limits of my involvement with them. I would not, could not, get intimately involved with anyone unable to accept my partner as a vital and special component of my life."

- **Practice Loving Yourself:** Loving yourself first fosters your self-esteem. Make a personal pact that you will always work on loving yourself versus making someone else responsible for your feeling loved. An active commitment to nurture, reassure, and look after yourself is the first step to building one's self-confidence. For example, I love myself by soaking in a hot bath after a stressful day and going to great lengths to pamper myself head to toe. I love myself daily by eating healthy foods, taking care of my aches or illnesses, being good to myself, giving myself the tenderness I deserve, and exercising at the gym. Self-love is defined differently by everyone, so get creative on this one.

Summary

Change is inevitable. Even the most stable and long-term relationships are subject to change. As we grow and evolve as beings, so do our needs, wants, desires, and pursuits. There are no simple answers or guarantees. Partners may some day face separation (permanent or temporary) or they may feel threatened by a secondary lover who will challenge the very core of their commitment. The scenarios are endless. We could spend a lifetime in the trenches of hypothetically painful outcomes. My best suggestion is to stay focused on the friendship of any and all relationships—a strong friendship will often outlive the sex or the cuddle partner or the emotions of the moment. By learning to accept and embrace the changing and transforming nature of relationships, we have less to fear.

The beauty of an open relationship of any kind is that you never have to break up in the traditional sense of the word. An open relationship will grow and evolve in a multitude of directions over time. Friends can become sexual lovers, then separate for a time and evolve into pen pals, then years later become soul mates, platonic or not platonic, long distant one year, live-in the next. There is no set path. Things might change in two days or two years down the line. And yes, it will be painful when a beloved cuddle partner breaks off this tie with you for whatever reason. It is an emotional let down when you've fallen in love with someone who may not feel the same way. Initially, it hurts, and it may even feel uncomfortable to be around them until the emotion passes. But who's to say that love can't be rekindled years later or that an old lover couldn't make a best friend later on? Who's to say that the painful experience of separation might make you both realize how much you truly need each other in your life in whatever capacity—friend, wrestling partner, massage buddy, 4AM crisis-hotline connection, and so on?

Loving openly and freely in this day and age, whether you're straight or queer, is a political act. We are conditioned by outmoded social norms that limit our perceptions and shackle us to unhealthy cycles of dissatisfying relationships. Yet we live in a time where we can choose our own gender or redefine our own sexual identity. Isn't it safe to assume that we also have a right to decide what kind of relationship is more suitable to our lifestyle? Declare yourself a revolutionary of the heart. Find out how you can expand your potential to love, radicalize your lifestyle, and together we can threaten the social fabric of patriarchy!

Facing the Fear of Being Misunderstood

"Polyamory is still so socially unacceptable that we don't even have a widely understood *name* for it. This may be because variations in relationship orientation are perceived as even more of a threat to the established social order than variations in sexual orientation." Dr. Deborah M. Anapol, *Polyamory: The New Love Without Limits*

Many non-monogamous people are in the "closet" about their lifestyle and multipartner relationships. This is true in the workplace, or with friends, and especially with family members. The reality of not being understood by others, harsh criticism from friends and outsiders who do not fully comprehend what you're doing, and the lack of acceptance by others who do not have an open mind about your chosen lifestyle, are what continue to keep us in the closet. Negative outside judgments can be painful and may even disrupt the solid groundwork that took you years to construct. For those of us who love in non-conventional ways, we have experienced firsthand how our way of loving threatens the established social order.

Be aware of the things that trigger your insecurities and doubt. There may be days when you question the very foundation of your relationships and everything you believe in, but don't be misguided by rumors from likely jealous outsiders. Let's face it, monogamy is no guarantee that people will like or dislike you. Choosing an open relationship means that even your friends may pass judgment and not agree or accept your alternative choice.

It's no wonder why so many of us are in the closet about non-monogamous practices. Learn to pick and choose carefully to whom you wish to disclose such information. For me, this topic of "coming out" is a touchy one. I only just recently came out about my non-monogamy to my parents and family. Though I have always been adventurous and I have frequently broken the socially-accepted norms set down by our culture, there is no easy answer for facing your fears about being misunderstood by loved ones. Only you can decide who you will be open with and with whom you choose not to.

We live in a time where we can choose our sexual identity or decide for ourselves if we want to be religious or not. We can choose to have a live-in partner and never marry and we can choose to have children or not. It is safe to assume that we also have a right to decide if multiple relationships are more suitable to our lifestyle. It is time to stop letting society convince you that you should feel bad or guilty about how many people you choose to love. This is your opportunity to form new households for the future and foster healthy and responsible relationships. There is nothing stopping you from finding the courage to love as many people as possible and inviting them to helping you raise a family, form friendships with your children, live in separate rooms, share lovers, share laundry, set boundaries, and start a mini-revolution in the privacy of your own home.

References

Allison, Dorothy. *Skin: Talking about Sex, Class & Literature*. Ann Arbor, MI: Firebrand Books, 1994.

Anapol, Dr. Deborah M. *Polyamory: The New Love without Limits*. San Rafael, CA: Intinet Resource Center, 1997.

Blue, Violet. *The Ultimate Guide to Sexual Fantasy: How to Turn Your Fantasies into Reality*. San Francisco, CA: Cleis Press, 2004.

Easton, Dossie and Catherine A. Liszt. *The Ethical Slut: A Guide to Infinite Sexual Possibilities*. San Francisco, CA: Greenery Press, 1997.

Goldman, Emma. *Living My Life: An Autobiography*. Salt Lake City, UT: Gibbs Smith, 1982. *The Traffic in Women and Other Essays on Feminism*, Albion, CA: Times Change Press, 1971.

King, Paul. *Polyamory: Ethical Non-Monogamy*. http://alternet.org/story/11808/. 2001.

Kipnis, Laura. *Against Love: A Polemic*. New York: Pantheon, 2003.

Lano, Kevin and Claire Parry (eds.). *Breaking the Barriers to Desire: New Approaches to Multiple Relationships*. Nottingham, England: Five Leaves Publications, 1995.

Munson, Marcia and Judith P. Stelboum (eds.). *The Lesbian Polyamory Reader: Open Relationships, Non-Monogamy, and Casual Sex*. Binghamton, NY: Haworth Press, 1999.

West, Celeste. *Lesbian Polyfidelity: A Pleasure Guide for the Woman Whose Heart Is Open to Multiple, Concurrent Sexualoves, or How to Keep Non-Monogamy Safe, Sane*. San Francisco, CA: Booklegger Press, 1995.

Bringing Parents Together in a "Happy" Divorce

23

CHAPTER

Ilana Kramer

I am a wildfire of curls and freckles, sitting in the backseat of my mother's broken-down station wagon. We are parked by the side of the road heading east, somewhere between California and New Jersey, and all I know is that I am three years old and on a terrific adventure. I watch as one of our tires bounds down a ravine, a skittish jackrabbit. Heat and fumes are rising from our hood, making the skyline tremble ahead. My sister, two years my senior and already in charge, is sitting in the front seat.

My mother is outside the car, frantic; she is looking for a spare she knows she doesn't have, but she is looking just the same. She and my father have just divorced, and now she has two daughters to raise and a car to push to the other side of the country.

Five years later, the chaos has subsided in a rare and curious way. I am on a family vacation at Universal Studios with my mom, my sister, and my dad. My sister and I are biting the bottoms of sugar cones and sucking out the soft ice cream. We are all waiting on line for an Alfred Hitchcock ride, when the attendant asks for a male participant. My mom immediately volunteers my father. Twenty minutes later my father stands on stage wide-eyed in a dress, playing the mother's role in "Psycho." When he's asked to introduce his family, we proudly stand up from the audience and wave. To onlookers in the park, we might look like your typical nuclear family, but if someone asked me for the low-down, I would have to explain I come from a happy divorce.

Growing up, my divorced family was unusual. My parents made a decision to make our family still act as a "family." While my friends in "intact" families hung out with both parents, and my friends of divorce had strict separate time with each parent, we fell into

From LILITH, Spring 2004, Vol. 29, Issue 1 by Ilana Kramer. Copyright © 2004 by Lilith Magazine. Reprinted by permission. Lilith is the independent Jewish feminist magazine. www.Lilith.org

an uncharted no-man's land. Since my two parents lived with an entire country dividing them, this resulted in a lot of family vacations. My mother and father planned lobster dinners in Connecticut, swimming with dolphins in Key West, skiing in the Catskills, and endless Amtrak trips to Florida to my paternal grandparents. With my mom, sister, and me all in a king-sized bed in one hotel room and my dad snoring next door in another, I felt my family all around me. Despite my having no recollection of their marriage together, I have a lot of memories of my parents, well, together. And our arrangement didn't end when my mother remarried.

Once we became a blended family, my dad would not only call on the phone for my sister, mom, and me, but would often ask to speak to his "husband-in-law," my step-dad. They would chat about business, cars, and exchange jokes. One Thanksgiving on the East Coast, my father and step-dad took my sister, step-siblings, and me to the Macy's parade in New York City. When my dad got remarried, during my first year of college, his new wife became yet another addition to the family. I remember my dad and step-mom staying at our home in New Jersey (with my mom and step-dad); in the mornings, we would all swarm around the table like fruit flies for lox-and-bagel breakfasts.

My college graduation this past spring was the real clincher. There was an option for parents to stay in the college dormitories, so my mother secured two rooms next door to each other. While friends maneuvered social plans to minimize their divorced parents' interactions, my four parents were coordinating theirs. My mom and step-mom were fussing over hors d'oeuvres parties between the two rooms, while my step-dad helped my father reconfigure the single dorm beds in his room to make up a larger one. Sunday morning, when I checked in with all of my parents in the dorm, I saw my step-dad watching a baseball game and my dad writing out bills at a study table, tufts of white hair flying out behind each ear and in one of his striped long t-shirts that my mother called his "nightgowns." My mom and step-mother were kibbitzing, making fun of my father together.

Walking out of the elevator, my family memories hit me like flashcards turning over: the time we drove in my grandparents' car in Florida, my grandpa stubborn, lost, and nearly deaf in the front seat, my mom and dad laughing hysterically in the back; or the time my mom threw pillows at my dad, hollering to him, "I hate men!" after an especially bad date. I think of my family holding hands, walking in to the song "We are Family!" at the reception after my bat mitzvah. And then I think back to my father taking me to my JCC nursery school classroom to say goodbye to my friends before my postdivorce journey east. I remember my father was a giant then, and I reached my hand up to hold his thick fingers and watch his peppery moustache, and I felt small and uncertain. Are all these memories, then, what comprise my definition of a happy divorce?

I know I'm simplifying a complex process. Every moment didn't sparkle with Brady-Bunch zing. I missed my father at soccer games and summer school plays. On vacations, when both parents tucked me into bed, I felt a pinch of that childhood gingerbread dream that maybe, just maybe my parents would fall back in love. And I imagine that in my own absorbed and eager youth, it was difficult in quiet ways for them both, especially my mother, the sensitive one who single-handedly raised my sister and me. But I believe my parents sustained our family unit in a unique and inventive way.

When I ask my father about it, he remembers how difficult it was when the divorce first happened. Apparently it never occurred to him that by separating from my mother he might live 3,000 miles away from his children. He feared we wouldn't remain close. That didn't happen. When I questioned my parents recently, he had great memories of fun times with my sister and me. On winter break from college, the three of us driving down the Baja peninsula in Mexico to drink piña coladas and set off fireworks ("Girls, don't tell your mother"). The time he helped me catch a six-foot sailfish. Or how my dad would give us the same lecture at the beginning of every summer to Be Nice to his long-term girlfriend ("She loves you very much, girls"). Meanwhile, we plotted like devilish twins, buying whoopee cushions and black soap, all for a woman who, in truth, did appear to love us even though we seemed to need to play tricks on her to keep solidarity with our mother. In a way, while my mother dealt with the less-glamorous tasks of raising us during the school year, my father was able to reap the benefits of having smart, well-adjusted little daughters fly out to him every summer.

Perhaps it was because my parents had a great expanse of geography between them that helped to cool the landscape of hostility inherent in divorce. Maybe it was that they divorced when I was an infant, and neither remarried until I was a teen, enabling them to free up time for vacations. Or maybe, by living with distance between them, my sister and I could easily adopt the lifestyle and values of my mother, which may have conflicted with my father's and caused confusion if we were all located in the same town. Whatever the case, my parents shared a love for large mishpocha gatherings and—most importantly—for their children. When my mom calls me now in Manhattan for Saturday morning "Plan Ahead" lectures or my dad calls late at night to mimic impressions of my mother fretting, "Your father...," both calls make me sigh and laugh.

I shared my perspective of my parents' divorce with my mother the other evening in a phone call. Turns out that her reality was less sugar-coated than I'd perceived it. In interest of full disclosure, I share with you the e-mail I got the next morning from my Mom:

Lani...Was thinking about our conversation...I guess it changed your idea of a "happy" divorce a little and I'm sorry, but the truth is that no divorce is painless or easy. I'm glad your perception of it was happy. That shows that despite my stress, you still perceived things between Dad and me as not too bad. Guess that was good for your development.

Divorced people go through the same stages as grief/loss people do: shock, denial, anger, sadness, and finally resolution. It can take many years to get through, particularly if one person is at a financial disadvantage. Also it's a loss of dreams and hopes. When you marry you think it is forever, and then it's not. The way I answered you last night was purely honest, and maybe you are now old enough to hear the truth. When I was a single-parent, I was in survival mode, both financially and emotionally. I sometimes acted in ways that were not always sincere, but I did it to survive. When I met your stepfather, some of the survival mode left, and then it didn't matter. Does this all make sense to a 22-year old? Don't know. Well, you asked.

Again, let me know your plans for Friday. I have a 3 pm. nail appt. but will be done by 4.

Love, Mom

Part

Conflict

If You Don't Feel Jealous Does It Mean You Don't Love Your Partner?

24

CHAPTER

Marina Cantacuzino

I have always—perhaps recklessly—prided myself on having a strong and harmonious marriage. Which is why I was nonplussed the other day when a friend intimated that because my husband and I aren't jealous of each other, perhaps our relationship isn't as strong and harmonious as I'd assumed. How could I have dinner with a male friend and he not be a little jealous? How could I not be threatened when a woman finds him attractive? But I don't. We don't.

As far as my friend is concerned, this absence of jealousy is a signal that my husband and I don't feel passionately about each other. Not as passionately as those who put limits and restraints on their partners do, anyway. I have told her it was a matter of trust. I have told her we are not afraid of each other having intimate friendships with anyone, even with members of the opposite sex. I have told her we do not feel we have ownership of each other, or the right to dictate who we can or cannot be friends with. While being extremely close, we allow each other to be more than just half of a whole. But she doesn't buy it.

Jealousy among married couples is commonplace. Some couples don't even like their partner to have a good time if they are not there with them: it undermines their sense of security. There are wives who do not like to see their husband chatting enthusiastically to a woman, and husbands who worry if their wife works closely alongside a male colleague. Plenty of people prefer to keep their partner on a leash, monitor their every move. But I have always believed that the tighter the leash, the greater the tendency toward infidelity. It presupposes that there must be something to be jealous of, that with freedom comes danger. By restraining a person's individuality, you make them eager to break out.

In 1947, Boris Sokoloff wrote in *Jealousy—A Psychological Study*: "Jealousy is not only inbred in human nature, but it is the most basic, all-pervasive emotion which touches man in all aspects of every human relationship." And it seems that it isn't limited to the early, vulnerable stages of relationships. Happy, loyal, loving couples in very long-term relationships suffer, too.

In an evolutionary sense, a man feels jealous because a woman's sexual infidelity jeopardizes his confidence that he is the genetic father of her children. If a deceived man invests decades of care, love and resources in another man's children, all his efforts in selecting and attracting his partner will have been wasted. On the other hand, while women can be certain they are the mothers of their children, jealousy erupts at the fear of losing a partner's protection and commitment.

Perhaps because of this, most women find a single lapse in fidelity without emotional involvement easier to forgive than the nightmare of another woman monopolizing their partner's tenderness, time and affection. Men are not quite so tolerant. A recent study from Yale University supports and reiterates the views of many similar studies—that while men are indiscriminately jealous about their mate's sexual misdemeanors, women object to their lover's close friendships with other women more than they would a brief sexual affair.

In *The Dangerous Passion*, David Buss, author and professor of psychology at the University of Texas, describes jealousy as an evolved solution to a recurrent problem of survival or reproduction. "Jealousy is necessary because of the real threat of sexual treachery. In a hazardous world where rivals lurk, partners harbor passions for other people and infidelity threatens to destroy what could have been a lifelong love, it would be surprising if evolution had not forged elaborate defences to detect and fend off these threats."

But while sexual jealousy may motivate us to ward off rivals, drive us to keep partners from straying and even communicate commitment to a partner who may be wavering, it can also, says Buss, sometimes be an "explosive solution."

The paradox is that jealousy—an emotion which evolved to protect love—can also rip a relationship apart. Battered women often report that their husbands seethe with jealousy, limit their contact with friends and family, and insist on knowing where they are at all times. The dark side of jealousy is pathological and can destroy previously harmonious relationships. But most marital jealousy is more moderate and, though often irrational, it is tolerated because it signals commitment.

Jealousy comes from fear of change, fear of losing control in a relationship, fear of abandonment. It comes from anxiety about being adequate as a lover/friend/parent, or doubts about enduring desirability.

To ward off these ugly emotions, some couples endeavour to hermetically seal their relationship. "Emotional infidelity" is the latest relationship paranoia sweeping America. In his book *Emotional Infidelity: How To Avoid It*, therapist Gary Neuman argues that the more male friends a woman has, the worse her marriage will fare. Neuman strictly adheres to this philosophy. "I don't touch women other than my wife and mother. I will return a handshake from another woman to avoid being rude...I don't "do coffee" alone with other women, or have lunch or dinner, unless it involves a short-term business deal. This may sound bizarre but it has helped me maintain complete physical and emotional focus on my wife."

Consultant psychologist Richard Beckett wonders if Neuman is advocating this degree of exclusivity because he doesn't want to provoke his wife's jealousy. "It suggests he's done it before, and all hell broke loose. Alternatively, he may not be coming to terms with his own desires and feelings."

According to Beckett's own evidence, most couples do not tolerate intimacy with others; even a close friendship can feel threatening. "Most couples don't have high levels of closeness outside their family and children," comments Beckett, "and sometimes even children provoke jealousy."

But as long as couples are compatible, desire similar amounts of attention from each other or seek equal degrees of seclusion, none of this poses much of a problem. Indeed, some people like their partner to feel jealous because it makes them feel wanted.

According to Simon Gelsthope, consultant clinical psychologist for Bradford District Care Trust, "on-going, low-level jealousy is a fairly useful way of keeping couples together and maintaining closeness."

So where does that leave couples who don't feel jealous? "Risky," says Gelsthope, "because it might mean you're so very confident in the love of that partner that in the end you take them for granted." I don't think my husband and I have yet taken each other for granted because we like the challenge of the "risky" path, treading that fine line between jealousy and complacency.

The Evolution of Jealousy

Christine R. Harris

CHAPTER

Love wasn't the only thing in the air on Valentine's Day 2003. A Texas jury had just found C. Harris guilty of killing her husband in a "sudden passion." After encountering him at a hotel with a mistress, she had driven the car over his body again and again. As others were exchanging tokens of love, the "Mercedes murderer" was sentenced to spend 20 years in jail.

Clara Harris was hardly the first woman to stand accused of murdering in a jealous rage. In various studies, jealousy is often ranked among the top three motives for nonaccidental homicides where motive is known—along with rage arising from a quarrel and murder during the commission of a crime. Across the ages the confounding power of sexual jealousy has inspired poetry, novels, drama, art and opera. It has also captured the attention of psychologists, who have used a variety of theoretical approaches in their pursuit of scientific understanding.

Early work focused on Freudian interpretations, the influence of which can still be seen in the psychiatric literature. As in other domains of psychology, however, recent research has followed a rather different direction. For some years now, a small but persistent group of investigators has attempted to uncover the nature and origin of this painful and dangerous counterpart of romantic love.

Most of us know jealousy from experience as a deeply negative emotion that arises when an important relationship is threatened by a rival. Given the inherent intricacies of social relationships, a simple theory that adequately captures the complexity of jealousy is unlikely. Hence research has focused on the interplay between social and cognitive factors in the incidence and expression of this emotion. Some psychologists have explored cultural differences and have found that jealousy is more pronounced in cultures that attach social importance to marriage and sanction sexual gratification only in the marriage bed and in cultures that place a premium on personal property. Others have tried to account for why some individuals show strong jealousy at the slightest provocation and others seem less susceptible. (Factors examined in these studies range from personality and parental-attachment styles to who has the better "deal" in a relationship.)

One relatively straightforward idea about jealousy in romantic relationships is at the center of a hot debate among psychologists. During the 1990s, as evolutionary psychologists began applying Darwin's theories to human behavior in novel ways, a new theory of the origins of jealousy developed. Jealousy, it was suggested, might have given a fitness advantage to men and women in our ancestral environment. But the selective pressures on males and females struggling to survive and reproduce in this environment were asymmetrical. Thus jealousy, like many of the emotions associated with mating, came to have a different character in men and women. The notion that jealousy evolved into an "innate module"—a wired-in brain circuit that has different primary triggers in men and women—is one of the most celebrated applications of an evolutionary approach to psychology.

Debate over this hypothesis continues. In fact, newer evidence raises questions about whether there is a fundamental difference between the male and the female experience of jealousy in romantic relationships. After reviewing the evidence in light of other theories, I believe an evolutionary explanation for this emotion may turn out to be more subtle and complex than the recent view suggests. Jealousy could certainly be an innate and adaptive emotion, but its form may be better explained by social-cognitive approaches, as well as developmental theory, than by theories based on proposed sex differences in our ancestors' mating strategies.

The Specific Innate Module Theory

As I mentioned above, evolutionary psychologists seek to explain the peculiarities of human psychology in terms of the selective pressures that operated on our ancestors in the Pleistocene Epoch—the pressures that determined whose progeny survived and whose did not. The wired-in emotions we have now, these writers maintain, are not necessarily ones that increase our inclusive evolutionary fitness (the survival of our genes) today. But they tended to provide a payoff in the very different environment of our forebears. This framework has been used in attempts to understand such diverse features of human nature as pregnancy sickness and depression.

According to David Buss at the University of Texas at Austin and several other evolutionary psychologists, a specific set of brain circuits guides our emotional reaction to threats in the context of sexual relationships. This emotional-cognitive module, they argue, makes men innately predisposed to jealousy over a mate's *sexual* infidelity. It makes women innately predisposed to jealousy over a mate's *emotional* infidelity.

This difference in the sexes' response to specific triggers is present now, according to these theorists, because people once faced different inclusive fitness risks during the Pleistocene. According to the theory of natural selection, mutations that increase fitness are favored and survive, because future generations inherit these mutations from successful individuals.

Ancestral man purportedly faced a grave Darwinian threat from cuckoldry—a result of the fact that eggs are fertilized internally and paternity is always somewhat uncertain. Should a man's mate be impregnated by another man, he might easily expend his scarce resources on genetically unrelated children, thus making his own Darwinian fitness plunge. Hence, natural selection shaped the male brain to respond specifically to sexual infidelity with intense jealousy—an emotion that would motivate actions to defend against cuckoldry.

Ancestral woman, knowing that she was the mother of her children, faced no such risk, and thus was not under the same selection pressure to respond to sexual infidelity. Rather, she faced the threat that a philandering male might divert his resources to another woman and her children. Because human children require years of care, these resources were supposedly critical to her inclusive fitness. Therefore, according to the theory, women developed an innate psychological module that is particularly sensitive to emotional infidelity (the assumption here being that men expend resources on the women they love).

This evolutionary theory of jealousy has received a great deal of general media attention in the past few years. However, as this article will show, there are other accounts that would be entirely consistent with evolution by natural selection.

Self-Report Studies

The innate-module theory has come to have a strong following among psychologists largely because of an outpouring of research that relies on self-reports of college students. Subjects are asked to imagine a romantic relationship in which their partner is either having sex with someone else or is falling in love with someone else, and then are required to choose which of the two types of infidelity would be more upsetting to them.

This forced-choice method was first designed by Buss and his colleagues in 1992 and has since been used in more than two dozen studies. In the United States, the method almost invariably produces a significant sex difference: Most women (usually 70 percent or more) indicate that emotional infidelity would be more disturbing, whereas more men (usually between 40 and 60 percent) report that sexual infidelity would be worse.

Figure 25.1

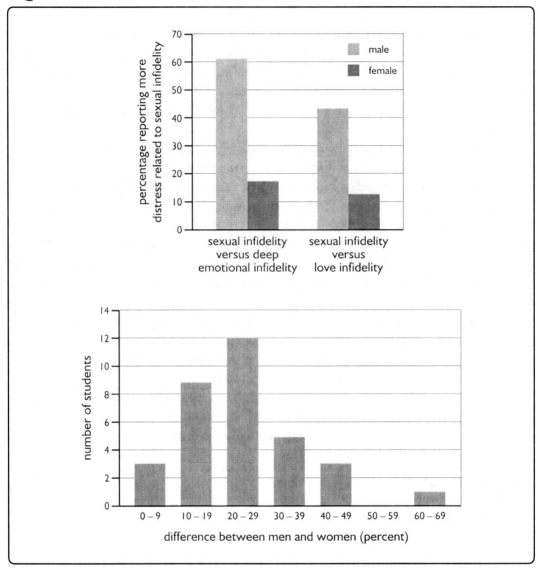

Jealousy's nature has been examined through forced-choice studies in which subjects describe their responses to imaginary scenarios involving a mate's infidelity. Imagined sexual infidelity might be expected to trigger jealousy in men because jealousy provided a payoff to ancestral man, whose inclusive fitness was threatened by cuckoldry. In contrast, ancestral woman might have responded more strongly to emotional infidelity because it implied a threat to the resources needed for the care of her children. When David Buss and his colleagues asked 202 college students for their reactions to infidelity scenarios involving sex, "deep emotional attachment" and "falling in love," their responses fit the predicted pattern (*top*). Since that 1992 study, more than two dozen similar studies have been published. The difference between the proportions of heterosexual men and women choosing sexual infidelity as the stronger trigger has ranged in these studies from 8 percent, in a study of Austrian adults, to 69 percent, in a United States college-student sample (*bottom*).

Recently I conducted an integrative review (or "meta-analysis") surveying these data. I found that the sex effect is robust and moderate in size but tends to be smaller among older subjects or in samples that include homosexuals. A sex effect has also been found in samples from other countries. However, in comparison to their counterparts in the U.S., far fewer European or Asian men seem to choose sexual infidelity as worse (often as few as 25 to 30 percent). This is an effect of culture comparable in size to the effect of sex.

Some of us have pointed out that such sex differences need not reflect innate modules. One possibility is that men and women may simply draw different conclusions about the hypothetical infidelity and what other unpleasantnesses it would likely imply. These inferences, then, produce the sex effect on the found-choice scenario. According to one view (nicknamed the "double-shot" or "two-for-one" hypothesis), men tend to think sexual infidelity would be more distressing because they infer that if a woman has sex with another man, she is probably also in love with him. Women tend to believe that men can have sex without being in love. Hence, sexual infidelity does not necessarily imply emotional infidelity. Instead, women reason that a man in love is likely to be having sex, and therefore they choose emotional infidelity as worse.

Evidence supporting this explanation for the sex difference in answers to the forced-choice question is somewhat mixed. Some investigators have confirmed that these differences in inferences mediate sex differences on forced-choice jealousy measures; others have not found support. Thus, such inferences probably play some role but cannot completely account for the difference.

David DeSteno and his colleagues at Northeastern University used an additional approach on the forced-choice question. They reasoned that if sex differences reflect wired-in, sex-specific evolved modules, then depriving people of the opportunity to reflect on the choice should increase the sex difference, polarizing the responses of men and women. They imposed a "cognitive load manipulation" on study subjects by asking them to remember a string of seven digits while answering questions. The cognitive load did not change males' responses, but females' responses shifted toward picking sexual infidelity as the more powerful jealousy trigger. This suggests that females' responses to the forced-choice questions may reflect inferences, along the lines of the double-shot hypothesis, or self-presentation strategies—the natural tendency of subjects to give answers that present a desired impression of themselves.

A number of investigators have tried presenting sexual and emotional infidelity scenarios separately, and assessing jealousy reactions with continuous rating scales rather than the forced-choice measure. Curiously, this tends to get rid of the predicted sex differences altogether, and on occasion it has even shifted them in the opposite direction (with women reporting *stronger* reactions to sexual jealousy). All in all, then, the forced-choice question clearly reveals some sort of sex difference, and one superficially in line with the evolutionary analysis. However, it is far from clear that it really reflects any sort of innate bias of the sort that evolutionary psychologists have proposed, rather than some other, more cognitively sophisticated kind of difference.

Physiological Measures of Jealousy

Scientifically minded readers will be wondering whether this question couldn't be studied in a way that circumvents the issues raised by self-report measures. Buss and his colleagues have used measures of autonomic nervous system activity to do so. In 1992, they recorded physiological activation as people contemplated being victims of different kinds of infidelity. Increases in male undergraduates' heart rates and electrodermal activity were in fact higher when they imagined a possible mate engaging in sex with someone else, compared

Figure 25.2

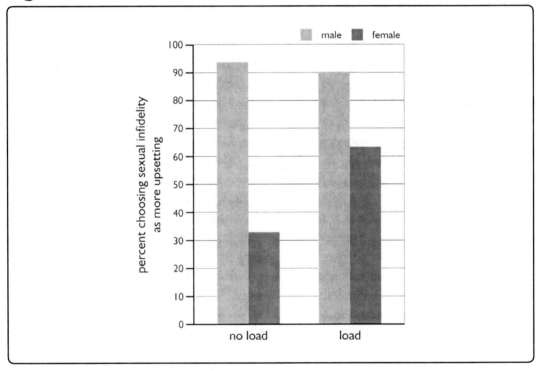

To help determine whether the sex differences in Figure 25.1 reflected "wired-in," innate modules of male and female jealousy, David DeSteno and his colleagues imposed a cognitive load. Subjects were asked to retain in memory a string of seven digits while answering questions. The load had no effect on males' responses, but females' responses shifted toward picking sexual infidelity as the more powerful jealousy trigger. This shift suggests that women's responses to forced-choice scenarios may reflect inferences or self-presentation strategies.

with the increases measured when these subjects imagined her falling in love with someone else. Female undergraduates showed a hint of the opposite pattern. These results have been interpreted as providing evidence for the predicted sex differences in jealousy.

Unfortunately, physiological arousal (reactivity) can reflect many different emotions— one reason lie detectors are not considered terribly trustworthy. Rises in blood pressure, increases in heart rate and sweating can accompany a variety of emotional states, such as fear, anger or even sexual excitement. Therefore, given that subjects are simply imagining infidelity, increases in reactivity might reflect other emotional or cognitive states besides jealousy.

This concern has been brought to the forefront in the jealousy debate by recent research conducted here at the University of California, San Diego, as well as in the laboratory of James Grice at the Southern Illinois University. Our lab found that men showed the same degree of increased physiological reactivity when they imagined *themselves* having sex with their girlfriends as they experienced when imaging someone else having sex with their girlfriends—that is, the same increase relative to their responses to imagined emotional entanglements. Thus, men's increased reactivity may reflect sexual arousal rather than, or as well as, sexual jealousy.

This newer work also failed to support the contention that women, in general, show stronger reactions to imagined emotional infidelity. Sexual experience appeared to modulate women's responses: Women who had actually experienced sexual relationships showed greater reactivity not to emotional infidelity, but rather to sexual-infidelity imagery. In other words, they showed a pattern of arousal resembling that of males.

At best, the psychophysiological data give an equivocal answer to questions about the innate-module hypothesis. Perhaps these studies fail to provide a good test of the hypothesis simply because the measures used are not picking up jealousy or distress. At worst, these measures *do* tap distress, but women and men both react more strongly to sexual than to emotional infidelity (at least when one examines individuals with actual relationship experience). Because investigators cannot randomly assign subjects to experience infidelity and then record their reactions when they learn about it, the issues raised by testing responses to imagined infidelity are not easily circumvented.

Jealousy, Murder and Mayhem

Some have argued that the strongest evidence for a sex-specific jealousy module can be found in patterns of violent behavior observed in many different cultures. In 1982, Martin Daly and Margo Wilson at McMaster University reviewed studies that looked at the motives behind murder. They concluded that more men than women committed homicide inspired by sexual jealousy. However, men commit all forms of violent crimes, in-

Figure 25.3

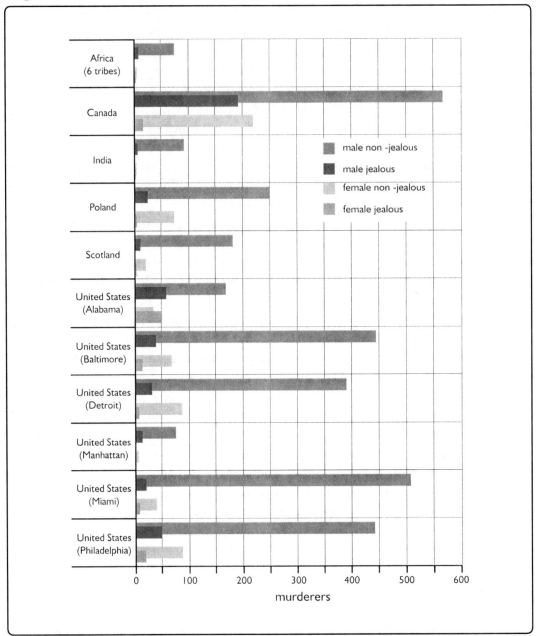

More men than women commit murders motivated by jealousy, various studies have found. However, men commit violent crimes of all types more frequently than women do. In an attempt to determine whether a sex difference could be demonstrated, the author examined 20 studies of murder motives from various cultures. The relative numbers of jealousy-motivated homicides by male and female murderers in these samples are shown here. No overall sex difference emerged, suggesting that murder studies do not provide evidence for a sex-specific jealousy module.

cluding murder, at far higher rates than women. So comparisons drawn from the sheer numbers of jealousy-inspired murders could be misleading. Two new studies have looked at jealousy as a motivating factor, taking differences in overall murder rates into account. The results paint a strikingly different picture. Recently I looked at murder motives across 20 cross-cultural samples (totaling 5,225 murders) and found no overall sex difference. Earlier, Richard B. Felson of the State University of New York at Albany examined 2,060 murders recorded in a database of 33 large, urban U.S. counties and found that women were twice as likely to murder out of jealousy as were men (a significant difference).

Fitting well with the revised view of the violence studies, other recent studies have asked adults to describe their reactions to real infidelity in their lives. In a sample of heterosexual and homosexual individuals of diverse ages who had experienced actual infidelity, both men and women reported that they focused significantly more on the emotional aspects of a mate's actual affair than on the sexual aspects. Other work examining college students' experiences with real infidelity also failed to show a sex difference.

Morbid Jealousy

Another line of evidence that has been offered to bolster the innate-module hypothesis comes from clinical cases of "morbid jealousy." Psychiatrists use this term to describe patients who display a conviction, most often delusional, that their mate is cheating on them. Often they experience anger and depression and feel compelled to check up on and spy on their mate. In some cases, morbidly jealous people attempt to prevent infidelity in an aggressive fashion. Some have even imprisoned their mates.

Aggregating across the five published studies that include both females and males, one finds 228 men (64 percent of the total) versus 127 women (36 percent) diagnosed with morbid jealousy. In an early analysis, Daly, Wilson and Suzanne J. Weghorst interpreted the preponderance of male patients in such studies as indicating the existence of a sexual-jealousy mechanism in men that is not present in women.

Assuming for the moment that a roughly 65:35 preponderance of male cases reflects the true incidence, and that the males' obsessions focus on sexual betrayal, what can be concluded? For many mental disorders, sex ratios are not 1:1. Men are overrepresented in several disorders ranging from substance abuse to autism. Australian psychiatrists Gordon Parker and Elaine Barrett have suggested that morbid jealousy is often a form of obsessive-compulsive disorder, or OCD. A number of clinical groups have reported successful treatment of morbid jealousy with fluoxetine, a serotonin reuptake blocker widely used in treating OCD. For example, in a study at Columbia University, Dan J. Stein, Eric Hollander and Stephen C. Josephson found the response of patients with obsessive jealousy to

Figure 25.4

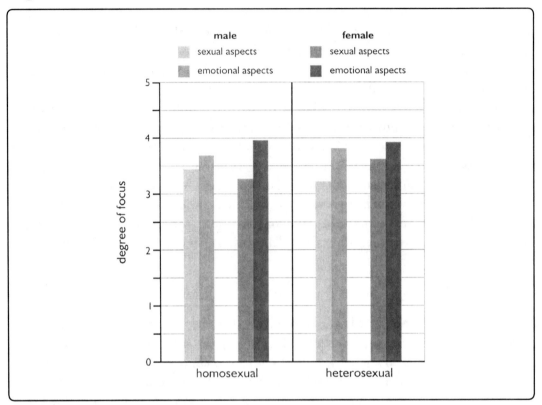

One of the author's studies suggests that male and female responses to real (rather than imagined) infidelity may be similar. In this study, both men and women focused more on the emotional aspects of a mate's actual affair than on the sexual aspects.

be as robust as one typically finds with traditional symptoms of obsessive-compulsive disorder.

The overall incidence of OCD seems to be about the same in men and women, although some studies have found that men are slightly overrepresented. There appears to be general agreement, however, that OCD with sexual obsessions occurs much more frequently in men than it does in women. For example, Patrizia Lensi and her colleagues at the University of Pisa reported a more than 2:1 male:female ratio for these symptoms within a large sample of consecutive patients admitted to an Italian psychiatric hospital for evaluation of obsessive-compulsive disorders.

If morbid jealousy is a manifestation of OCD, and males are prone to suffer from the same disorder with sexual obsessions, it seems questionable to draw general conclusions about male psychology based on the occurrence of this disorder. Symptoms found in male OCD patients might reflect male-female differences in the general population, or they might not. "Exactness and symmetry obsessions" are other OCD symptoms that show up much more often in men than women (ratio more than 3:1). It would be a mistake to infer from this that men in general have more appreciation of symmetry or exactness than do women.

In sum, when we leave the pallid laboratory studies behind and look at people dealing with real infidelity, people driven by jealousy to commit crimes or people morbidly obsessed with the possibility of infidelity, we do not find that particularly stark sex differences support the notion of a sex-specific innate module. Individuals of both sexes experiencing betrayal report that they focus more on the emotional rather than sexual aspects of the situation (in contrast to the physiological data). Men show a greater degree of violent or obsessional jealousy, but they do so only roughly in proportion to their general tendency toward violence and sexual obsession.

Jealousy and Natural Selection

At first blush, the basic tenets of the innate-module theory—that different selective pressures on men and women gave rise to different proximate mechanisms—are compelling. The theory offers an exciting opportunity to link human psychology to the ultimate driving force behind the design of all life on Earth, namely evolution by natural selection. The questionnaire data provided a tantalizing hint that such linkages could be sustained.

As the preceding discussion shows, however, the evidence for the fundamentally different wired-in jealousy mechanism in the two sexes weakens as one moves away from asking college students to choose among hypothetical alternatives toward real infidelity among adults. Why would this be the case? Alternative explanations at two levels, not mutually exclusive, occur to me and suggest a need for continued research.

First, it should be noted that almost nothing is known for certain about the social or cultural environment of the Pleistocene. The threats to Darwinian fitness that our ancestors faced did not necessarily present themselves in the way that biology alone might predict. Cuckoldry rates may not have been as high as evolutionary psychologists have assumed; for early hominids living in small bands, betrayal may have been far harder to achieve than in present-day urban societies. Males may not have expended enough resources on their offspring to impose the severe consequences of cuckoldry envisioned by evolutionary psychologists. In their review of present-day hunter-gatherer societies, Wendy Wood of Duke University and Alice Eagly at Northwestern University have shown that there is a great deal of cross-cultural variability in the relative contributions of men and women to subsistence, and women sometimes contribute more. Such variability makes it difficult to infer from evidence at hand what conditions prevailed in the Pleistocene.

Furthermore, even if our ancestors did pay a great price for cuckoldry and resource loss, evolution may have solved this problem in a somewhat different way than the innate-module account suggests. For one thing, focusing on a mate's sexual or emotional betrayal may not have been such an effective way to *prevent* infidelity. According to proponents of the hypothesis, the sex act *per se* is the trigger that most activates the male jealousy mechanism, whereas the female jealousy mechanism is most activated by evidence that a mate is falling in love. Buss and others have pointed out that signal detection among victims of jealousy can be quite accurate; that is, a jealous individual is often correct in believing that infidelity has taken place. If the cues that trigger jealousy were readily apparent to our Pleistocene forefathers only after the infidelity was a *fait accompli*, the sex-specific triggers would likely have rung alarm bells too late to avoid the Darwinian penalty. The fitness advantage of jealousy that follows sexual infidelity is somewhat unclear.

Instead, a more effective strategy for our ancestors may have been vigilance to the precursors of betrayal. Infidelity rarely occurs abruptly. Presumably, well before copulation, our ancestors—like modern-day humans—engaged in behavior that signaled the beginnings of sexual interest, emotional interest or both (an ambiguity that has occurred to more than one woman when trying to gauge her date's interest). Hence, there may be no need for men and women to have evolved different sex-linked jealousy triggers. Instead, both sexes might prevent infidelity by being alert to, and ill-disposed toward, flirtatious behavior and other common early warning signs of sexual or emotional interest. This hypothesis is consistent with evidence that men and women may not have innately different responses to the two forms of infidelity.

One might wonder how people compare with other animals. Cross-species comparisons can be quite enlightening in our search for knowledge about evolution and the human mind. Indeed, several evolutionary psychologists have bolstered their arguments for greater male sexual jealousy by pointing out that in many species, males engage in mate guarding when females are sexually receptive—that is, when they are in estrus and can conceive. In such cases, a male follows a female and attempts to repeatedly mate with her while trying to prevent other males from getting near her.

However, there are several striking differences between human beings and such species. For one, female humans are fairly unusual in that they are physically capable of having sex throughout their reproductive cycle but have hidden estrus: There are not clear signs when a female is most fertile. Another difference is that the males of many of these species do not engage in paternal investment, supporting the care of their offspring, a factor that is key in the theories of human mating. Even monogamous bird species with high paternal investment differ from humans in several ways, including the fact that they have clutches, whereas human babies generally enter the world in single file.

Might clearer insights into our own nature be obtained from data on other primates? As noted by Alan Dixson in his synthesis of primate sexuality, there is tremendous variability in sexual and mating behavior across primate species. Of the apes, gibbons are the only ones that form monogamous pair-bonds. It is of interest that a female gibbon will run off other female gibbons that stray into her territory, apparently without waiting to see whether they have sexual or emotional intentions toward her mate.

A Social-Cognitive Theory of Jealousy

Some of the liveliest moments in the classic situation comedies of early American television followed this formula: Husband (or wife) responds to the attentions of an attractive, admiring and perhaps openly flirtatious stranger with a flush of pleasure; this enrages a spouse (perhaps hidden behind the flowerpot), who in turn begins to act in irrational and hilarious ways. In early television, these jealousy plots added a touch of sexual spice to a medium where direct presentation of sex was forbidden. A single smile or fluttering of eyelashes could spark a riotous cascade of preposterous events.

The work of emotion theorists who take a social-cognitive perspective offers a dry but straightforward explanation for the actions that such a smile might trigger in the mind of an anxious mate. These theorists emphasize the importance of cognitive appraisal. They suggest that jealousy is particularly likely to arise over perceptions that a potential rival poses a threat to what one perceives to be valuable in oneself and in an important relationship.

Drawing on the work of the late psychologist Richard Lazarus at the University of California, Berkeley, one model distinguishes between what are called *primary* and *secondary appraisals*. In a primary appraisal, an individual assesses an event as having positive, negative or no consequences for himself or herself. If the appraisal is negative, the individual tries to determine the scope of the threat and engages in secondary appraisals designed to cope with the threat.

I have argued that in the case of jealousy the primary appraisal of threat might be elicited by an input as simple as a positive interaction between the beloved and any potential rival (in sitcom terms, an act of gallantry or a sideways glance at a swinging skirt.) Such an interaction between two others may elicit a vague sense of threat that does not have to be consciously assessed, may be innate and may occur in other animals. It functions to motivate actions that will break up the threatening liaison. At least in human adults, additional appraisals also come into play, including efforts to figure out what the liaison implies for one's relationship and oneself. These appraisals affect both the intensity and direction of jealous feelings.

This perspective on jealousy is consistent with a theoretical framework that has been applied to other social and "moral" emotions, such as anger. (What will make someone angry? No exhaustive list is possible: The answer depends on what the individual believes he or she is justly entitled to.) In this view, emotions have a "primordial" form that is hard-wired into the nervous system by evolution, but they also have an "elaborated" form that reflects cultural norms and meanings.

There is no conflict between such a view and the idea that jealousy serves an adaptive function by maintaining mating relationships, which are important to both sexes for many reasons. Contemplating the meaning and causes of a mate's infidelity might prove adaptive, by helping identify behavioral strategies that could help sustain this or a future relationship. Theories that view jealousy as a generally psychological mechanism have two advantages. For one, they readily provide flexibility to account for cross-cultural differences in jealousy. For another, they can encompass jealousy outside the context of mating (for example, jealousy between siblings or friends), obviating the necessity to define separately emotions that often can be quite similar.

The Ontogeny of Jealousy

It is even possible that jealousy originally evolved outside the mating context, as a response to competition between siblings—who from conception are rivals for a parent's resources—and was later usurped for the purpose of keeping friendships and mateships together.

Sibling rivalry is not an unfamiliar phenomenon in nature. In several avian species that typically have a clutch size of two, such as the black eagle, the older sibling routinely kills the younger one. In many more avian species, siblicide appears facultative, only occurring sometimes, such as when an older chick is not receiving enough food to maintain its body weight. Work examining proximate mechanisms leading to sibling rivalry and competition in other species, including primates, might help provide cues about the origins of jealousy in humans.

Because recent jealousy studies have focused on adult relationships, the experimental investigation of the ontogeny of jealousy is still in its infancy. To date, experiments with children have focused on the jealousy commonly observed when a sibling enters a family. The older child, usually a toddler, often displays a range of negative emotions, and parents often appear to be less positive in their interactions with the older child (showing less playfulness and more confrontation) than with the new arrival.

Although changes in parental behavior clearly contribute to the child's distress, it appears that jealousy in infants can be elicited simply by a parent directing attention to another. Sybil Hart at Texas Tech University and her colleagues found that infants as young as six months who did not themselves have siblings displayed greater negative facial expressions (furled eyebrows, downturned lips) when their mothers interacted with a life-like baby doll, relative to when their mothers behaved the same way toward a nonsocial toy. In another study, eight-month-olds verbally and physically attempted to distract their mothers to stop them from interacting with another child.

These findings suggest that complex cognitions are not needed to elicit at least some primitive form of jealousy in infants. However, with development, social and cognitive factors become increasingly important. Even by preschool age, the specifics of a social triangle influence whether jealousy arises. For example, two Canadian investigators, Sonia Masciuch and Kim Kienapple, found that four-year-olds demonstrated more jealousy when their mothers interacted with a similar-aged peer than when she interacted with an infant. Younger infants' jealousy did not appear to be affected by the rivals' age.

One issue raised by this research is whether the expressions and behaviors of infants in triads can be taken as evidence for jealousy in particular or whether such displays are simply unspecified distress. A similar issue confronts the adult literature: Is jealousy a basic emotion, a blend of various negative emotions or a label for a particular social situation? It is likely that a new definition of jealousy itself will emerge as various lines of evidence converge.

Conclusions

Exploration of the evolutionary roots of behavior and emotion can be a fruitful source of hypotheses for psychology. The research discussed here, however, suggests that robust sex differences in jealousy over infidelity probably do not exist. It seems more likely that natural selection shaped fairly general jealousy mechanisms designed to operate across a variety of interpersonal contexts. What sex differences do exist seem likely to reflect differences in cognitive judgments rather than sexually dimorphic hardwired structures. In sum, it seems altogether likely that the same green-ey'd monster may dwell within the hearts of men and women—a monster that might first arise in the minds of babes, long before sex and romance have emerged. It is as we emerge from under a parent's protective wing that, painfully, jealousy becomes what Havelock Ellis called "that dragon which slays love under the pretence of keeping it alive."

References

Buss, D. M. 1995. "Evolutionary psychology: a new paradigm for psychological science." *Psychological Inquiry* 6:1-30.

Buss, D. M., R. J. Larsen, D. Westen and J. Semmelroth. 1992. "Sex differences in jealousy: Evolution, physiology, and psychology." *Psychological Science 3*:251-255.

Daly, M., M. Wilson and S. J. Weghorst, 1982. "Male sexual jealousy." *Ethology and Sociobiology 3*:11-27.

DeSteno, D., M. Bartlett, J. Braverman and P. Salovey. 2002. "Sex differences in jealousy: Evolutionary mechanism or artifact of measurement?" *Journal of Personality and Social Psychology 83*:1103-1116.

Dixson, A. F. 1998. *Primate Sexuality: Comparative Studies of the Prosimians, Monkeys, Apes, and Human Beings.* New York: Oxford University Press.

Grace, J. W., and E. Seely. 2000. "The evolution of sex differences in jealousy: Failure to replicate previous results." *Journal of Research in Personality 34*:348-356.

Felson, R. B. 1997. "Anger, aggression, and violence in love triangles." *Violence and Victims 12*:345-362.

Hart, S., T. Field, C. del Valle and M. Letourneau. 1998. "Infants protest their mothers' attending to an infant-size doll." *Social Development 7*:54-61.

Harris, C. R. 2000. "Pscyhophysiological responses to imagined infidelity: The specific innate modular view of jealousy reconsidered." *Journal of Personality & Social Pscyhology 78*:1082-1091.

Harris, C. R. 2002. "Sexual and romantic jealousy in heterosexual and homosexual adults." *Psychological Science 13*:7-12.

Harris, C. R. 2003. "A review of sex differences in sexual jealousy, including self-report data, psychophysiological responses, interpersonal violence, and morbid jealousy." *Personality and Social Psychology Review 7*:102-128.

Lazarus, R. S. 1991. *Emotion and Adaptation.* New York: Oxford University Press.

Lensi, P., G. B. Cassano, G. Correddu, A. Ravagli, J. L. Kunovac and H. S. Akiskal. 1996. "Obsessive-compulsive disorder: Familiar-developmental history, symptomatology, comorbidity and course with special reference to gender-related differences." *British Journal of Psychiatry 169*:101-107.

Masciuch, S., and Kienapple, K. 1993. "The emergence of jealousy in children 4 months to 7 years of age." *Journal of Social & Personal Relationships 10*:421-435.

Mock, D. W., H. Drummond and C. H. Stinson. 1990. "Avian siblicide." *American Scientist 78*:438-449.

Parker, G., and E. Barrett. 1997. "Morbid jealousy as a variant of obsessive-compulsive disorder." *Australian and New Zealand Journal of Psychiatry 31*:133-138.

Wood, W., and H. A. Eagly. 2002. "A cross-cultural analysis of the behavior of women and men: Implications for the origins of sex differences." *Psychological Bulletin 128*:699-727.

Study Defines Major Sources of Conflict Between Sexes

26

CHAPTER

Differences Are Found in What Disturbs Men and Women

Daniel Goleman

In the war between the sexes, virtually all combatants consider themselves experts on the causes of conflict. But now a systematic research project has defined, more precisely than ever before, the points of conflict that arise between men and women in a wide range of relationships.

The new studies are showing that the things that anger men about women, and women about men, are just about the same whether the couple are only dating, are new-lyweds or are unhappily married.

The research is the most sophisticated yet conducted, and some findings are surprising. Although a vast body of literature cites heated arguments over money, child-rearing or relatives as frequent factors in disintegrating marriages, those conflicts seldom emerged in the new studies.

Instead, the research often found more subtle differences, like women's feelings of being neglected and men's irritations over women being too self-absorbed. There were also more pointed complaints about men's condescension and women's moodiness.

Upset by Unfaithfulness and Abuse

Some forms of behavior bothered both sexes about equally. Both men and women were deeply upset by unfaithfulness and physical or verbal abuse. But the most interesting findings were several marked differences between men and women in the behaviors that most disturbed them.

Sex, not surprisingly, was a major problem, but men and women had diametrically opposed views of what the problem was. Men complained strongly that women too often turned down their sexual overtures.

In contrast, the most consistent complaint among women was that men were too aggressive sexually. This conflict may be rooted deep in the impact of human evolution on reproductive strategies, according to one theory, or it may simply reflect current power struggles or psychological needs, various experts say.

Help In Counseling Couples

Understanding the sources of trouble between the sexes, psychologists say, could do much to help couples soften the impact of persistent problems in their relationships, and help therapists in counseling couples having difficulties.

"Little empirical work has been done on precisely what men and women do that leads to conflict," said David M. Buss, a psychologist at the University of Michigan who conducted the studies. The results were published in May in the *Journal of Personality and Social Psychology*.

Dr. Buss conducted four different studies with nearly 600 men and women. In the first, he simply asked men and women in dating relationships about the things their partners did that made them upset, hurt or angry.

The survey yielded 147 distinct sources of conflict, ranging from being disheveled or insulting to flirting with others or forcing sex on a partner.

In the second study, Dr. Buss asked men and women who were dating or who were newlyweds how often they had been irked by their partner's doing any of those things. From these results, Dr. Buss determined that the complaints fell into 15 specific groups. He then had another group of men and women rate just how bothersome those traits were.

Men said they were most troubled by women who were unfaithful, abusive, self-centered, condescending, sexually withholding, neglectful or moody.

Many men were bothered, for example, if their partner was self-absorbed with her appearance, spending too much money on clothes, and being overly concerned with how her face and hair looked.

Women complained most about men who were sexually aggressive, unfaithful, abusive, condescending, emotionally constricted, and those who insulted the woman's appearance, neglected them, or openly admired other women.

Many women were also bothered by inconsiderate men. For instance, they complained about a man who teases his partner about how long it takes to get dressed, or who does not help clean up the home or who leaves the toilet seat up.

'Basic Differences in Outlook'

Other research has produced supporting findings. "We've seen similar points of conflicts in marital rights," said John Gottman, a psychologist at the University of Washington whose research involves observations of married couples while they fight.

"Many of these complaints seem to be due to basic differences in outlook between the sexes," Dr. Gellman added, citing men's complaints that women are too moody, or that women dwelled too much on the feelings.

"That is the flip side of one of women's biggest complaints about men, that they're too emotionally constricted, too quick to offer an action solution to an emotional problem," he said.

"Generally for women, the natural way to deal with emotions is to explore them, to stay with them," he continued. "Men, though, are stoic in discussing their emotions; they don't talk about their feelings as readily as women. So conflict over handling emotions is almost inevitable, especially in marriages that are going bad."

For couples in the first year of marriage, Dr. Buss found the sexual issues to be far less of a problem than for most other couples. Instead, women tended to complain that their new husbands were inconsiderate and disheveled.

"You'd expect that sex would be the least troubling issue for a couple during the honeymoon year," Dr. Buss said. Even so, newlywed men were still bothered somewhat about their wives sexual withholding, but the wives didn't complain much about their husbands being sexually aggressive."

Nevertheless, the overall finding that men tend to see women as being sexually withholding, while women see men as too demanding, also fits with other findings. Researchers at the University of New York at Stony Brook found in a survey of close to 100 married couples that the husbands on average wanted to have sex more often than did the wives.

Problems Compounded

In the last of Dr. Buss's series of tests, married men and women were asked about their main sources of marital and sexual dissatisfaction. A new set of complaints emerged, along with the previous ones cited by dating couples and newlyweds. The more dissatisfied with the relationship, the longer the list of complaints.

For example, the more troubled the couple, the more likely the husband was angered by his wife being too possessive, neglecting him and openly admiring other men.

The dissatisfied wives, by contrast added to their list of complaints that their husbands were possessive, moody and were openly attracted to other women.

Sex was especially problematic for unhappy married men and women.

"The sexual complaints are standard in unhappy marriages," Dr. Gottman said. "But it tends to crop up even in otherwise happy marriages. Generally, women have more prerequisites for sex than men do. They have more expectations about what makes lovemaking OK. They want emotional closeness, warmth, conversation, a sense of empathy."

He added: "Sex has a different meaning for women than for men. Women see sex as following from emotional intimacy, while men see sex itself as a road to intimacy. So it follows that men should complain more that women are withholding, or women say men are too aggressive."

Investment in Reproduction

Dr. Buss sees his results as affirming the importance of evolution in shaping human behavior. "The evolutionary model that I use holds that conflicts occur when one sex does something that interferes with the other's strategy for reproduction," he said.

His view is based on the theory put forth by Robert Trivers, a social scientist at the University of California at Santa Cruz, who proposed that women are more discriminating than men about their sexual partners because biologically women have to invest more time and energy in reproduction than do men.

Men on the other hand stand to gain in terms of reproductive success for having sexual relations with as many women as possible, the theory holds.

"To some degree the sexes are inevitably at odds, given the differences in their strategies," Dr. Buss said.

Even so, Dr. Buss does not see evolution as explaining all his findings. "The sources of conflict between men and women are much more diverse than I predicted," he said.

Some of that diversity may be caused by sex roles. "Men and women are socialized differently as children," said Nancy Cantor, a social psychologist at the University of Michigan. "Men, for example, are not expected to be as open with their emotions as women, while women are expected to be less aggressive than men. So you'd expect a list very much like he found."

Dr. Gottman offered another explanation, saying: "The categories sound like much of what we see in couples' fights. But they miss what underlies all that: whether people feel loved and respected. Those are the two most important dimensions in marital happiness."

Box 15.1

The War of the Sexes: 2 Views of the Battlefield

Based on a new study of close to 600 men and women, many areas of conflict for couples are the same for both sexes. But here are the main areas where men and women diverge sharply over how upsetting certain behaviors are:

What Bothers a Woman About a Man

SEXUAL DEMANDS: Making her feel sexually used; trying to force sex or demanding it.

CONDESCENSION: Ignoring her opinions because she is a woman; treating her as inferior or stupid; making her feel inferior.

EMOTIONAL CONSTRICTION AND EXCESS: Hiding his emotions to act tough; drinking or smoking too much.

NEGLECT: Unreliability; not spending enough time with her or calling when promised; ignoring her feelings or failing to say he loves her.

THOUGHTLESSNESS: Being unmannerly, belching, for instance, or leaving the toilet seat up; not helping clean up the home; teasing her about how long it takes to get dressed.

What Bothers a Man About a Woman

SEXUAL REJECTION: Refusing to have sex; being unresponsive to sexual advances; being a sexual tease.

MOODINESS: Acting "bitchy" or otherwise being out of sorts.

SELF-ABSORPTION: Fussing over her appearance, worrying about her face and hair; spending too much on clothes.

Source: David A. Buss, Ph.D.,
University of Michigan

Preventing Failure in Intimate Relationships

Disrespect, mistrust, and alienation can create a brick wall between a couple. Forgiveness can tear it down.

CHAPTER 27

J. Earl Thompson Jr.

We live in a time when domestic violence is rampant and divorce is common. Every 15 seconds, according to the FBI, a woman is battered by her husband or lover. Domestic abuse is the leading cause of injury to women and accounts for more physical harm to them than automobile accidents, rape, and muggings combined. A conservative estimate is that at least 20% of the women in the U.S. are likely to be the victims of severe violence at the hands of men at least once in their lifetimes, a figure that has remained constant for the last decade.

One-half of first and 60% of second marriages end in divorce. Why does love turn sour? What causes marriages to fail? What factors lead to couple disaffection and the breakdown of committed relationship? Why is there so much violence in intimate relationships? Is there any hope for people to create and sustain nonviolent relationships that animate and fulfill them?

Fascination with the dynamics of intimate relationships is rife. There is a veritable flood of popular and scholarly books, articles, and TV talk shows about family and couple relationships. Self-proclaimed relationship gurus claim to have the answer to what makes for a good marriage. The degree of concern with this subject seems to be a direct response

Dr. Thompson is professor of pastoral psychology and family studies, Andover Newton Theological School, Newton Centre, Mass.

From *USA Today Magazine*, March 1996, pp. 40-42. Copyright © 1996 by the Society for the Advancement of Education. Reprinted by permission.

to the spread of domestic violence and the breakdown of marriages in American society, one which seldom has been grounded in and informed by solid empirical research.

A lot more is known about why intimate relationships fail than in the past. Then, knowledge about marital disaffection was based mainly upon ideological convictions, clinical intuition, structured interviews, or surveys. Thanks to researchers such as cognitive-behavioral psychologist John Gottman and sociologists of emotions Suzanne Retzinger and Thomas Scheff, there now is a trustworthy foundation of empirical evidence that solves many of the puzzles and clarifies much of the confusion about the causes of alienation and even violence in couple relationships.

Gottman studied 2,000 couples over 20 years and followed 484 of them for as long as a decade. While doing laboratory interviewing of the couples about neutral, positive, and negative topics, he measured electronically their physiological responses (heart rate, blood-flow rate, perspiration, and the presence of stress-related hormones in the urine and blood). Then, he followed up these interviews with questionnaires and conversations to determine what the spouses were thinking and feeling during the interviews and what they imagine their partners were thinking and feeling. He also used questionnaires and conducted an oral history about the state of their marriage through the years.

Gottman discovered that "human relationships, like other natural processes, are not random and unknowable, but appear to obey certain laws." In the face of popular misconceptions about what undermines relationships, he argues that there are four variables that, by themselves, do not lead to the failure of relationships and predict divorce. First, couples who create a volatile relationship characterized by a lot of conflict and anger do not necessarily end up divorced. Indeed, constructive anger focused on a particular issue and expressed without contempt or criticism is healthy, perhaps even necessary. It acts a lot like "spice that keeps the relationship from going flat." Gottman maintains that "blunt, straightforward anger seems to immunize marriages against deterioration."

Second, the other side of this coin is equally true. Couples who tend to minimize or avoid conflict at all costs do not face the inevitable breakdown of their marriages.

Third, couple incompatibility regarding central issues such as religion, politics, and the use of money does not lead to marital dissolution either. What is crucial is the way in which the spouses manage their incompatibilities.

Finally, sexual differences do not in themselves unravel marriages. Gottman found out that, in satisfying marriages, there are virtually no gender differences in the expression of emotions and that men who do housework are more likely "to be more happily engaged and involved in their marriages than men who did not, and less lonely, less stressed, and less likely to be sick four years" after his initial interviews of them.

What does lead to the dissolution of relationships and predicts divorce are what he calls the "Four Horsemen of the Apocalypse," a set of behaviors that attack and destroy the bonds of affection, trust, and commitment. These enemies are excessive criticism of the partner, defensiveness in the face of the partner's dissatisfactions and complaints, emotionally withdrawing and isolating oneself from one's partner (stonewalling), and contempt expressed verbally and nonverbally.

What is indispensable for the well-being of a couple's relationship and a lasting marriage is an "emotional ecological balance" that includes five positive emotional interactions to every one negative interchange. If a couple can create this sort of balance between their positive and negative interactions, they can weather conflict, anger, boredom, incompatibilities, and sexual problems.

From a different perspective, Scheff and Retzinger have come up with a remarkably similar conclusion. Their method was to videotape interviews with couples and subject these interviews to a sequential analysis of the spouses' discourse. The couple was asked to discuss three topics, each for 15 minutes: something neutral like the events of the day; an issue about which they frequently argue; and activities they enjoy doing as a couple. Using verbal, nonverbal, and visual cues, the researchers sought to infer the emotions communicated by the couple.

Scheff and Retzinger contend that the strength and vitality of the social bond between persons in an intimate relationship depends upon the extent of healthy or genuine pride awakened in the relationship. The opposite of genuine pride is shame (Gottman's "contempt"). Attention to the condition of the social bond cannot be optional, for the social bond is being strengthened, maintained, repaired, or weakened in every transaction. The emotions of genuine pride or shame are triggered in every interaction and signal the state of the social bond.

Partners communicate something about the other's worth by means of every word, gesture, facial expression, and action. When partners understand and acknowledge each other's "thoughts, feelings, and actions" as well as their "intentions and character," they increase healthy pride in each other and build secure bonds. When spouses misunderstand, fail to "ratify," and reject each other, they awaken shame in each other and damage their social bond.

Positive emotional messages strengthen the couple's solidarity, increase cooperation between them, and make for clear and unambiguous communication. In sharp contrast, critical, judgmental, and humiliating interactions lead to unremitting conflict, distorted, confused communication, and alienation.

Scheff and Retzinger agree with Gottman that anger and conflict in and of themselves are not injurious to lasting marriages. They go one step beyond him with their assertion that anger usually is the way people defend themselves against the shame activated by the interaction. Shame and anger go hand in hand. What leads to alienation and often domestic violence is that the shame is not acknowledged and the consequent alienation is not dealt with.

Couples frequently get swept up in shame-rage spirals that can escalate to physical violence. What causes marital breakdown is the couple's unwillingness or inability to address their shame and alienation and repair their damaged or severed emotional bond. The viability and permanence of a committed relationship hinges upon whether persons can acknowledge and resolve humiliating interactions.

Criticism, defensiveness, stonewalling, and contemptuous or shaming encounters attack the bonds of marriage and leave attachments fractured or broken. What is common to the first three of those negative behaviors is that they trigger shame. Of the "Four Horsemen," shame is the most deadly.

Shame is the most hurtful and debilitating of all emotions, "an inner torment" and "sickness of the soul," according to psychologist Silvan Tomkins. When people feel terrible about themselves in America's culture of narcissism, they are more likely to experience shame, not guilt. Shame is the companion to narcissistic injury. Exposing the self to itself, shame illuminates our profound alienation from ourselves and others. What this emotion discloses to us is our defectiveness, deficiency, inadequacy, unworthiness, weakness, and sense of failure. In addition, shame involves not only sobering self-exposure, but exposure of the self to others. Shame is a negative evaluation of the self from the perspective of others, "a vicarious experience of the other's scorn." No wonder this "affect of inferiority" is so corrosive to marriages.

> "Criticism, defensiveness, stonewalling, and contemptuous or shaming encounters attack the bonds of marriage and leave attachments fractured or broken."

Not all shame erodes intimate social bonds; only unacknowledged shame does. Indeed, a certain amount of shame is inevitable in close relationships. Marriages fail when couples cannot identify their own shame reactions, do not recognize or admit that they are humiliating each other, and do not communicate about it. In turn, unacknowledged shame triggers rage, leading to intractable conflict and, all too often, domestic violence.

What can repair and renew damaged social bonds? What can revitalize intimate relationships when the partners have become estranged, embittered, and hopeless? What can restore respect, trust, and affection after alienation has set in? What is powerful enough to heal the wounds of shame? The answer is forgiveness.

This claim is not accepted universally. Psychologists Michal McCullough and Everett Worthington, Jr. argue convincingly that, despite extensive research, there is insufficient empirical data "to conclude that forgiving has any clear physical or psychological benefits." Nor is the weight of therapeutic practice on the side of endorsing the value or utility of forgiveness in therapy. Neither secular nor religious counselors make extensive use of forgiveness techniques in their work. There is scant social scientific evidence that forgiveness actually reduces negative effects and none that it enhances a sense of well-being, leaving a dilemma wherein it is known what leads to social alienation and relationship failure, but not what transforms estranged relationships.

For their part, Gottman, Retzinger, and Scheff neither rule out forgiveness as an answer to marital breakdown nor make any claims for it. Yet, most individuals can attest from experience to the power of an apology and the offer of forgiveness to heal interpersonal injuries and repair fractured social bonds. Until more empirical research is done on forgiveness, it will be necessary to trust the wisdom that comes from religious traditions, clinical insights, and personal experiences informed by reason, intuition, and common sense.

What is forgiveness? The dictionary defines it as giving up resentment, vengeful feelings, and all claims to punishment. How do people forgive when the natural thing to do when they have been hurt and humiliated is to retaliate and settle the score? Can forgiveness really transform estranged relationships? Is it always safe to forgive? At the heart of the Judaeo-Christian tradition is the belief that God is a god of forgiveness who requires believers to forgive those who have betrayed, rejected, injured, and therefore shamed them. This tradition claims that forgiveness can resolve anger, resentment, and shame and reconcile damaged relationships. Of course, this is a value commitment and has not yet been *proven* by social scientific research.

From a psychological perspective, the most compelling and cogent expositions of forgiveness have been to approach it in terms of a series of stages. A case in point is the work of family therapist Terry Hargrave. He asserts that forgiveness is an arduous process that incorporates two stages: exoneration and overt forgiveness. Exoneration—setting someone free from the blame of wrongdoing—involves insight and understanding.

Insight identifies what concrete behaviors actually caused the injury, the extent of the damage, and who is responsible. It clarifies the bases of powerful emotional reactions of fear, shame, and anger when someone has been harmed, and it aids in protecting oneself by setting limits to further injury at the hands of the perpetrator of the hurt. Insight also can function as an effective restraint against retaliation and inflicting injury upon someone else.

Understanding opens the door to a greater comprehension of the offender's position, limitations, development, efforts, and intent. Individuals are able to comprehend better what led the offender to injure and humiliate them. The work of exoneration empowers people to hold the offender responsible and accountable for his or her actions while enabling them to identify with the offender's flawed humanity since they, too, have been or could be the inflictor of injury upon others. Hargrave claims that understanding can lessen the tendency to blame either the offender or ourselves, and therefore can dilute pain and shame.

Not everyone will move to the next phase of overt forgiveness. For whatever reasons, some will conclude that the broken relationship is not worth repairing or cannot be restored. The injured individual could conclude that the offender is unable or unwilling to make amends and change his or her ways; therefore, it is not safe to move to the next phase. In this case, the person offended could decide that he or she is unwilling to make himself or herself vulnerable even in small, measured ways to the offender.

Overt forgiveness has two parts. In the first, the injured person offers the offender opportunities to prove gradually that he or she can be trusted. The offender has to acknowledge his or her wrongdoing and take responsibility for it in a way that is congruent with the offended one's understanding of the injury. This surely will involve an apology by the wrongdoer and acceptance of it by the hurt one. The apology functions as a method of promise of restitution for the injustices of the past. This move is risky and could lead to more hurt and deeper alienation.

In part two, the one offended has to extend overt forgiveness to the person who has hurt him or her. The offended one, in effect, gives up any claim to injustice and moves beyond resentment and the desire to punish. For this to happen, both individuals have to want to overcome their alienation and restore a relationship of love, trust, and fairness.

Forgiveness is not the only force that can dilute or dissolve shame and repair and renew the "interpersonal bridge," but I believe it is the most powerful and effective means. Much more empirical research is needed to test this proposition, though. The way of forgiveness is not easy or likely to become popular and widespread. It requires a disciplined commitment to the value and belief that the most meaningful and enduring relationships thrive in this way of life.

Shame is a painful part of close relationships and can shatter intimate bonds if it is not acknowledged and processed. The most effective way to cope with shame and undercut its corrosive consequences is with disciplined forgiveness.

Part VII

Terminating a Relationship

Cupid's Covenant

Andrew J. McClurg

CHAPTER

A Truly Minority View on the Law

With Valentine's Day looming, it's a good time to get some legal perspective on the whole relationship thing, especially the breaking-up part. We need to face the fact that despite our hopelessly unrealistic expectations, most relationships don't last.

Breaking up has serious consequences for both parties that need to be considered in advance, while equal bargaining power still exists. Never enter into a relationship unless both parties have executed the Relationship Termination Agreement.

The Contract

The undersigned Prospective lovebird, being of sound mind but probably not for long, enters into the following agreement to govern his/her respective rights and responsibilities in the event of a partnership dissolution:

1. I agree not to go around blabbing the embarrassing secrets and quirks you confessed to me in strict confidence on the silly assumption that I wasn't going to someday hate your guts. Breach of this paragraph shall constitute tortious interference with prospective advantageous relationships.

2. Within 10 days following the contract termination, I covenant to place 25 melodramatic phone calls to you, at least half of which shall occur late at night while I

am intoxicated. Just to remind you that I still have strong feelings for you, at least five of these calls shall qualify as harassment under applicable law.

3. I shall retain any and all cards, gifts and other items of endearment supplied during the contract term for one full calendar year, at which time I may dissolve them in sulfuric acid. I shall reread all cards on at least five occasions, and hereby bind myself to feel nostalgic, wistful and wonder whether we made a mistake on each such occasion.

4. When asked why the contract was terminated, I shall falsely represent: "It was a mutual decision. We're still good friends."

5. Upon breakup, you shall return all items of personal property belonging to me, with immediate attention to any videotapes made during the course of said contract.

6. It is understood that the next person I date shall be less attractive than you and that this provision shall be strictly construed against the datee. I agree not to date your best friends, even though I think a couple of them are really hot.

7. Friends shall be split as follows: —— is my friend. Do not even attempt to speak to him/her, as he/she is subject to an express condition subsequent to curse you loudly in the event of a contract breach. —— can be your friend, since I've always found him/her affected and annoying.

    Other mutual acquaintances are my friends on (specify one) odd/even numbered calendar dates, alternate weekends and every other major holiday.

8. I agree not to hang out on your turf, including but not limited to your front porch and the alley behind your house, especially while on a date.

9. I covenant not to refer to any future contracting party as "Puppytoes," "Yum-yum" or (add appropriate pet name here).

10. I shall have the option of temporarily resuming the contract on at least two occasions after the breakup, at least one of which shall be initiated by a romantic chance encounter, preferably at someone's wedding. It is understood that these contract renewals will be for short periods and end badly.

Signed, with love (subject to change without notice).

Why Breaking Up Is So Hard to Do— Gay Divorce

Jyoti Thottam, Nathan Thornburgh, Betsy Rubiner, and Wendy Cole

29

CHAPTER

At least for a while, Shanon Delaney enjoyed the sweet thrill of marriage. On Valentine's Day 2001, the hair stylist, 32, and his partner wed in a civil-union ceremony. Three years later, that formal recognition made their breakup a little easier to bear. They went to family court and made it official again. Delaney kept the cats; his partner kept the car. "I call it my divorce," Delaney says. "That way everyone can understand what I went through."

Of the 954 civil unions performed for Vermont residents, 29 have so far been formally and clearly dissolved in that state. But the vast majority of Vermont's civil-union licenses, 5,770, have gone to people outside Vermont, and those gay couples who don't wind up happily ever after could enter the same legal no-man's-land they were trying to escape by getting married.

In Texas, a lower-court judge in Beaumont allowed two men who had been wed in Vermont to dissolve their union, but he reversed himself after state attorney general Greg Abbott argued that because Texas law prohibits gay marriage, the state cannot grant a gay divorce. If mediation fails, the only other alternative, says Houston attorney Jerry Simoneaux, is district court, where a judge might, for example, divide assets according to how much each partner contributes. Family court judges can weigh what is fair. "The person who stayed at home would lose a lot," Simoneaux says.

But some states are carefully opening the door to gay divorce. In a closely watched case in Sioux City, Iowa, district court Judge Jeffrey Neary allowed two women to terminate the civil union they got in Vermont. But rather than call it a divorce, his ruling simply dissolved their union and reverted the women to single status. Several Republican lawmakers and a church pastor are challenging the ruling in the Iowa Supreme Court, arguing that that kind of dissolution would implicitly recognize such unions and pave the way to same-sex marriage.

Gay couples who do not have civil unions or "relationship agreements" have few protections. And gay parents can find themselves with no legal right to see the children they helped raise—only biological and adoptive parents have legal standing. On that basis, in 1999 an appeals court in Illinois denied visitation rights to a woman who had raised a daughter with her partner from birth and continued to support the child after their split. "It's sometimes as though the other parent never existed, which is a horrible thing for a child," says Suzanne Goldberg, a professor of law at Rutgers University. Some gay lawyers have complained that clients have wanted to employ anti-gay arguments—like insisting on a biological connection to secure custody—against their estranged partners. Gay divorce, it turns out, is as painful as the straight kind, and a lot more complicated.